LABORATORY BIOLOGY

A basic companion for
advanced students

C. J. Hendrickse

BASIL BLACKWELL

FOR JOHN

ACKNOWLEDGEMENTS

I should like to thank Davies, Laing & Dick College for the use of the equipment, apparatus, microscope slides and specimens reproduced in this book. Also Dr Graham Clingbine for his advice and encouragement.

The author and publishers would like to thank the following organisations:

Commonwealth Agricultural Bureaux, SL2 3BN, UK, for permission to reproduce the Table of Relative Humidity which appeared in M. E. Solomon, Control of humidity with potassium hydroxide, sulphuric acid and other solutions, *Bulletin of Entomological Research*, 42 (1951).

Longman for permission to reproduce the Table of χ^2 which appeared as Table IV of Fisher and Yates, *Statistical Tables for Biological, Agricultural and Medical Research*, published by Oliver & Boyd, Edinburgh.

The cover photograph shows a cross-section of a human sciatic nerve and is reproduced courtesy of A. Buckingham, Sir William Dunn School of Pathology, Oxford.

First published 1986

Published by Basil Blackwell Ltd.
108 Cowley Road
Oxford OX4 1JF
England

British Library Cataloguing in Publication Data

Hendrickse, C. J.
Laboratory biology: a basic companion for advanced students
1. Biology — Technique
I. Title
575'.028   QH324

ISBN 0 631 90059 4

Typeset by Oxprint

Printed in Great Britain

CONTENTS

LIST OF EXPERIMENTS

PREFACE

This book is intended as a practical guide for students following a two-year course for A-level biology. The text emphasises particularly the material required for assessed practicals and practical examinations. It covers the practical requirements for the core of most examining board syllabuses. For reasons of space, some organisms required by a single board have been omitted.

In my experience, students seem to feel a need to refer to a text in class. Even with the relatively small classes at A-level, the teacher cannot always reach every student the minute help is required. I hope that this text will enable a student to find the advice or example that he or she needs, as and when it is needed.

Every session that a student spends in the laboratory should have some sort of record. This text aims to show the student how to compile the various sections of his or her record — first for assessment by the teacher as a requirement of the examination and, secondly, as a necessary aid to revision for practical (and theory) examinations.

C. J. Hendrickse 1986

Abbreviations, units and variables

ABBREVIATIONS

conc.	concentrated
concn.	concentration
dil.	dilute
GD	general diagram
HP	high power
log	logarithm
LP	low power
LS	longitudinal section
OD	optical density
OP	osmotic potential
RQ	respiratory quotient
SD	standard deviation
SE	standard error
sp.	species
STP	standard temperature and pressure
TP	turgor pressure
TS	transverse section
VS	vertical section
WP	wall pressure

UNITS

mm^3	cubic millimetres
cm^3	cubic centimetres
dm^3	cubic decimetres
μm	micrometres
mm	millimetres
cm	centimetres
m	metres
min	minutes
h	hours
mg	milligram
g	gram
kg	kilogram
atm.	atmosphere
Pa	Pascals
kPa	kilopascals

VARIABLES

d	distance
i	intensity
r	radius
t	time

1 HOW TO USE AND CARE FOR YOUR MICROSCOPE

The optical axis of the microscope must pass through the centre of each lens. The mirror beneath the microscope stage where the transparent object a–b is situated reflects light through that object to the objective. The objective actually contains several lenses, and projects an exact image up to the eyepiece. The lens system in the eyepiece gives an enlarged, but reversed image, a_I–b_I. This means that you must move the slide, when necessary, in the opposite direction from that which your eye tells you is required.

The microscope is probably the most expensive piece of equipment that you will use frequently. It must be looked after properly and treated with care.

Optical arrangement and light rays in a microscope

Eyepiece lens system

Optical axis

Lens system of objective

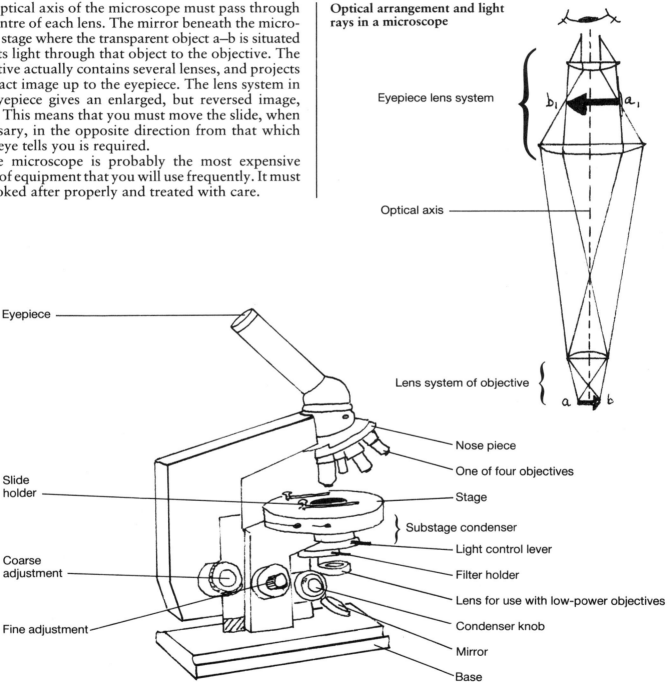

Eyepiece

Slide holder

Coarse adjustment

Fine adjustment

Nose piece

One of four objectives

Stage

Substage condenser

Light control lever

Filter holder

Lens for use with low-power objectives

Condenser knob

Mirror

Base

The microscope

Checklist

SETTING UP THE MICROSCOPE FOR USE

1 Wipe the eyepiece, the surface of the condenser and the mirror with a lens tissue. If they are heavily marked, moisten the lens tissue with a little alcohol and wipe the surfaces carefully.

This will remove dust particles and grease from fingerprints — these impede the passage of light, reduce the quality of the image you can see and cause difficulties in focusing.

2 Check the surfaces of the lenses at the base of each objective, particularly the highest power lens. Wipe them carefully. Glycerol may be removed using a tissue moistened with water; Canada balsam may be removed using a tissue moistened with xylol.

Glycerol from temporary preparations or even Canada balsam from deteriorating permanent preparations may stick to the lenses. (Take care! Do not use too much solvent or the lens mounting may be affected.)

3 Set up a lamp at the correct distance. Using the plane (straight) side of the mirror, view through the eyepiece without a slide. Adjust the mirror to give maximum brightness.
Check that the diaphragm is fully open and that the condenser is completely racked up.

A curved mirror is used only with daylight. Beware of using direct sunlight because of the potential damage to the eyes.

Often the condenser becomes unknowingly lowered by someone feeling for the fine adjustment and finding the condenser knob instead.

THE MICROSCOPE IN USE

4 Check that the slide preparation is dust and fingerprint free. Wipe, if necessary.

5 Place the slide in position and adjust, viewing externally, until the specimen is centrally placed.

6 View through the eyepiece, using the lowest power objective. Focus, first with the coarse and then with the fine adjustment. Control the light, if necessary, by closing down the diaphragm. If low power is sufficient, make your drawing. Always avoid 'empty magnification' (see Chapter 3).

7 If necessary, proceed through the increasing objective powers until you reach the magnification required or, if this is not sufficient, change to a higher magnification eyepiece.

Focusing the specimen at each increasing magnification ensures that you do not lose track of the specimen and waste time trying to find it. High-power magnification sees only a very small field of view.

8 Always focus carefully at high power. Rack downwards to the slide, viewing from the *side*. Then rack *upwards* while viewing through the eyepiece.

This should prevent you from putting the objective through the slide, and breaking the slide!

If your slide looks fuzzy and you cannot focus clearly, check that the glass and lens surfaces are clean.
Try not to let the objective come into contact with the slide.

This may damage the slide, or dirty the objective.

Using the oil immersion lens

This is used for seeing bacteria and small algae that cannot be seen under normal lenses. If the organisms are smaller than the resolving power of the microscope when using air between the lens and the slide, they will be invisible. The **resolving power** is the ability of the microscope to separate two lines which are very close together, seeing each line clearly (rather than both lines merging into one). This power determines how small an organism the microscope can detect; it is dependent on the **refractive index** of each component. The refractive index of air is not the same as glass, and so the light rays are bent at the glass–air interface. By using oil with the same refractive index as glass, this bending can be eliminated, and the resolving power increased. A special oil immersion objective, ×90, is used.

PROCEDURE

1 Place a small drop of immersion oil on the coverslip area of the slide.
2 Rack down slowly, viewing from the side and using the coarse adjustment, until the situation resembles that in the diagram:

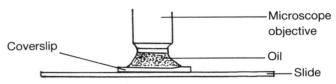

3 Viewing through the eyepiece, rack fractionally upwards, using the fine adjustment, until you are satisfied with the focus. Make sure that the objective lens does not lose contact with the oil drop.
4 Clean the objective lens carefully with a lens tissue after use, ensuring that it is free from oil.
5 Clean the slide preparation.

Checklist

AFTER USING THE MICROSCOPE

1 Check that the slide has been removed from the stage.	
2 Check that the *lowest* power objective is in position, *not* the high power.	*Another student may use the microscope without checking, and may rack downwards carelessly, thinking that the low-power objective is in position. This may damage the condenser.*
3 If you have an eyepiece tube cover, put it in position and place the eyepiece in its rack. Otherwise, leave the eyepiece in position to prevent dust falling into the open tube. Cover carefully with a plastic cover, or place the microscope in its box.	*Always try to minimize the dust and fingerprints that can get onto the instrument.*

2 MAKING STAINED MICROSCOPE PREPARATIONS

When examining live unstained material under a microscope, some structure can be seen as a result of the differing densities of varying parts of the cytoplasm. Stains accentuate the distinction between the various components of a tissue or an organ. Different components may stain with varying intensity, or even different colours, with a single dye. Each component may stain only with a dye peculiar to it, e.g. haematoxylin for a nucleus, and eosin for the cytoplasm. The difficulty with stained material, which is therefore dead, is to know whether or not the killing and staining procedures have altered the structure of the original specimen, or have introduced artefacts.

Fixing is the term used to denote the rapid killing of cells in such a way as to minimise any alteration in their structure. **Hardening** of the tissues makes possible the cutting of thin sections with little distortion, and enables the tissues to withstand treatment with solutions of varying osmotic strengths. 70% alcohol will carry out both these stages, but does cause a certain amount of shrinkage. It is quite satisfactory, however, for most purposes. Many specimens or sections, when you are

Stains most commonly used in the preparations that you will come across

Stain	Result	Notes and examples
1 Single stains		
Iodine in potassium iodide solution	Brown cytoplasm; dark brown nuclei	Temporary preparations of plant tissue, e.g. lettuce or onion epidermis
Methylene blue	Blue cytoplasm; dark blue nuclei	Plant or animal temporary preparations, e.g. squamous cells from cheek, onion epidermis
Methyl green acetic	Green cytoplasm; dark green nuclei	
Borax carmine	Red cytoplasm; dark nuclei	Temporary or permanent preparations of animal tissue, e.g. whole mount of *Obelia*, teased muscle
Aniline sulphate	Lignified tissues stain yellow	Provide tests for the presence and distribution of lignin in plant tissue sections
Schultze's solution (chlor-zinc-iodine)	Lignified tissues stain yellow	
Acid phloroglucin	Lignified tissues stain red	
2 Double stains		
Haematoxylin and safranin	Lignified tissues stain red; non-lignified (i.e. cellulose) tissues stain blue	Plant histology sections, e.g. TS stem or root of Angiosperms
Safranin and light green	Lignified tissues stain red; Cell walls and cytoplasm stain green	
Haematoxylin and eosin	Blue nuclei; pink cytoplasm	Animal tissues, e.g. blood, teased striped muscle
Leishman's stain (methylene blue and eosin in methanol)	Erythrocytes stain pink; nuclei of white cells stain blue; platelets stain purple	Specifically for blood

required to stain them, are already placed in 70% alcohol.

You will not be required to cut your own sections; this can really only be done satisfactorily by embedding the material in wax and cutting very thin sections with a microtome. You may, however, be required to strip the epidermis from a leaf, make a smear of blood, tease a muscle preparation or mount a whole specimen. Examples of these will be given later.

Permanent preparations that you use ready-made are mounted in Canada balsam, a resin from a conifer. This resin is transparent, and will not evaporate. It has a refractive index very near to that of glass, an essential property if you are to see your section clearly, and is dissolved in a solvent, such as xylol. Minute traces of water in the plant or animal tissue cause cloudiness in the xylol, so every preparation must be thoroughly **dehydrated**. This is achieved by passing the specimen through ethyl alcohol of increasing concentration until it reaches absolute alcohol. Subsequent transfer to xylol or clove oil causes the specimen to become transparent, when it is said to be **cleared**. It may then be mounted in glycerol, if only a temporary preparation is needed, or in Canada balsam for permanency. Some other mounting preparations, e.g. 'Cellusolve', remove the need for clearing and dehydration.

All these procedures must be carried out in making a permanent preparation, but the staining procedures may vary according to the type of specimen. The staining is carried out before the specimen is dehydrated. For plant specimens the stain is used mainly to distinguish between different types of cell walls.

Points to note when mounting temporary preparations

N.B. Presentation counts!

1 Ensure that the coverslip and slide to be used are clean and free from dust and fingermarks.
2 The mounting fluid should be placed centrally on the slide. The amount should be correct — neither too much (coverslip slides around) nor too little (air enters empty spaces).
3 Any excess mounting fluid should be cleaned up carefully. Filter paper moistened with water is suitable for glycerol.

4 Check your mounting fluid for air bubbles. If present, prick them with a sharp seeker. If there are too many, start again. Try to avoid *squirting* the mounting fluid from the pipette.
5 Place the coverslip gently on the mounting fluid, avoiding further air bubbles.

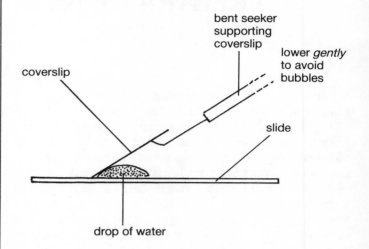

Some bubbles may be removed by a gentle side-to-side movement of the coverslip, but if there are too many, you may have to remount the specimen.
6 Ensure that the specimen is as central as possible under the coverslip.
7 Clean up the slide and label neatly.

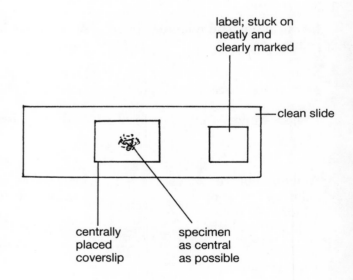

Examples of temporary preparations that you may be required to make

1 Using methyl green acetic to make a preparation of squamous epithelial cells from cheek lining

A combined fixative (acetic, i.e. ethanoic acid) and stain (methyl green). Useful also for temporary preparations of Protozoa or other small organisms.

  a Scrape cheek carefully to obtain living cells.

Use the blunt end of a well-washed scalpel.

  b Smear onto a slide and add a drop of physiological saline solution.

Saline (physiological, i.e. 0.09%) is similar in osmotic potential to the cell contents, and so should not distort tissues.

  c Mount with a coverslip and examine under low power.

Try to achieve a smear of several cells, fairly well spread out, not clumped together (yet easy to find).

  d Stain by irrigation:

If your drop of stain is not large enough, you may find the colour too pale at the right-hand side — use plenty of stain.

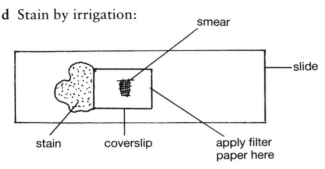

smear — slide — stain — coverslip — apply filter paper here

Pull stain through slowly and patiently to avoid unstained spaces in the centre.

Do not forget to clean up slide neatly afterwards!

---

2 To stain onion epidermal cells

*You may also use methylene blue or iodine in procedures **1** and **2**.*

  a With fine forceps, strip off a thin layer from the inside of a fleshy scale of an onion bulb.

  b Place flat on slide, cut a suitable square and reject the rest.

  c Cover quickly with physiological saline, if the irrigation technique is to be used, or a drop of methyl green acetic, for direct staining.

Take care to avoid air bubbles, either from specimen drying out, or as a result of it not adhering properly to the slide.

  d Add coverslip and label.

---

3 Whole mount of *Obelia*, using borax carmine

This is an example of **differentiation**, i.e. differential destaining. Dense structures should appear red; cytoplasm and less dense structures should appear pale pink.

(N.B. Set out your solutions in watch glasses before you start, as the specimen must be moved quickly at exactly the right moment.)

  a Place in 70% alcohol and leave for 5 minutes

Use a brush or section lifter for transferring specimens, so as to avoid damage; 70% alcohol will kill and fix if your specimen was fresh.

  b Transfer to borax carmine and leave till overstained, i.e. until the entire specimen is a very dark red. This may take 15 minutes or longer.

Remove the specimen into a fresh watch glass of 70% alcohol and view under the low-power objective of the microscope to determine the degree of staining. (Unlike methyl green acetic, the alcohol will not affect the stain.)

  c When it is ready, transfer it to a watch glass of acid alcohol (see Appendix 1).

This will quite quickly remove the stain — first from the cytoplasm, later from the denser areas. Follow progress carefully under the microscope until proper differentiation is reached.

d Transfer quickly to fresh 70% alcohol.

This stops further removal of stain. (If you have over-done things, and your specimen is now understained, i.e. pale pink all over, put it back into the stain and repeat the procedure until you are satisfied.)

e Mount in glycerol for a temporary preparation.

You may use this procedure for teased mammalian muscle. The procedure is identical except that, just prior to mounting, a few strands of muscle (i.e. individual fibres) are selected for presentation on the slide.

---

4 Insect mouth parts, e.g. cockroach or locust

These do not require staining but individual parts must be separated from each other.

a Soak in 10% potassium hydroxide for 1 hour.

More, if necessary — you may have to deal with the entire insect head.

b Gently tease with blunt seekers until you are able to separate the parts.

c Mount in glycerol and put on a coverslip.

Arrange the mouth parts neatly in the correct relative positions.

(You might also have to mount insect trachea, legs or wings.)

---

5 To make a blood smear

For safety, and reasons of hygiene you are no longer permitted to use your own blood. A specimen will be provided.

a Place a small drop of blood on a slide

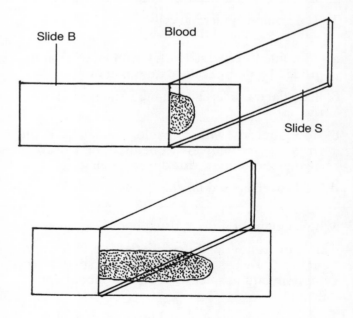

Allow slide S to contact the blood drop, which will spread along the base of slide S.

b Push slide S along slide B, drawing the droplet out into a thin smear.

c Dry by warming in air. Do not heat — it distorts the cells.

d Add a few drops of Leishman's stain; this will fix and stain in about 20 seconds.

e Dilute by adding a few drops of distilled water. Mix by rocking the slide gently and leave for 10 minutes.

f Rinse off excess stain with distilled water.

g Dry in air.

h Mount in glycerol and add coverslip.

3 HOW TO DRAW YOUR PLANT AND ANIMAL SPECIMENS

You should always keep a record of all work carried out in a practical class, whether it is in the laboratory or in the field. All the plant and animal types that you study should therefore be faithfully recorded in detail. (Not least because you need to revise for your examinations!)

Your drawing record should have the following aims:

1 To show clearly the external and often also the internal appearance of the specimen, or part of the specimen.
2 To show the relative positions of all structures in proportion to each other.
3 To indicate the magnification or reduction.
4 To label each anatomical structure.
5 To annotate, so as to add information extra to that capable of being shown in the drawing.

You will need:

1 A fairly hard pencil, H or even 2H, that will keep a sharp point for drawing fine detail. (HB is sometimes recommended, but it does not keep a sharp point for very long, the lines are dark and thick, and it leaves marks when rubbed out.)
2 A good quality rubber (a soft 'putty' rubber is ideal) so as not to tear or mark the paper.
3 A blade (preferably) for sharpening the pencil (not your dissecting scalpel!)
4 A ruler for labelling.
5 Loose-leaf paper. This may not be within your control, but it should be of as good a quality as is economically possible. Firm typing paper is excellent. Loose sheets will enable you to arrange your drawing record in a taxonomic fashion — you may not make your drawings in sequence. If you keep the sheets in a hard-backed ring file, then you can arrange each practical section to your satisfaction.

General hints and tips for making your diagrams

1 For whole specimens:
   a Rough out the outline of your specimen first, in light pencil.
   b Use a ruler, or dividers if you have them, to check the proportions — you may have to draw smaller, or larger than your actual specimen.
   c Use your common sense on sizing — a very large specimen may take up a full page, but more generally it will take up half a page; use less than this for small specimens. (It is *not* necessary to make every diagram fill the page; see the section on how to compute the magnification.)
   d When you are satisfied, draw in the lines firmly; keep the outlines simple.
   e Shading is not required — it takes up too much time. Labelling makes details clear.
   f Indicate any fine detail, e.g. skin patterning or cilia, on a small portion of the specimen only (label accordingly!).
   g There are no perfectly straight lines in nature, so never use a ruler for drawing.

Right!	*Wrong!*
Lines should be smooth and continuous	Sketched

Always use double lines to indicate blood vessels, nerves etc.

	Right!	*Wrong!*
Keep the thickness constant, especially at branches.		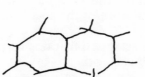
Such structures should 'grow' out of each other		

2 For microscopic sections, there are some extra points to remember.

	Right!	*Wrong!*
Lines should always meet *exactly*, e.g.		
plant cells	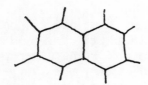	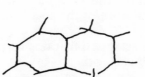
animal cells		
Put in the cut edges of cells not fully drawn — cells are not usually in isolation.		

Nuclei, if shown, are granular, not 'blobs'.

Low-power plans, or low-power diagrams, e.g. of plant anatomy or mammalian organs, must show areas *only*, *never* cells , e.g. TS plant stem

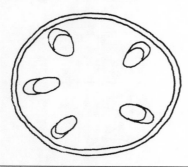   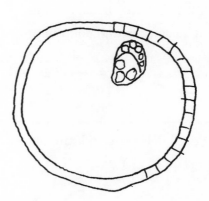

etc.

Right!	*Wrong!*

ciliated cells

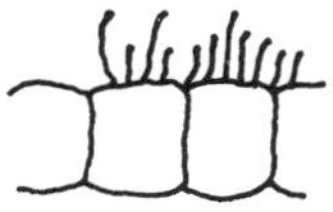

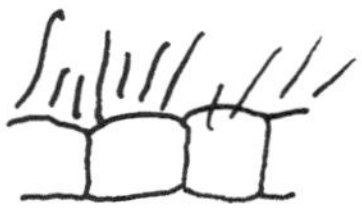

For thickening, i.e. lignification, on plant cell walls:

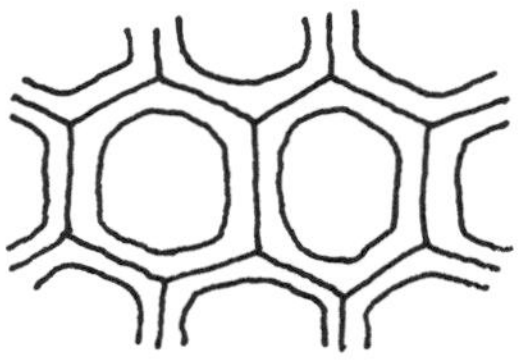

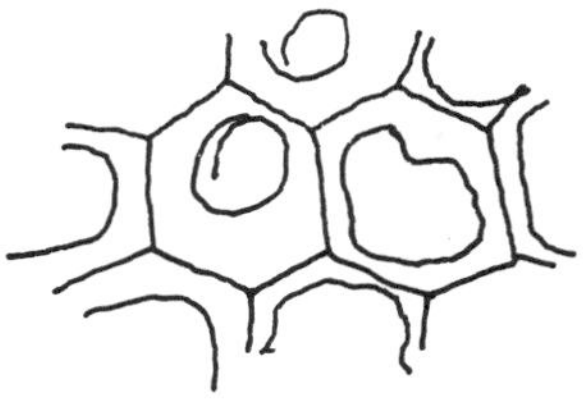

LABELLING YOUR DIAGRAMS

Thin, neat, ruled lines in pencil (so that you can correct mistakes!).

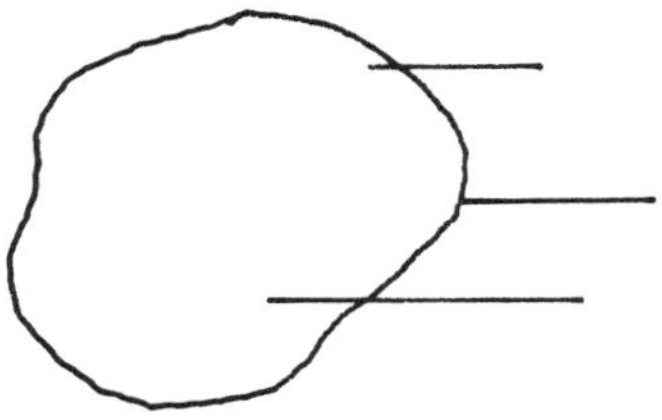

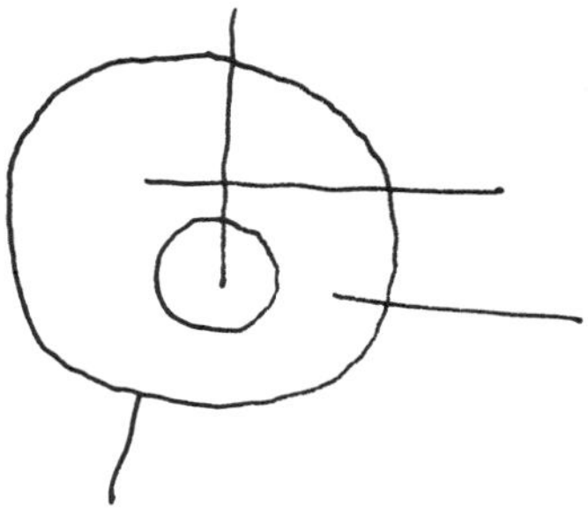

Arrowheads are not necessary.
Cut across as little of the drawing as possible.
Label lines should *never* cross.

Keep label lines parallel (if possible) or evenly radial (if possible).

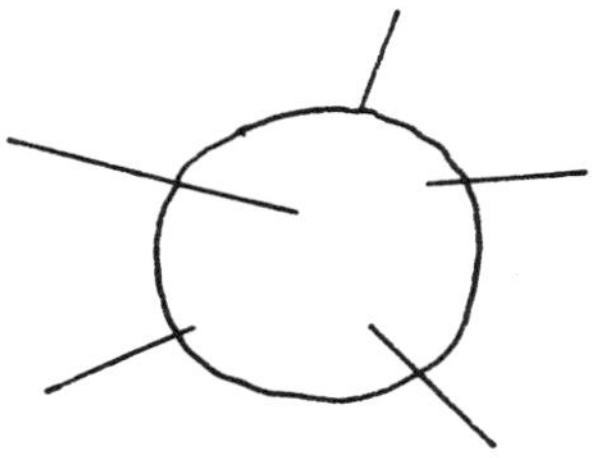

Whole phrases may be used in annotations to make structure perfectly clear.

If a structure is lost, damaged, or cut by accident, e.g. during dissection, label 'position of' and draw with dotted lines.

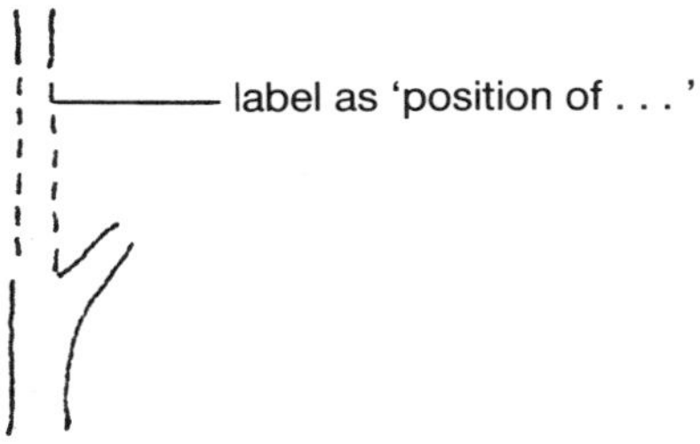

———— label as 'position of . . .'

HOW TO COMPUTE THE MAGNIFICATION Whole specimens may be drawn lifesize, enlarged or reduced. Use a ruler to measure the specimen and the drawing. Write the appropriate figure, i.e. ×1, ×4 or ×⅛, by the title. A hand-lens magnifies from ×2 to ×10 — this is usually stated on the frame. If you are using a microscope, multiply the value on the eyepiece in use by the value on the objective, e.g. ×15 eyepiece with a ×40 objective magnifies ×600.

If your drawing is larger than the specimen seen under the microscope, be careful to include this in your calculations. Try never to make 'empty magnification'. For example, if you draw *Euglena*, a microscopic protozoan, a little larger than you see it under high-power (×600), your total magnification might be ×900 or even ×1200. At this magnification, you would only expect to see what is shown by the microscope. If you draw that same specimen to take up half a page, the magnification might be ×9000! At this magnification, structures would appear which are invisible at ×900, and which you would thus not be able to show. Your drawing would therefore be inaccurate.

ANNOTATION
1 Any structure known to be present, but not seen, should be indicated beside the drawing. Always be totally honest and draw *only* what you see — not what you think should be there! But be sure that the structure is really 'not seen', and not just 'overlooked'.

2 A specimen should always be classified — usually beside the title. Identifying and classifying features should be included.
3 For whole specimens the habitat and life history should be indicated.
4 Special points of biological interest should be noted, e.g. adaptation to environment (for whole specimens) or adaptation of cell structure to function (for a microscopic section of tissue). This could be placed alongside the appropriate label. Allow room in the layout of your labels.
5 Compare and contrast similar types if necessary, e.g. a free-living member of a group of animals and a parasitic member of the same group, a monocotyledonous and dicotyledonous stem structure, striated, cardiac and smooth muscle, and so on.

You will find examples of the way in which all this could be carried out in the taxonomy chapters.

Your drawings require care and attention to detail in order to pass an assessment or an examination with good marks. Practise will enable you to make your drawings fairly quickly. Bear in mind that you do not have to be 'able to draw'. Accuracy and neatness with correct relative proportions and relative positions of individual structures are much more important in a diagram. Sloppy and untidy work will lose you marks. Remember to put in the magnification and, if it is a whole specimen, to classify it.

Never leave a drawing without a title and labels; make sure that you do this before leaving the laboratory, while you still have the specimen to look at.

4 ANIMAL TAXONOMY

Outline classification of Kingdom Animalia (only one classification of a number acceptable to the examining boards)

Phylum	Sub-group (usually designated 'Class')	Examples
Protozoa	Sarcodina (Rhizopoda)	*Amoeba*
	Mastigophora (Flagellata)	*Euglena*
	Ciliata (Ciliophora)	*Paramecium*
	Sporozoa	*Plasmodium*
Porifera		The sponges
Coelenterata	Hydrozoa	*Hydra*; *Obelia*
	Anthozoa	*Actinia*
	Scyphozoa	Jellyfish (*Aurelia*)
Platyhelminthes	Turbellaria	*Planaria*
	Trematoda	*Fasciola*
	Cestoda	*Taenia*
Nematoda		*Ascaris*
Annelida	Oligochaeta	*Lumbricus*
	Polychaeta	*Nereis*; *Arenicola*
	Hirudinea	*Hirudo*
Arthropoda	Crustacea	*Carcinus*; *Daphnia*
	Myriapoda	*Lithobius*
	Arachnida	*Epeira*
	Insecta	*Pieris*, *Apis*, *Locusta*
Mollusca	Gastropoda	*Helix*
	Lamellibranchiata	*Mytilus*
	Cephalopoda	*Octopus*; *Sepia*
Echinodermata	Asteroidea	*Asterias*
	Echinoidea	*Echinus*
	Crinoidea	The sea lilies
	Ophiuroidea	The brittle stars
	Holothuroidea	The sea cucumbers
Chordata Sub-phylum Protochordata (*Acrania*)	Hemichordata	*Saccoglossus*
	Urochordata	*Ciona*
	Cephalochordata	*Amphioxus*
Sub-phylum Craniata (Vertebrata)	Cyclostomata	The Hagfish; lampreys
	Pisces	*Bony fish; cartilaginous fish
	Amphibia	*Rana*, *Triturus*
	Reptilia	The snakes, *lizards and turtles
	Aves	*Birds
	Mammalia	*Mus* (Rodentia) and other groups

* Required for study.

PHYLUM: PROTOZOA

Single cells. Organelles only present.

CLASS: SARCODINA (RHIZOPODA)

Protoplasm divided into ectoderm and endoderm. Possess pseudopodia. One nucleus. Holozoic nutrition. No sexual reproduction.

AMOEBA SP. (× 400)

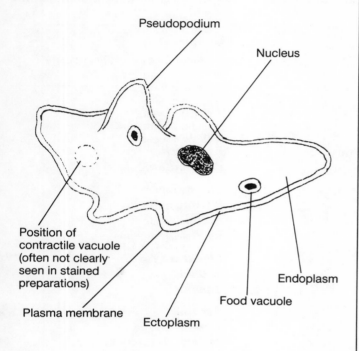

Live in soil, fresh or marine waters, and damp places generally. Feed by phagocytosis (engulfing of food by pseudopodia).

Life history

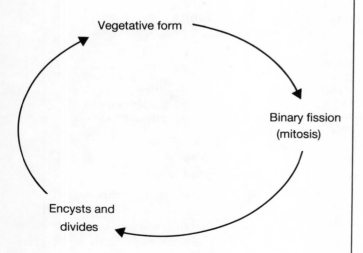

PHYLUM: PROTOZOA

CLASS: MASTIGOPHORA (FLAGELLATA)

All members are characterized by the possession of one or more flagella. May contain chloroplasts. Usual reproduction by binary fission.

EUGLENA SP. (2 × 400)

(Subgroup Phytomastigina — contain chloroplasts.)

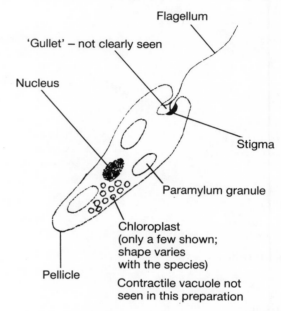

Found in ponds, puddles and polluted waters. Body is covered with a thick flexible pellicle. Paramylum is the reserve carbohydrate. Chloroplasts enable photosynthesis to take place in the light; in the dark, or in the absence of chloroplasts, large organic molecules may be utilized heterotrophically. Exhibits euglenoid movement: alternate lengthways contractions and relaxations of the body.

Life history

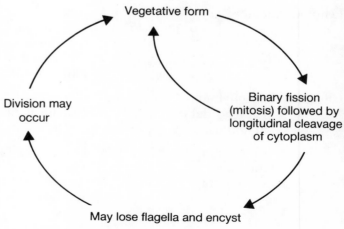

PHYLUM: PROTOZOA

CLASS: CILIATA (CILIOPHORA)

All members possess cilia on some parts of the cell. Also possess a pellicle. Two nuclei. Reproduction usually by binary fission. May also conjugate and exchange nuclear material.

PARAMECIUM SP. (2 × 400)

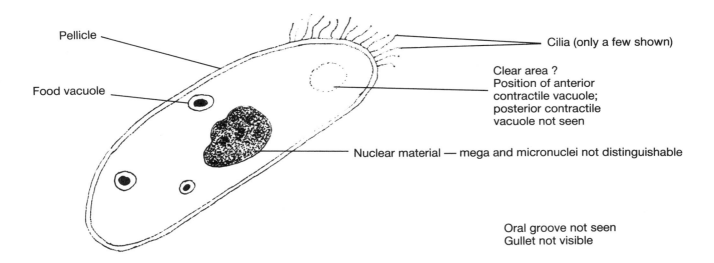

Found in stagnant ponds. Feed on small particles. Rather larger than other ciliates. Spiral swimming action.

Life history

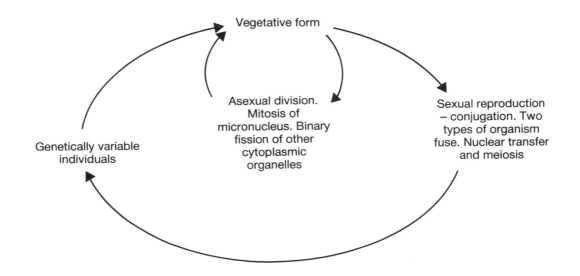

PHYLUM: COELENTERATA

Diploblastic metazoan; body wall with mesogloea. Radially symmetrical. Single body cavity — the enteron. Nervous system a network. Tentacles with nematocysts.

CLASS: HYDROZOA

Both hydroid and medusoid forms.

HYDRA SP. (× 30)

Whole mount, with bud

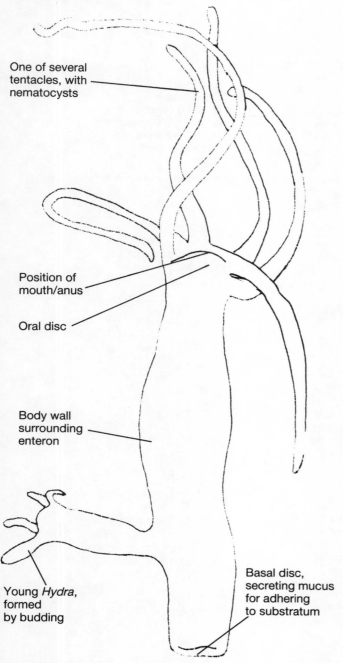

One of several tentacles, with nematocysts

Position of mouth/anus

Oral disc

Body wall surrounding enteron

Young *Hydra*, formed by budding

Basal disc, secreting mucus for adhering to substratum

Solitary types. The polyp form only is present. Enteron is undivided. Freshwater, attached to weed. May contain symbiotic brown or green algae in the endoderm. Some forms are hermaphrodite; in some the sexes are separate. Ovary and/or testis borne on the body.

TS body wall of *Hydra*: GD (× 50)

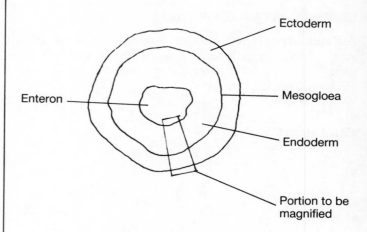

Ectoderm

Enteron

Mesogloea

Endoderm

Portion to be magnified

HP portion of body wall (× 600)

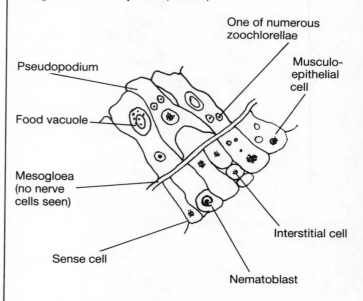

Pseudopodium

One of numerous zoochlorellae

Musculo-epithelial cell

Food vacuole

Mesogloea (no nerve cells seen)

Sense cell

Interstitial cell

Nematoblast

Flagellate cells not seen

Life history

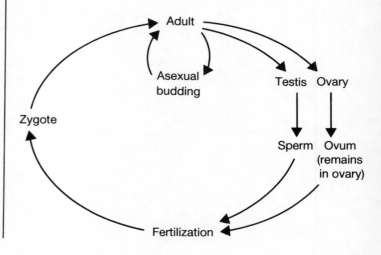

Adult

Asexual budding

Testis   Ovary

Zygote

Sperm   Ovum (remains in ovary)

Fertilization

PHYLUM: COELENTERATA

CLASS: HYDROZOA

***OBELIA* SP. (× 30)**

Portion of colony

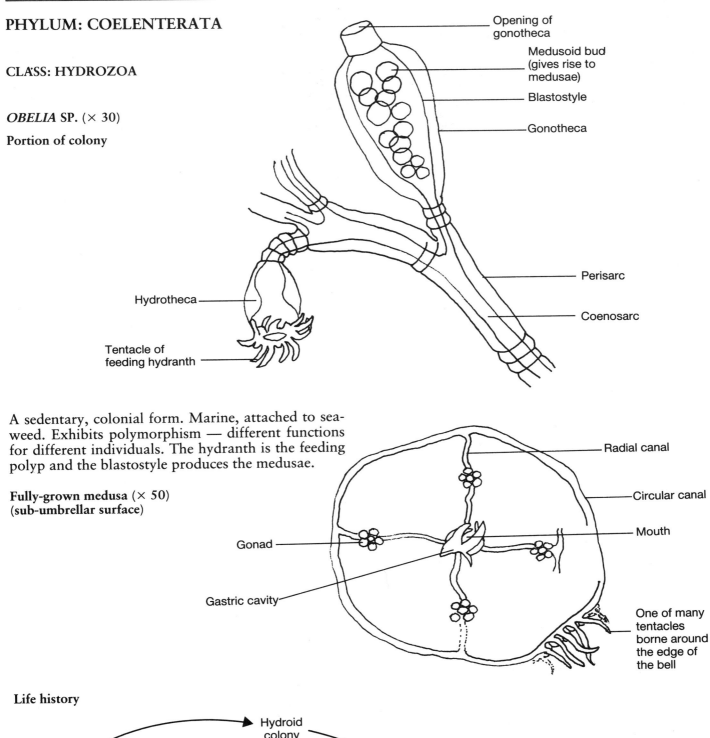

Opening of gonotheca

Medusoid bud (gives rise to medusae)

Blastostyle

Gonotheca

Perisarc

Coenosarc

Hydrotheca

Tentacle of feeding hydranth

A sedentary, colonial form. Marine, attached to seaweed. Exhibits polymorphism — different functions for different individuals. The hydranth is the feeding polyp and the blastostyle produces the medusae.

Fully-grown medusa (× 50)
(sub-umbrellar surface)

Radial canal

Circular canal

Mouth

Gonad

Gastric cavity

One of many tentacles borne around the edge of the bell

Life history

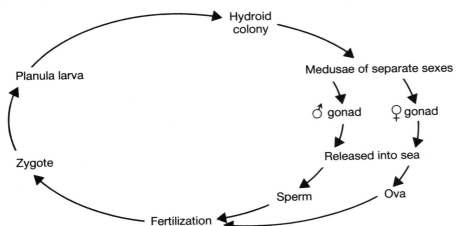

Hydroid colony

Planula larva

Medusae of separate sexes

♂ gonad   ♀ gonad

Released into sea

Zygote

Sperm   Ova

Fertilization

PHYLUM: COELENTERATA

CLASS: ANTHOZOA

Hydroid form only, solitary or colonial. Enteron divided up with vertical partitions.

ACTINIA SP. (× 1)

(Sea anemone)

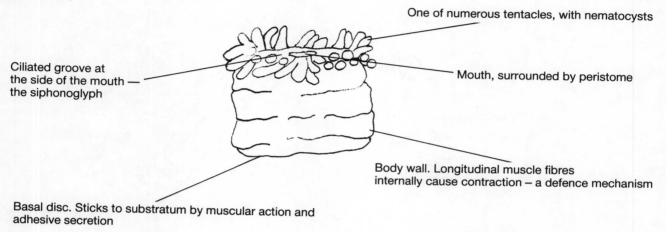

One of numerous tentacles, with nematocysts

Ciliated groove at the side of the mouth — the siphonoglyph

Mouth, surrounded by peristome

Body wall. Longitudinal muscle fibres internally cause contraction – a defence mechanism

Basal disc. Sticks to substratum by muscular action and adhesive secretion

Sessile, marine, solitary types. Found on rocky shores and in deeper water. Feed on, e.g. small crustaceans. Tentacles, when retracted, give a bead-like effect — hence the common name — the beadlet anemone.

Life history

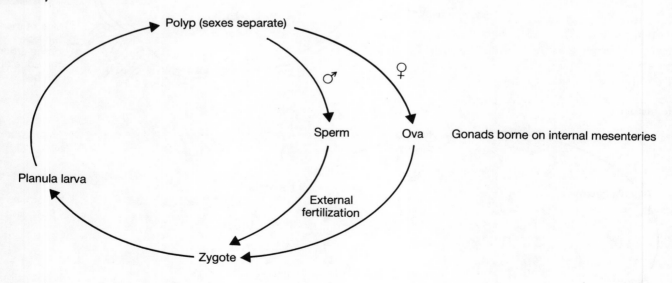

Polyp (sexes separate)

♂   ♀

Sperm   Ova   Gonads borne on internal mesenteries

Planula larva

External fertilization

Zygote

PHYLUM: PLATYHELMINTHES

Triploblastic, acoelomate (no perivisceral coelom). Space between gut and body filled with loose mesodermal parenchyma. Bilaterally symmetrical. Organ grade of organisation. No metameric segmentation. Body flattened dorsoventrally. Excretion by flame cells.

CLASS: TURBELLARIA

Free-living, aquatic. Glide over surfaces by action of cilia on epidermis, or by rippling action of muscles in the body wall.

PLANARIA SP. (× 10)

Whole mount, GD

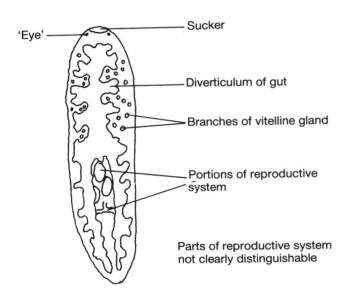

Body entire, unsegmented. Carnivorous, mouth ventral. Simple intestine. Hermaphrodite, but cross-fertilising. Sperm are exchanged for internal fertilisation. Eggs with yolk cells are deposited in a capsule to be shed. Hatch after several weeks.

Life history

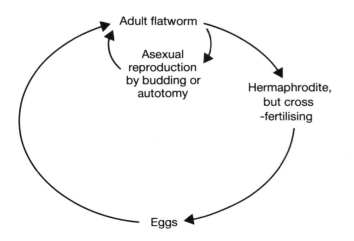

PHYLUM: PLATYHELMINTHES

CLASS: TREMATODA (THE 'FLUKES')

All endoparasitic. Thin, leaf-like. Thick cuticle; suckers. No cilia. Hermaphrodite. Cross fertilising. Several stages in the life history.

FASCIOLA SP.: THE LIVER FLUKE (× 5)

Parasitic in the bile ducts of sheep.

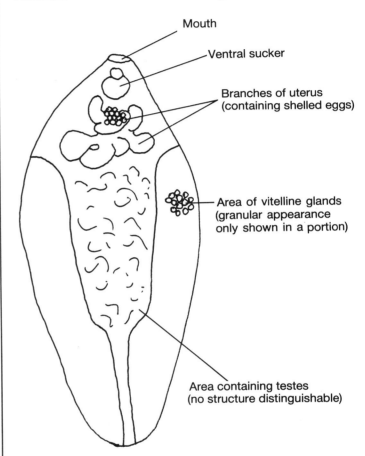

Structure of reproductive organs not distinguishable

Life history

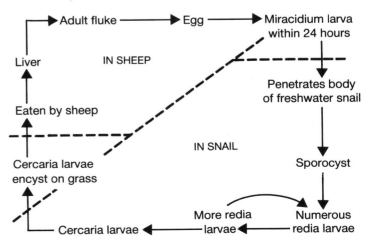

PHYLUM: NEMATODA

Bilaterally symmetrical. Triploblastic. Acoelomate, but a pseudocoel present, produced by giant cells in the mesoderm, with large vacuoles. Elongated, pointed at both ends. No cilia. Alimentary canal has mouth and anus. Sexes separate.

ASCARIS SP. (× 1)

Parasitic in the small intestine of mammals.

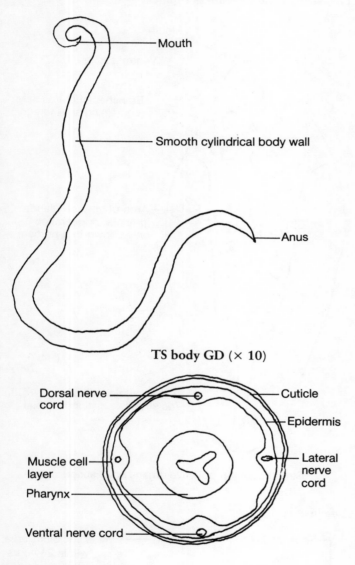

TS body GD (× 10)

Life history

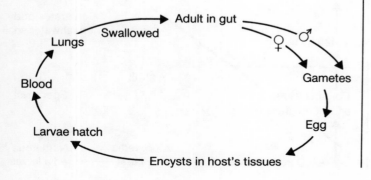

PHYLUM: ANNELIDA

Triploblastic, coelomate. Bilaterally symmetrical. Metameric segmentation (i.e. every segment the same age). Cylindrical; thin cuticle. Body wall with longitudinal and circular muscle. Double ventral nerve cord. Excretion by nephridia. Chaetae present.

CLASS: OLIGOCHAETA

Head undifferentiated; no appendages, no parapodia. Two pairs of chaetae per segment. Hermaphrodite. Internal fertilisation. Eggs laid in cocoons.

LUMBRICUS SP.: THE EARTHWORM (× 2)

Lives in damp soil in burrows. Eats soil and deposits casts on surface after digesting the soluble material.

Side view

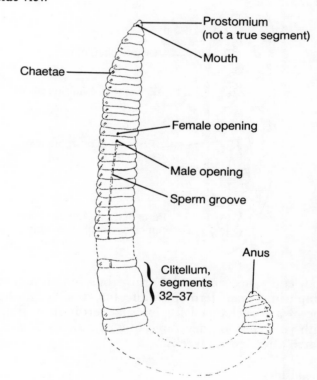

Life history

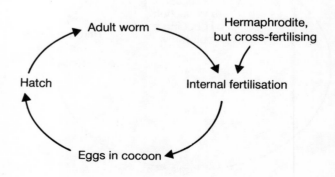

PHYLUM: ANNELIDA

CLASS: POLYCHAETA

Chaetae numerous, borne on parapodia. Cephalization
well marked. Sexes separate. External fertilisation.

NEREIS SP.: THE RAGWORM (× 3)

Marine form, lives in burrows in the sand. Casts seen
on the surface.

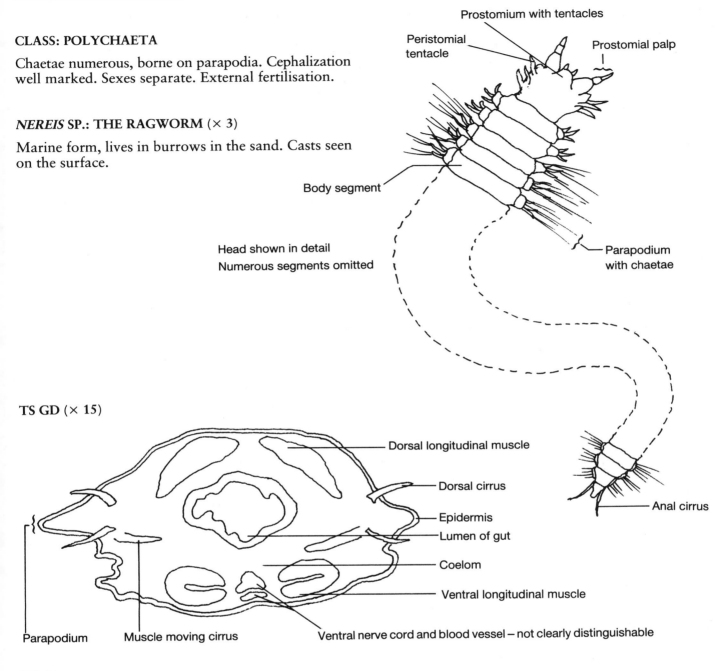

Head shown in detail
Numerous segments omitted

TS GD (× 15)

Life history

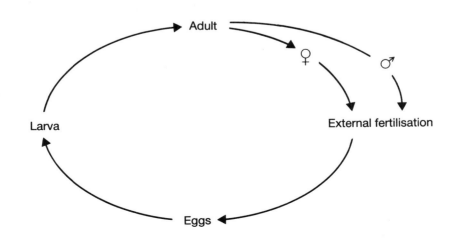

PHYLUM: ARTHROPODA

Coelomate (a haemocoel); metamerically segmented.
Appendages not on every segment. Triploblastic.
Bilaterally symmetrical. Exoskeleton, often of chitin.
Jointed limbs, some pairs of which function as jaws.
Central nervous system with ganglia and paired ventral
nerve cords. Contractile 'heart' lying dorsally in
haemocoel.

CLASS: CRUSTACEA

Gills. Two pairs of antennae. Calcareous exoskeleton.
Head often fused with thorax, forming a cephalothorax.

CARCINUS SP.: THE SHORE CRAB

Dorsal view (× 1)

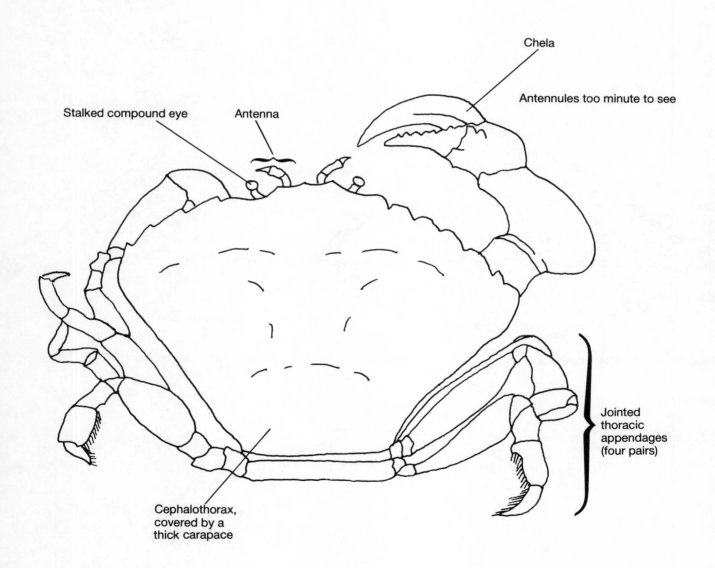

Chela

Antennules too minute to see

Stalked compound eye

Antenna

Jointed
thoracic
appendages
(four pairs)

Cephalothorax,
covered by a
thick carapace

Ventral view ($\times$ 1)

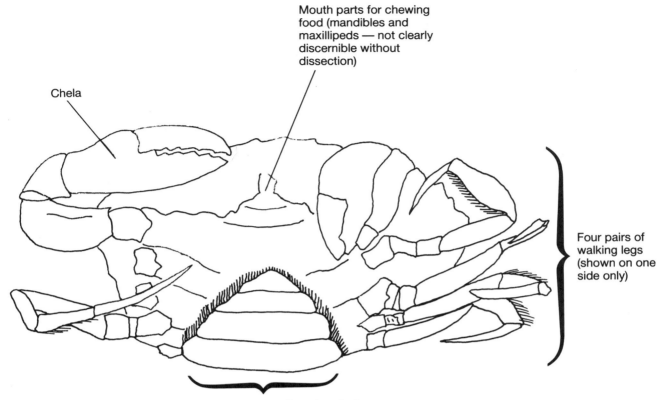

Chela

Mouth parts for chewing food (mandibles and maxillipeds — not clearly discernible without dissection)

Four pairs of walking legs (shown on one side only)

Abdominal segments, flexed ventrally

Crabs (Decapoda: five pairs of limbs). Four pairs of walking limbs; segment of first limb modified to a chela, or claw. Stalked mobile eye. Head and thorax covered by a carapace. Inhabits beaches and rocky shores.

Life history

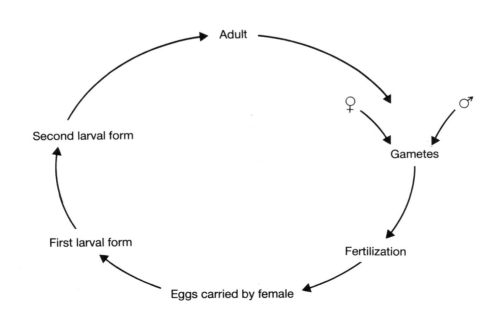

Adult

♀   ♂

Second larval form

Gametes

First larval form

Fertilization

Eggs carried by female

PHYLUM: ARTHROPODA

CLASS: CRUSTACEA

DAPHNIA SP.: THE WATER FLEA (× 50)

Gas exchange through body surface. Carapace enclosing thoracic limbs. Lives in the surface waters of ponds and lakes. Biramous antennae. Parthenogenetic, producing haploid eggs. In adverse conditions, males *are* produced and fertilise large yolky eggs. These hatch into females in the spring.

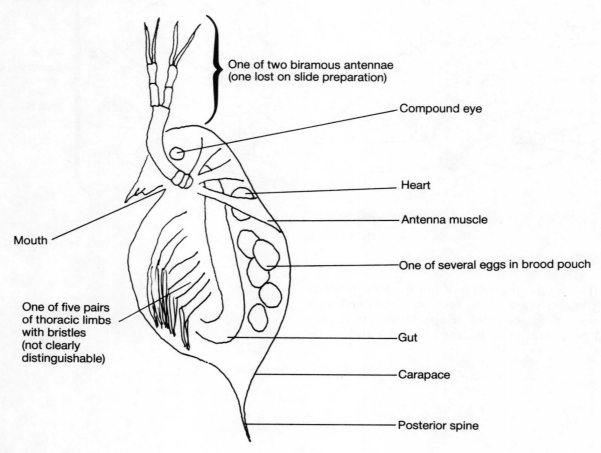

Life history

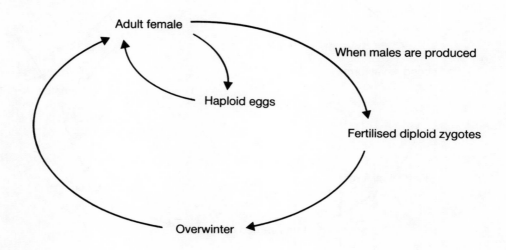

PHYLUM: ARTHROPODA

CLASS: ARACHNIDA

Two divisions to the body — prosoma with head and four pairs of legs, the opisthosoma with no appendages. Gas exchange by lung 'books'. Mouth parts are chelicerae and pedipalps.

EPEIRA SP.: THE GARDEN SPIDER (× 5)

Terrestrial form. Spins web to trap insect prey. Exoenzymes injected and resulting liquid sucked out.

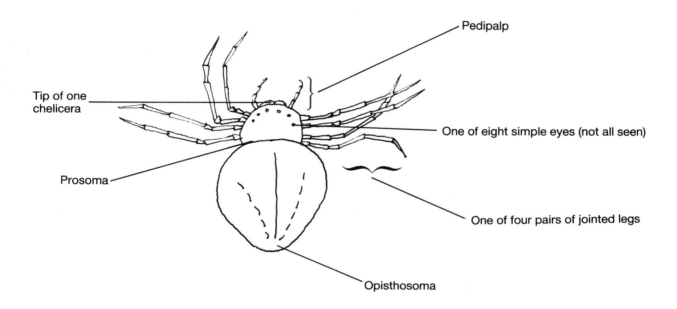

Life history

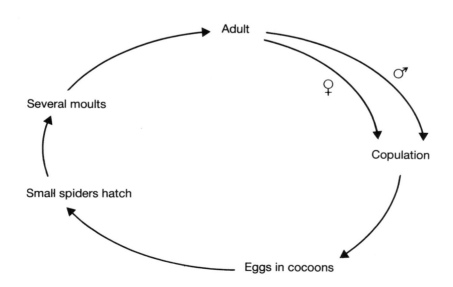

PHYLUM: ARTHROPODA

CLASS: INSECTA

Three pairs of walking legs. Usually two pairs of wings. Body divided into head, thorax and abdomen. One pair of antennae. Compound eyes. Complete or incomplete metamorphosis occurs. Respiration by tracheae, guarded by spiracles.

ORDER: LEPIDOPTERA

Maxillae form proboscis. Complete metamorphosis egg → larva → pupa → imago. Wings large and covered in scales.

PIERIS SP.: THE CABBAGE-WHITE BUTTERFLY

Large curled proboscis. Not covered in hairs. Wings brightly coloured. Two generations per year.

Life history

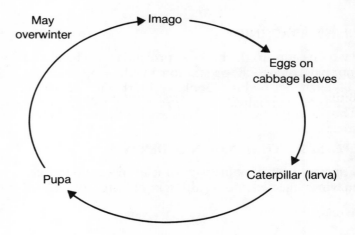

Imago (adult) (× 2)

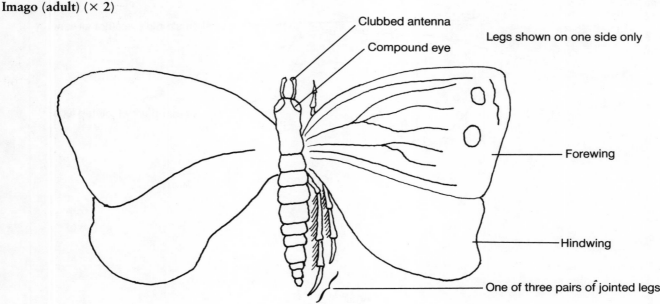

Clubbed antenna
Compound eye
Legs shown on one side only
Forewing
Hindwing
One of three pairs of jointed legs

Larva (caterpillar) (× 2)

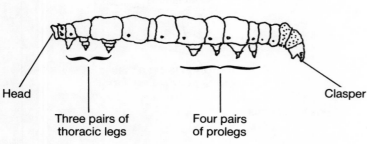

Ocelli on head not visible

Head

Three pairs of thoracic legs

Four pairs of prolegs

Clasper

Pupa (× 2)

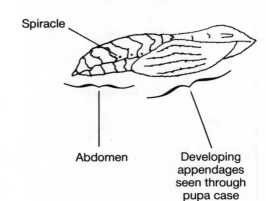

Spiracle

Abdomen

Developing appendages seen through pupa case

PHYLUM: ARTHROPODA

CLASS: INSECTA

ORDER: HYMENOPTERA

Biting or sucking mouthparts. Two pairs of wings. Thorax and first abdominal segment fused. Colonial; social.

APIS SP.: THE HONEY BEE

Worker (× 2)

Worker: Sterile female; ovipositor modified to form sting. Sucking mouthparts. Produce wax for comb; feed larvae, collect pollen and nectar, clean and ventilate hive. Life span, 6 weeks.

Drone: Fertile male. Larger, with no sting. Fed by workers; fertilise queen. Killed in autumn.

Queen: Larger body than worker. Sting with no barb. Fed by workers. Lays eggs. May set up new colony. Lives several years. Fertilised in flight by drone. Lays eggs in comb cells → female larvae. If these are fed on royal jelly → queens, if on honey and pollen → workers. Unfertilised eggs → drones. Secretes a substance which inhibits the production of a new queen. If queen dies, or colony enlarges, a new queen can develop. Leads a swarm to form a new colony.

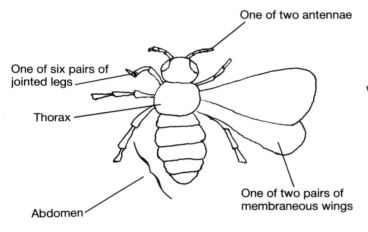

Life history

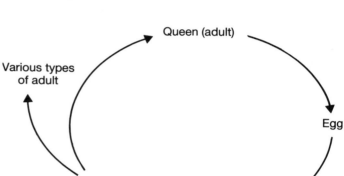

Leg of worker bee   3rd leg (× 10)

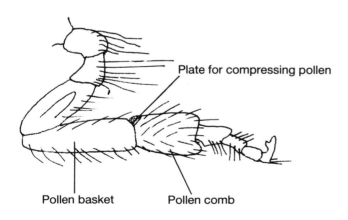

**Wing (× 10)
(to show arrangement of veins)**

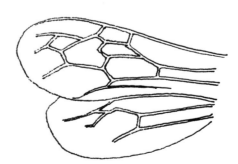

The two wings are attached by microscopic hooklets to act as one unit

PHYLUM: ARTHROPODA

CLASS: INSECTA

ORDER: ORTHOPTERA

Biting mouthparts. Third pair of legs enlarged for jumping. Bear organs for stridulation – a mating call.

LOCUSTA SP.: THE LOCUST

Hemimetabolous. Egg → nymphal stages → adult. Feed on vegetation in warm regions of the world. Swarms, triggered off by overcrowding, are of economic importance.

Locust wing (× 2)

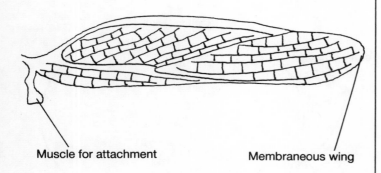

Muscle for attachment   Membraneous wing

LOCUST: INSTRUCTIONS FOR A GENERAL DISSECTION

1 Remove the wings. You can remove the first two pairs of legs as well if you feel it is necessary.
2 Make a cut dorsally along the right-hand side of the abdomen, fairly near the last segments, and continue up dorso-laterally to the anterior end of the thorax.
3 Place ventral surface down on a dissecting tray with wax. Put a pin through the last segment of the abdomen.
4 Put a pin through each femur of the last pair of legs. Flood dish with water.
5 Carefully deepen your incision through the cuticle of the thorax, cutting the muscles lying dorsoventrally below.
6 Cut across laterally at the anterior end of the thorax and the posterior end of the abdomen to make a flap which you can turn over to the left-hand side and pin down. You will see along the length of this flap the 'heart' – a long tube with dilations in each segment.
7 Remove the whitish-yellow fat body and most of the tracheal system.
8 Pin the hind gut to one side just above the last abdominal segment. This exposes the reproductive system and the ventral nerve cord.
9 If you wish to trace the nervous system into the head, make two incisions, one on each side of the head capsule.
10 Remove the cuticle between the cuts.
11 Carefully remove as much muscle as possible.
12 Trace out the various ganglia and connectives. (70% alcohol applied to the nerves in a freshly-killed insect enables them to be more clearly seen.)

Locust mouth parts (× 4)

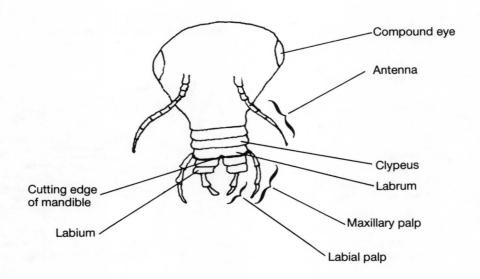

Compound eye

Antenna

Clypeus

Labrum

Maxillary palp

Labial palp

Cutting edge of mandible

Labium

Stages in the life history of instars
See page 30.

LOCUST: GENERAL DISSECTION OF THE FEMALE
(× 3)

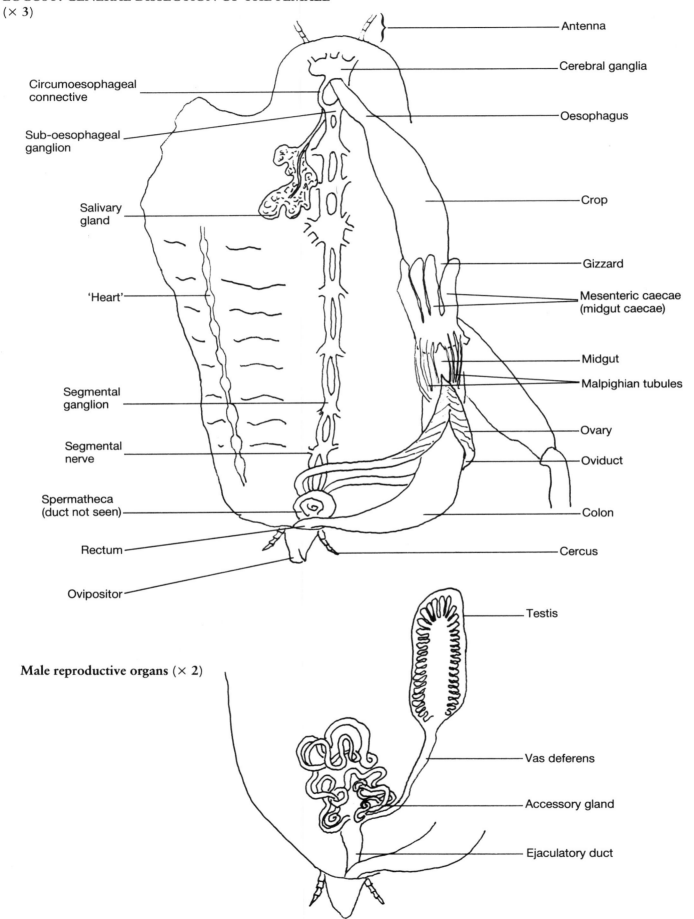

Antenna

Cerebral ganglia

Circumoesophageal connective

Oesophagus

Sub-oesophageal ganglion

Salivary gland

Crop

Gizzard

'Heart'

Mesenteric caecae (midgut caecae)

Midgut

Malpighian tubules

Segmental ganglion

Segmental nerve

Ovary

Oviduct

Spermatheca (duct not seen)

Colon

Rectum

Cercus

Ovipositor

Testis

Male reproductive organs (× 2)

Vas deferens

Accessory gland

Ejaculatory duct

LOCUSTA MIGRATORIA (× 2)

Instars: stages in life history

Appendages shown
on one side only

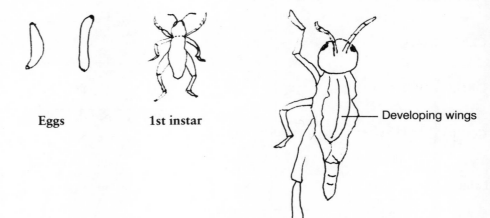

Eggs   1st instar

Developing wings

3rd instar

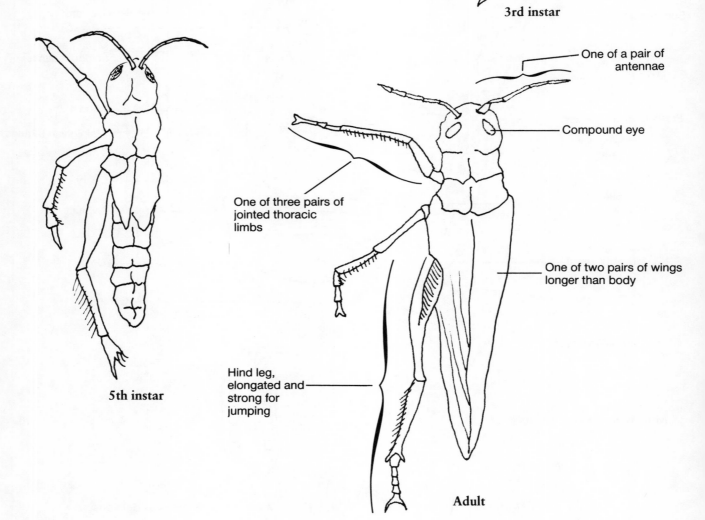

5th instar

One of a pair of
antennae

Compound eye

One of three pairs of
jointed thoracic
limbs

One of two pairs of wings
longer than body

Hind leg,
elongated and
strong for
jumping

Adult

Abdominal segments (× 2)

Male

Ovipositor
valves

Female

PHYLUM: ARTHROPODA

CLASS: INSECTA

ORDER: ORTHOPTERA

COCKROACH MOUTH PARTS (× 20)

Labium

Maxilla

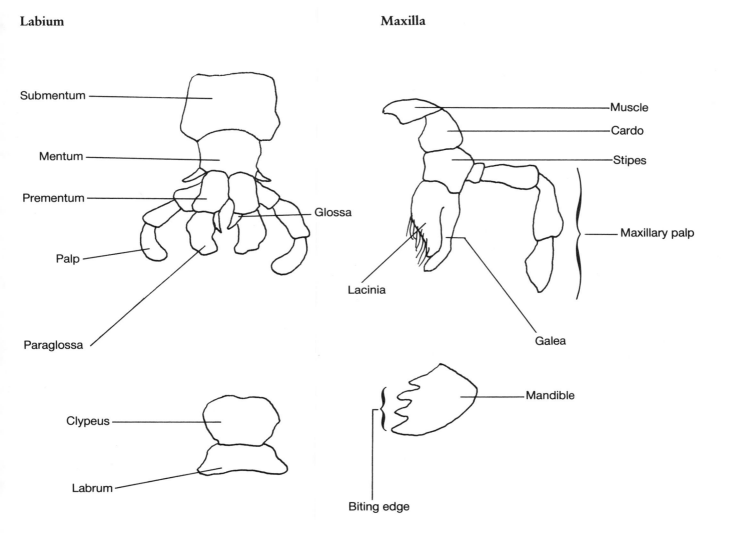

PHYLUM: MOLLUSCA

Unsegmented, often bilaterally symmetrical. Triploblastic. Head, muscular foot, and visceral hump. May be covered with shell, secreted by the mantle — an extension of the visceral hump. Coelom reduced — haemocoel.

CLASS: GASTROPODA

Tentacles — visceral bump twisted (torsion) so that anus lies above the head. Radula present.

HELIX SP.: THE SNAIL (× 1)

Terrestrial forms, feeding on vegetable matter. Hibernate in winter by sealing the shell.

Life history

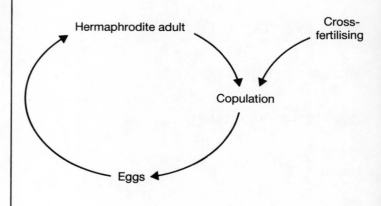

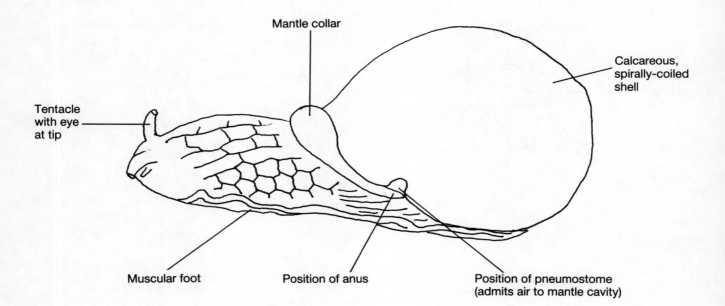

Dorsal view of shell

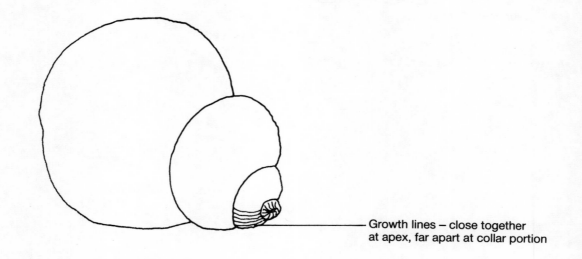

PHYLUM: MOLLUSCA

CLASS: LAMELLIBRANCHIATA

Bivalves. Head reduced; no tentacles or eyes. Gills. All
aquatic.

MYTILUS SP.: THE MUSSEL (× 2)

Marine or freshwater. Attached to rocks or stones by
byssus threads.

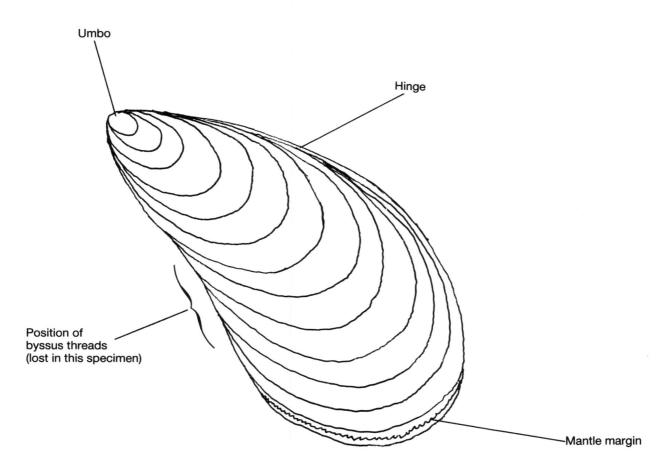

Life history

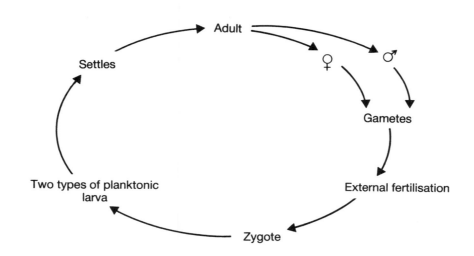

PHYLUM: ECHINODERMATA

Radially symmetrical (often pentamerous — radiating in five directions). Coelomate; not segmented. No head. Water-vascular system, dilating tube feet. Exoskeleton of calcareous plates. Sexes separate.

CLASS: ASTEROIDEA

Star-shaped; flat body. Pouches of gut into each 'arm'. Mouth ventral. Gills, pedicellariae and spines on outer surface.

ASTERIAS SP.: THE STARFISH

Dorsal view (× 1)
(aboral surface)

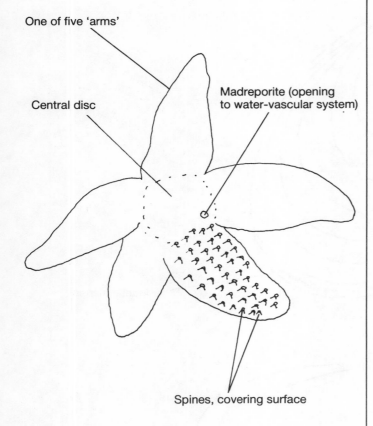

One of five 'arms'

Central disc

Madreporite (opening to water-vascular system)

Spines, covering surface

Skin gills and pedicellaria not seen

Ventral view (× 1)
(oral surface)

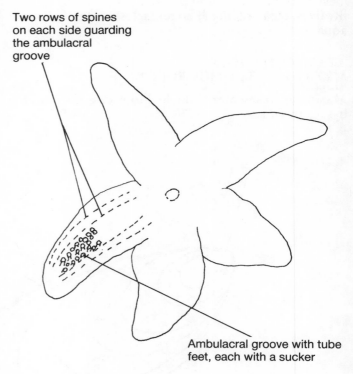

Two rows of spines on each side guarding the ambulacral groove

Ambulacral groove with tube feet, each with a sucker

Live on rocky and sandy surfaces, just below the intertidal zone. Feed off bottom-living molluscs, usually bivalves, using tube feet to pull them apart. Sexes separate. External fertilisation.

Life history

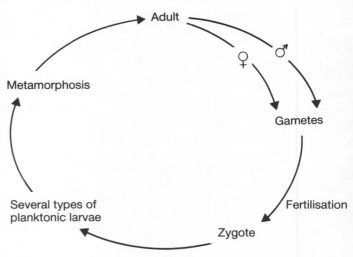

Adult

Metamorphosis

Gametes

Several types of planktonic larvae

Fertilisation

Zygote

PHYLUM: CHORDATA (VERTEBRATA)

Possess notochord at some time of life. Dorsal hollow nerve cord. Closed blood system. Post anal tail. Well-developed brain. Skeleton internal — bone or cartilage. Kidneys; heart. Usually two pairs of limbs.

CLASS: OSTEICHTHYES

Bony fish. Covering of bony scales. Air bladder as outgrowth of the gut. Visceral clefts persist as gills. Lateral line system.

CLUPEA SP.: THE HERRING (× ½)

Pelagic. Plankton feeders when young, later other small fish and crustaceans.

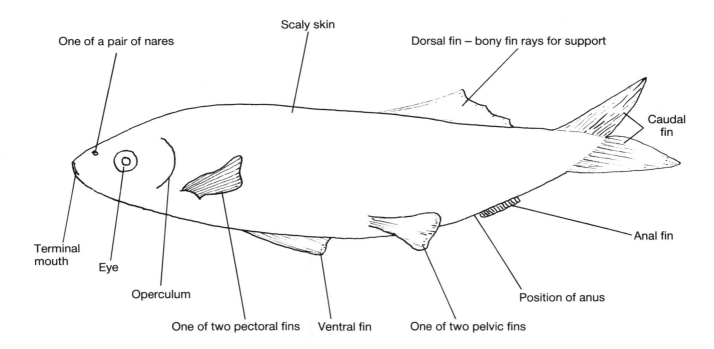

Life history

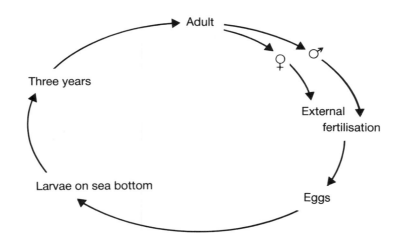

PHYLUM: CHORDATA

CLASS: AMPHIBIA

Pentadactyl limbs. Soft skin with mucous glands. Gills in larvae, lungs in adult.

ORDER: ANURA

No tail in adult, nor gills. Hind limbs modified for jumping.

RANA SP.: THE FROG

Found in damp vegetation near ponds and ditches. Feed on invertebrates, e.g. snails, worms and grasshoppers. Hibernate at the bottom of the pond in winter.

Life history

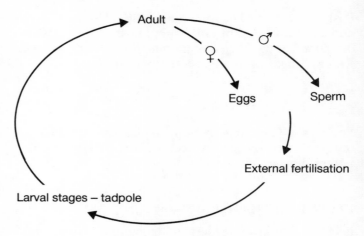

(Order Urodela: e.g. Triturus, the newt. Retains gills and tail.)

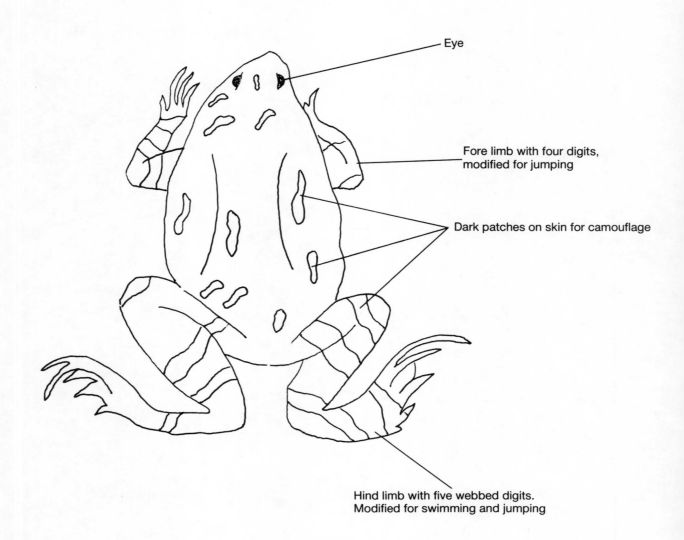

RANA TEMPORARIA: STAGES IN LIFE HISTORY (× 1)

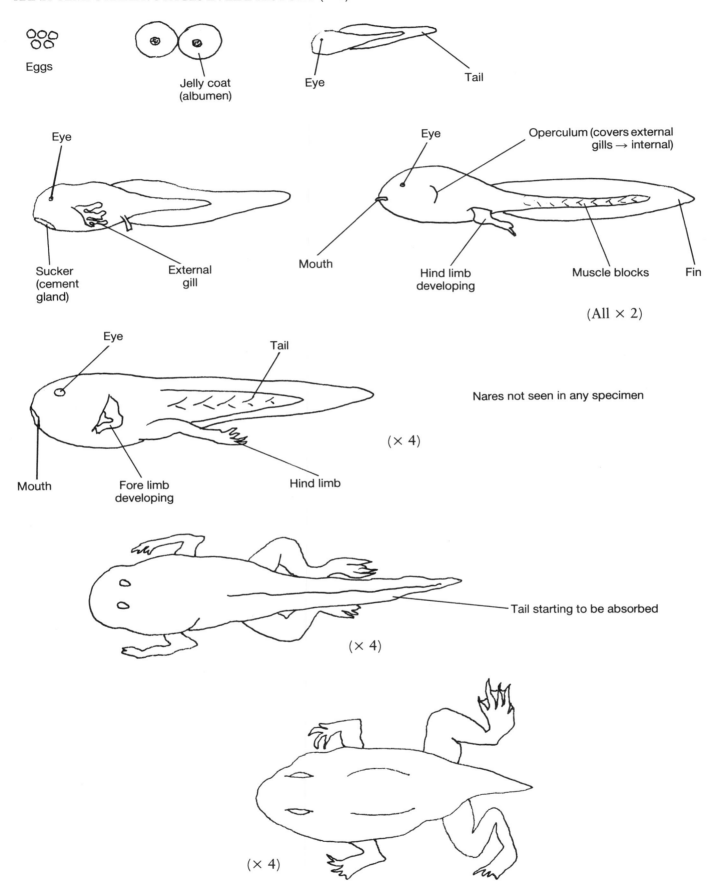

Eggs

Jelly coat (albumen)

Eye

Tail

Eye

Sucker (cement gland)

External gill

Eye

Operculum (covers external gills → internal)

Mouth

Hind limb developing

Muscle blocks

Fin

(All × 2)

Eye

Tail

Nares not seen in any specimen

Mouth

Fore limb developing

Hind limb

(× 4)

Tail starting to be absorbed

(× 4)

(× 4)

Tadpole at later stage of metamorphosis

PHYLUM: CHORDATA

CLASS: REPTILIA

Skin with horny scales. Lungs. Lay large yolky eggs with horny shell. No larval stage.

LACERTA SP.: THE LIZARD

Feed on insects and spiders. Colonize dry sunny areas. Internal fertilization. Some species are viviparous, giving birth to live young after eggs develop inside the female for 3 months.

($\times$ 1)

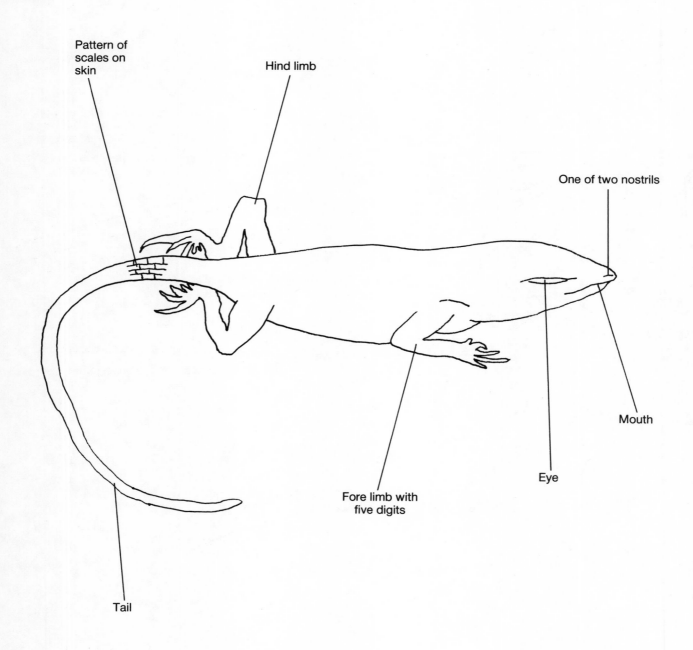

PHYLUM: CHORDATA

CLASS: AVES

Homiothermic. Fore limbs modified to wings. Feathers over body, except for the legs with scales. Lungs. Large yolky eggs in calcareous shells. Various habitats and feeding methods. Build nests in which to rear young. Parental care.

BIRD, e.g. ROBIN (× 1)

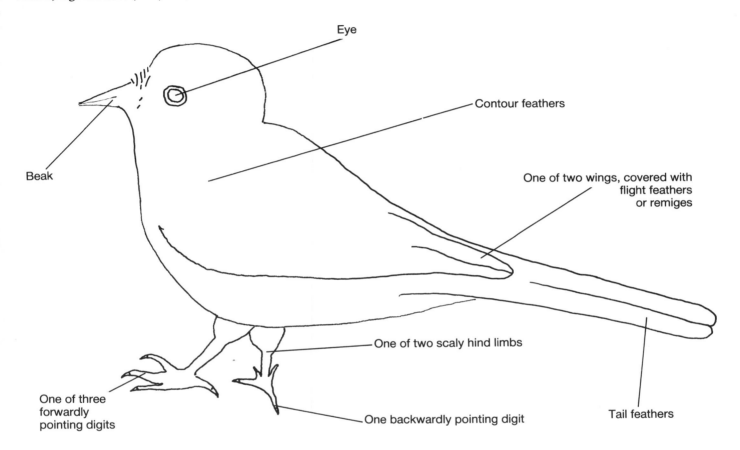

Skeleton of fore limb (× 1)

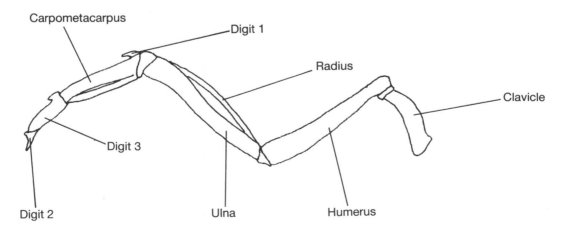

5   MAMMALIAN ANATOMY AND HISTOLOGY

PHYLUM: CHORDATA

CLASS: MAMMALIA

Homiothermic. Skin with hair. Young fed on milk
from mammary glands. Development internal, in uterus.
Lungs. External ears (pinnae). Diaphragm.

EUTHERIA: TRUE PLACENTAL MAMMALS

ORDER: RODENTIA

One pair of upper incisors — enamel on front only.
No canines. Plantigrade limbs.

***MUS MUSCULUS*: THE MOUSE (× 1)**

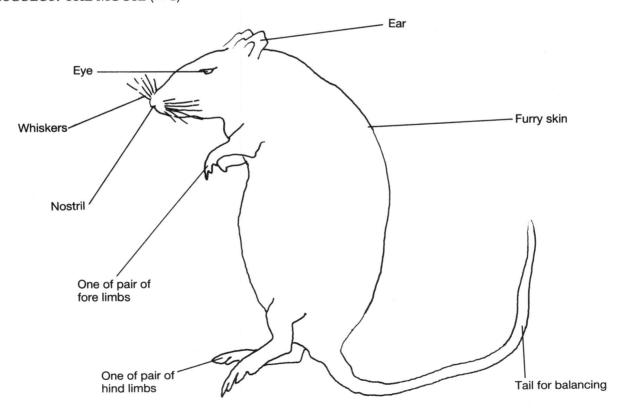

Herbivorous; several litters of young per year.

DISSECTION OF THE MOUSE

INSTRUCTIONS FOR DISSECTION

1 Damp the fur of the mouse to reduce risk of it becoming loose and interfering with the dissection.

2 Lay the animal on its back in a dissecting dish with wax. Secure the limbs with awls placed in position just below the paws. Be *very* careful at this stage not to stretch the arms too far — the blood vessels from the heart to the upper limbs are very easily broken by doing so.

3 Make an incision over the middle of the abdomen in the mid-ventral line. Lift up the skin, which is quite loose, with coarse forceps and insert the point of the scissors.

4 Continue cutting up the mid-ventral line between the lower abdomen and the thorax. Keep the points of your coarse scissors upwards so as not to cut the underlying body wall.

5 At the level of the sternum, take your cut laterally into each upper limb. Just above the position of the bladder, cut laterally along the skin of the lower limbs. This will give you two flaps of skin to pin out sideways.

6 Carefully loosen the skin from the body wall by gently tearing away the underlying connective tissue with a needle or a scalpel.

7 Repeat this pattern of cuts in the body wall, still keeping the points of your fine scissors upwards to avoid damaging the gut.

8 Take care to avoid damaging the diaphragm with your lateral cuts at the level of the rib-cage. Pin out the body wall. The gut is now visible *in situ* and may be drawn, if wished.

9 Flood the dish with water to make the display of the gut somewhat easier.

10 Normally, the aim is to display the gut and its associated organs. This includes mesenteries in which there are blood vessels supplying the gut, e.g. branches of the coeliaco-mesenteric artery and vein. In order to display the gut properly, it must be untwisted as far as possible, while endeavouring to leave most mesenteries intact. It is usually easier to displace the folds of the small intestine to one side, and the folds of the large intestine to the other. As the mouse is so small, it is sometimes allowable to leave one loop of the large intestine passing over the small intestine, rather than try to disentangle it completely.

11 Make sure that you have clearly displayed the junction of the stomach and duodenum.

12 In the mesentery in this area you should be able to see the tiny leaf-shaped pancreas.

13 It is here, where the large and small intestine cross, that you should try to display the hepatic portal vein. Gently pull the strand of the small intestine away from the loop of the large intestine, and twist the bulk of the large intestine over and away, to your right. This should free the two parts of the intestine from each other, and still leave the hepatic portal vein intact. However, in some small specimens this blood vessel is not clearly visible.

14 Make sure that the caecum is well displayed, as well as the area where the rectum passes into the anus.

15 Because the mouse is so small, you may not be able to see the bile duct.

16 Pin out the loops of the gut to display them to the best advantage, without destroying too many mesenteries. Draw your dissection.

17 Make special note of any structures that you know to be present but could not see. You will probably have to leave the fatty tissue surrounding the blood vessels in the mesenteries — this may be quite pronounced in a well-fed specimen, and is too difficult to remove.

**DISSECTION TO SHOW ALIMENTARY CANAL AND
ASSOCIATED ORGANS** (× 1)

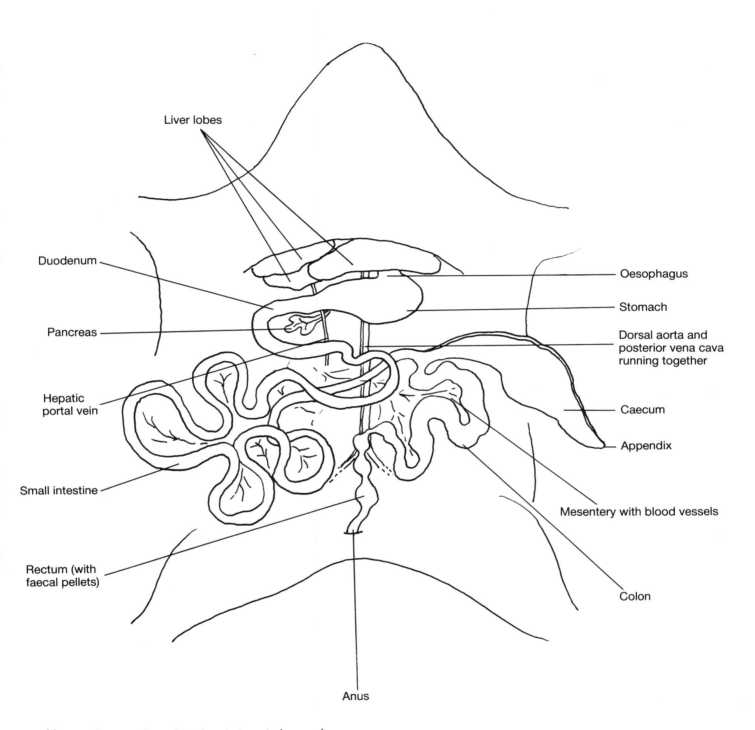

Liver lobes

Duodenum

Pancreas

Hepatic
portal vein

Small intestine

Rectum (with
faecal pellets)

Oesophagus

Stomach

Dorsal aorta and
posterior vena cava
running together

Caecum

Appendix

Mesentery with blood vessels

Colon

Anus

Mesenteric artery from dorsal aorta to gut obscured

PREPARING TO DISSECT THE URINOGENITAL SYSTEMS OF THE MOUSE

1 Carefully remove the gut by first cutting through the rectum just above the anus. Take care not to damage the bladder or the reproductive organs while doing this.
2 Cut across the oesophagus just above the cardiac end of the stomach.
3 Cut through the major blood vessels joining the gut to the dorsal aorta and the posterior vena cava. Remove the entire gut.
4 The liver may also be removed.
5 Clear away the fatty tissue surrounding the ureters. Remove also the fat obscuring the bladder region.
6 Dorsal aorta, posterior vena cava, renal arteries and veins must be cleared of mesentery and other debris. The examiners expect that a seeker could be slid underneath a blood vessel or ureter along its length (at least on one side, where paired structures are involved).

MALE URINOGENITAL SYSTEM

1 Cut open one testis sac, and display testis *in situ*. (In the mouse it frequently happens that the testes come out of their sacs and are lying free in the body cavity.)
2 Try not to detach the epididymis from the testis.
3 Turn the bladder to one side and pin so as to show the opening of at least one ureter into the bladder.
4 Make sure that the way the vas deferens loops over the ureter before entering the top of the urethra is clearly shown.
5 Make two cuts, one on either side of the lower part of the urethra, through the pelvic girdle.
6 Remove the small piece of bone and dissect out the underlying tissues.
7 Turn the seminal vesicles over to the same side as the bladder. Secure with a pin, if necessary.

In the mouse you may not be able to see all the accessory reproductive glands, like the prostate, or Cowper's glands, especially if the animal is young.

MOUSE: MALE URINOGENITAL SYSTEM (× 1)

Dissected from ventral surface

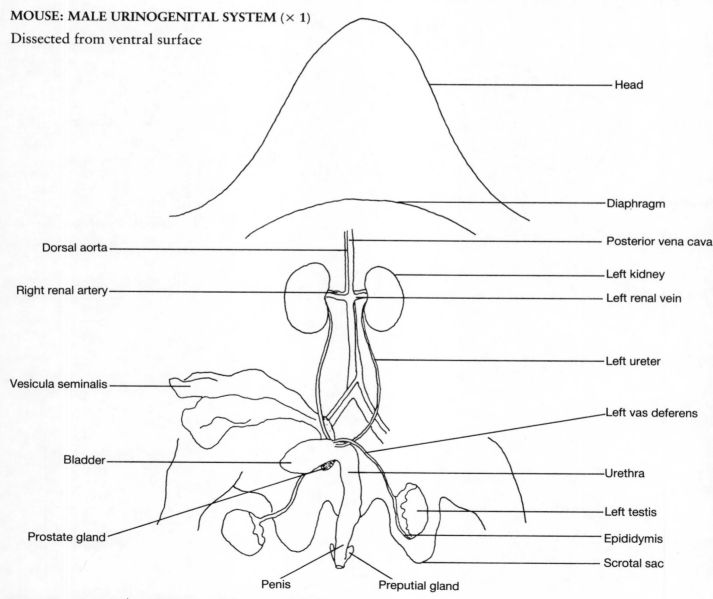

Spermatic cord not seen. Adrenal and Cowper's glands not seen (generally too small to see in the mouse)

FEMALE URINOGENITAL SYSTEM

Most of this will be displayed *in situ* when you remove the gut. The uterus may be very small, quite large, or contain embryos. You may have difficulty in seeing the ovary. In any case, the ovarian vein is very rarely seen.

As in the male, cut through the pelvis, extend the hind limbs out a little further, and dissect out all the underlying tissues.

DISSECTION OF THE THORAX

(Nerves are not usually taken into account in the mouse — they are too fine to be seen.)

1 Cut carefully along the base of the rib-cage, but *above* the diaphragm, endeavouring to leave that intact.
2 Cut anteriorly along the ribs as near as possible to the dorsal surface, on each side. Turn back the flap of the rib-cage.
3 Carefully cut through the top (anterior end) of the sternum and remove the rib-cage.
4 The brachial and subclavian veins are very near the surface and must be traced out first. Trace them backwards from the front of the fore limb, where you can usually see them clearly through the body tissue, to the heart. (The vessels are very small — a dissecting lens will help.)
5 Trace out all the vessels *as far as you can* into the fore limbs and up into the neck.
6 Displace the heart to the right side (left as you look at the dissection). Hold it in position by wedging with a pin.
7 You should now be able to see the pulmonary veins returning from the lungs, together with the main aorta, and the branches arising from it. (If your mouse is freshly killed, a little alcohol pipetted onto the vessels will help to harden them and stop any bleeding. Remove water from the dish first.)

Always draw your dissection as it is — marks are awarded for the way in which the drawing resembles the dissection. In some examinations, only the drawings are marked by the examiner, after previously being assessed for their degree of similarity to the dissection. If you should cut or lose anything, show its original position by dotted lines, and label accordingly.

MOUSE: FEMALE URINOGENITAL SYSTEM (× 1)

Dissected from ventral surface

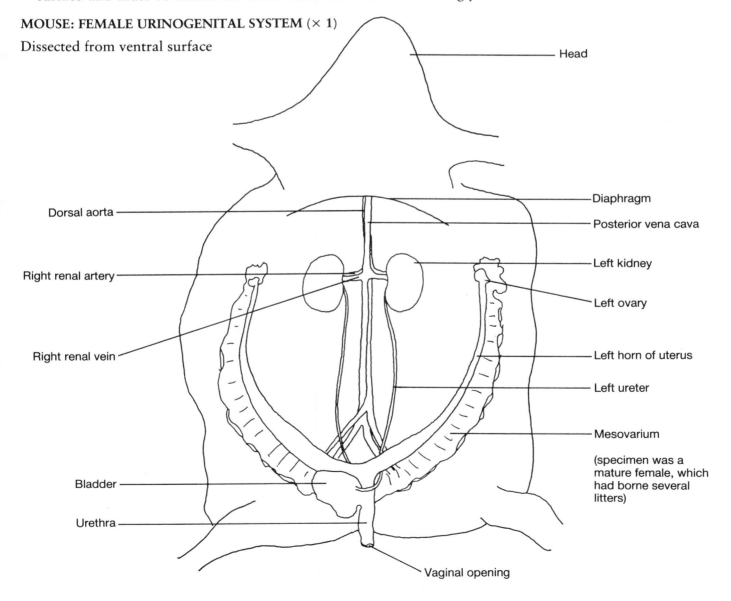

- Head
- Diaphragm
- Posterior vena cava
- Left kidney
- Left ovary
- Left horn of uterus
- Left ureter
- Mesovarium

(specimen was a mature female, which had borne several litters)

- Dorsal aorta
- Right renal artery
- Right renal vein
- Bladder
- Urethra
- Vaginal opening

MOUSE: THORAX DISSECTION (INCLUDING
LOWER REGIONS OF NECK) (× 1)

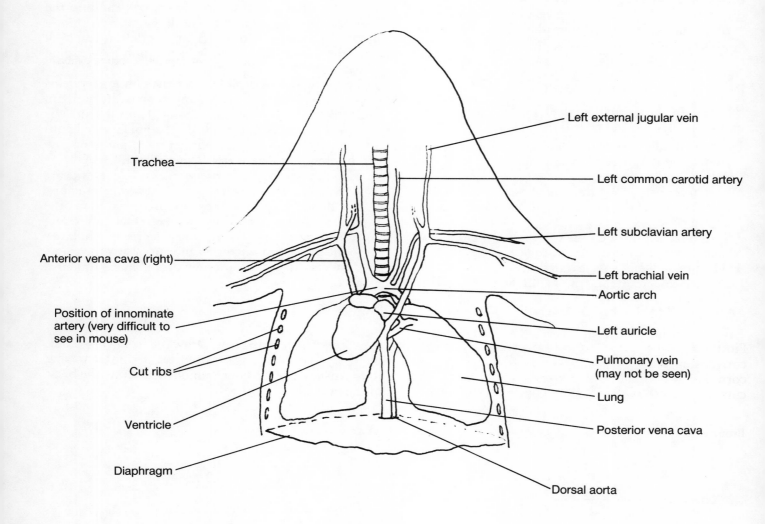

Trachea

Anterior vena cava (right)

Position of innominate
artery (very difficult to
see in mouse)

Cut ribs

Ventricle

Diaphragm

Left external jugular vein

Left common carotid artery

Left subclavian artery

Left brachial vein

Aortic arch

Left auricle

Pulmonary vein
(may not be seen)

Lung

Posterior vena cava

Dorsal aorta

Ductus arteriosus and azygos vein too small to see. Division of
common carotid arteries into internal and external branches too
small to follow.

DISSECTION OF THE MAMMALIAN EYE,
e.g. OX (× 1)

Draw the external features.

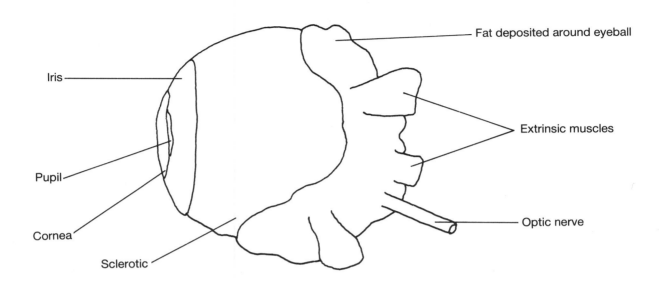

Pin the eye to the wax of a dissecting dish with the cornea directed upwards. Make an incision into the cornea in front of the pupil. Extend out into four radial cuts towards the sclerotic. Keep your scissors upwards to avoid damage to the lens. Draw the front view when the four flaps of tissue are deflected backwards. Remove lens and vitreous humour and draw the back of the eyeball.

Front view (× 1)

Internal view (× 1)

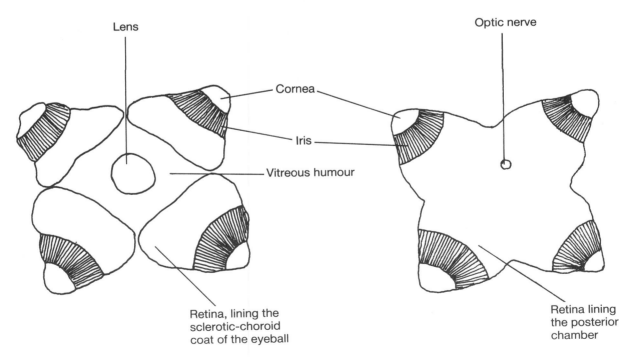

DISSECTION OF THE MAMMALIAN HEART, e.g. LAMB

Remove as much fat as possible to expose the blood vessels. Your specimen may or may not have a complete set of blood vessels; complete specimens are a little difficult to obtain. Draw the external features.

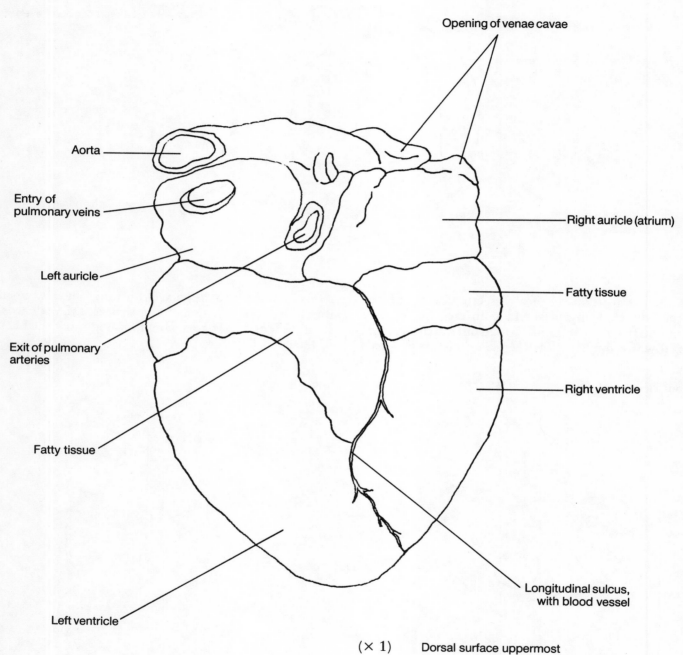

Opening of venae cavae

Aorta

Entry of pulmonary veins

Left auricle

Exit of pulmonary arteries

Fatty tissue

Left ventricle

Right auricle (atrium)

Fatty tissue

Right ventricle

Longitudinal sulcus, with blood vessel

(× 1)   Dorsal surface uppermost

The left ventricle has a thicker wall than the right ventricle. Having identified the right ventricle, make a longitudinal incision through it just to the right of the longitudinal sulcus (the fatty groove separating the two ventricles). Continue the incision up through the right auricle. Wash out any blood. Cut open the pulmonary artery to display the three semilunar valves where the artery leaves the ventricle. Make a similar incision through the left auricle and ventricle. Cut open the aorta to display the semilunar valves at the point where it leaves the ventricle. Make drawings of more than one view so as to show as much structure as possible.

HEART DISSECTED: VENTRAL VIEW (× 1)

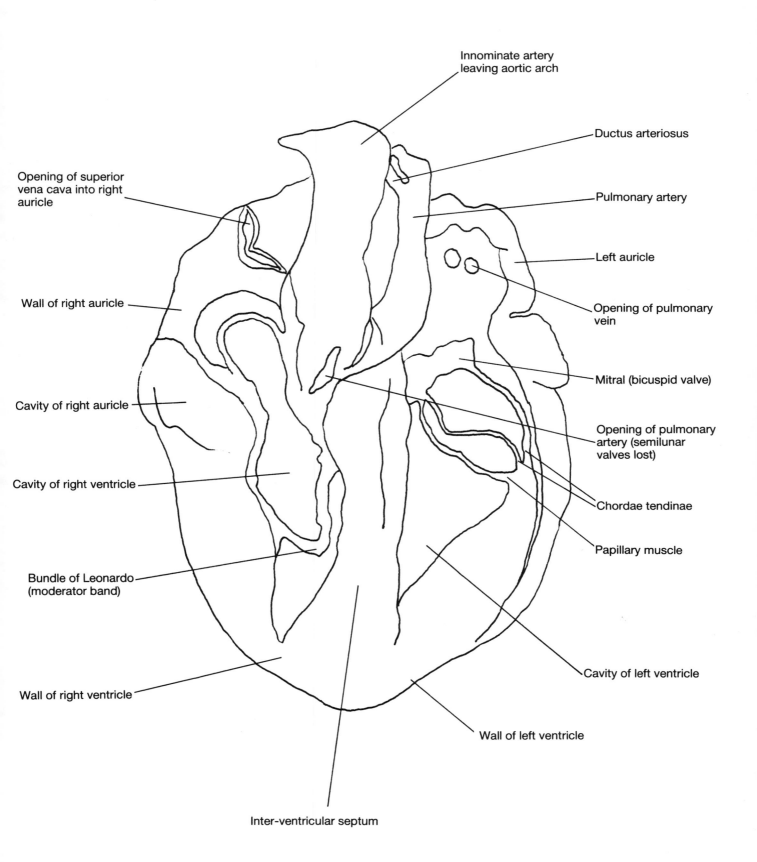

Innominate artery
leaving aortic arch

Ductus arteriosus

Pulmonary artery

Opening of superior
vena cava into right
auricle

Left auricle

Opening of pulmonary
vein

Wall of right auricle

Mitral (bicuspid valve)

Cavity of right auricle

Opening of pulmonary
artery (semilunar
valves lost)

Cavity of right ventricle

Chordae tendinae

Papillary muscle

Bundle of Leonardo
(moderator band)

Cavity of left ventricle

Wall of right ventricle

Wall of left ventricle

Inter-ventricular septum

HEART DISSECTED: VIEW FROM LEFT SIDE (× 1)

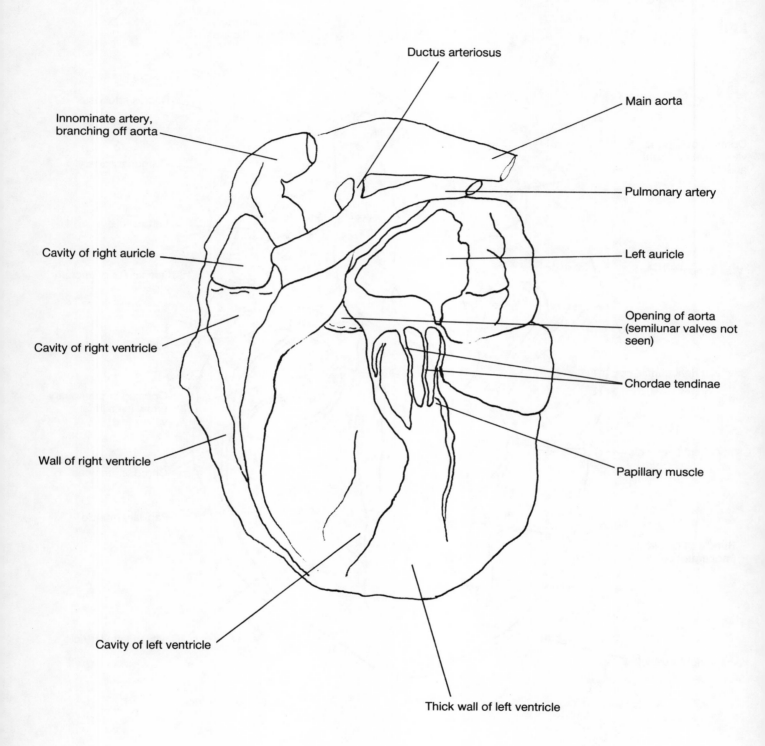

Ductus arteriosus

Main aorta

Innominate artery, branching off aorta

Pulmonary artery

Cavity of right auricle

Left auricle

Opening of aorta (semilunar valves not seen)

Cavity of right ventricle

Chordae tendinae

Wall of right ventricle

Papillary muscle

Cavity of left ventricle

Thick wall of left ventricle

DISSECTION OF THE MAMMALIAN KIDNEY e.g. PIG

Divide the kidney into right and left halves, leaving the ureter on one half. Draw this cut surface.

LS (× 1)

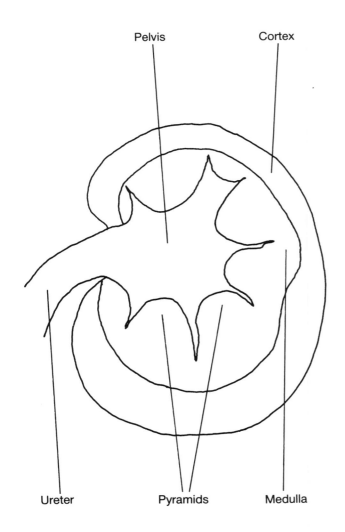

Pelvis

Cortex

Ureter

Pyramids

Medulla

MAMMALIAN FOETUS, e.g. RAT (× 1)

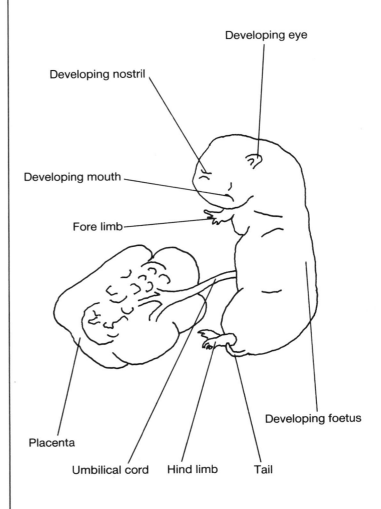

Developing eye

Developing nostril

Developing mouth

Fore limb

Developing foetus

Placenta

Umbilical cord

Hind limb

Tail

MAMMALIAN SKULLS

DOG (× 1) (EXAMPLE OF A CARNIVORE)

Dental formula $\dfrac{3142}{3143} = 42$

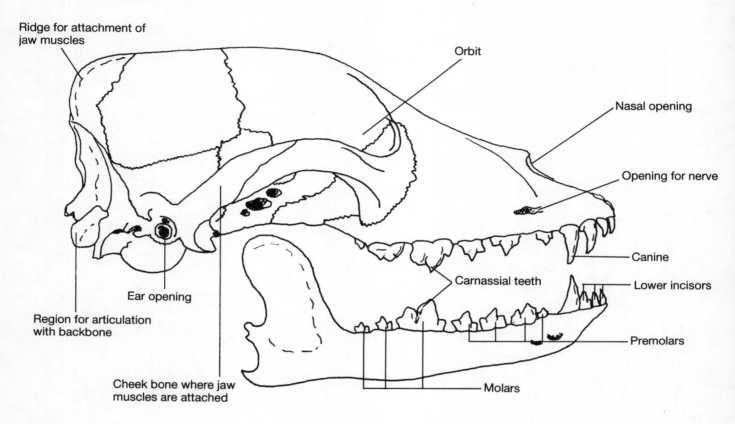

Ridge for attachment of
jaw muscles

Orbit

Nasal opening

Opening for nerve

Canine

Carnassial teeth

Lower incisors

Ear opening

Premolars

Region for articulation
with backbone

Cheek bone where jaw
muscles are attached

Molars

SHEEP (× ½) (EXAMPLE OF A HERBIVORE)

Dental formula $\dfrac{0033}{3133} = 32$

Teeth with open roots

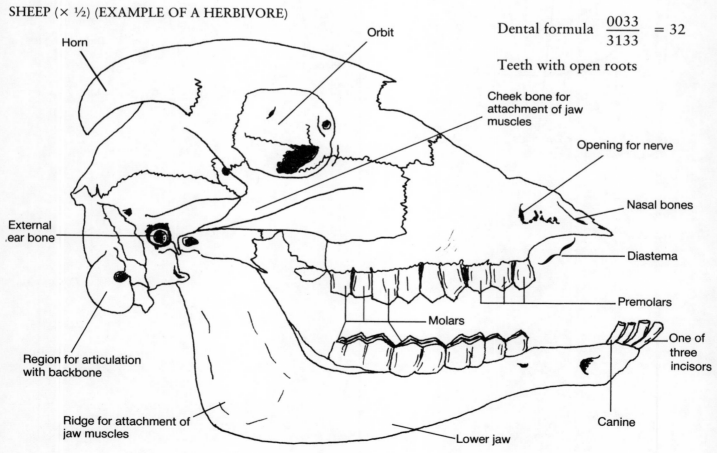

Horn

Orbit

Cheek bone for
attachment of jaw
muscles

Opening for nerve

Nasal bones

External
ear bone

Diastema

Premolars

Molars

One of
three
incisors

Region for articulation
with backbone

Ridge for attachment of
jaw muscles

Lower jaw

Canine

MAMMALIAN VERTEBRAE, e.g. RABBIT (× 2)

CERVICAL

Anterior view

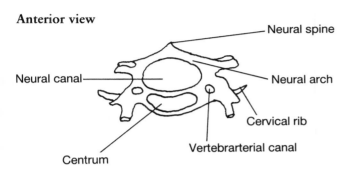

Left lateral view

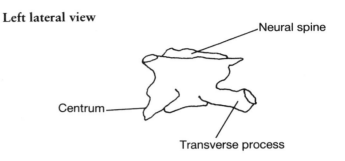

THORACIC

Anterior view

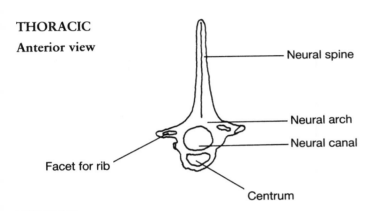

Left lateral view

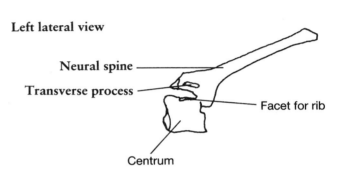

LUMBAR

Anterior view

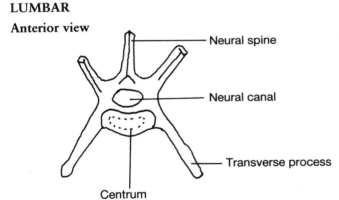

Left lateral view

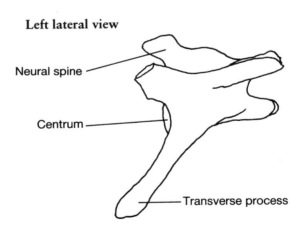

Vertebra	Neural spine	Transverse processes (zygapophyses)
1 Cervical	Very short	Very wide and flat in first cervical (Atlas); odontoid process in second cervical (Axis). Cervical ribs
2 Thoracic	Long and backwardly directed; thin	Very short
3 Lumbar	Short and thick; forwardly projecting	Very long and stout. Lower ones pointing forwards; upper ones on both anterior and posterior ends

MAMMALIAN VERTEBRAE, e.g. RABBIT (× 2)

ATLAS
Anterior view

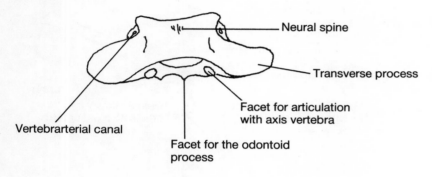

- Neural spine
- Neural arch
- Transverse process
- Facet for articulation with skull
- Neural canal

AXIS
Left lateral view

- Neural spine
- Odontoid process
- Surface for articulation with Atlas vertebra
- Centrum

From above

- Neural spine
- Transverse process
- Facet for articulation with axis vertebra
- Facet for the odontoid process
- Vertebrarterial canal

SACRUM (four vertebrae fused)
Dorsal view   Left lateral view

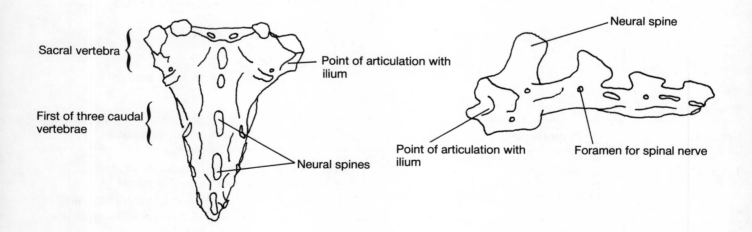

- Sacral vertebra
- First of three caudal vertebrae
- Point of articulation with ilium
- Neural spines

- Neural spine
- Point of articulation with ilium
- Foramen for spinal nerve

MAMMALIAN LIMB GIRDLES, e.g. RABBIT

PECTORAL GIRDLE

Clavicle very much reduced in rabbit. In a running or jumping animal the clavicle would be too easily damaged.

Dorsal view (× 2)
Left Scapula

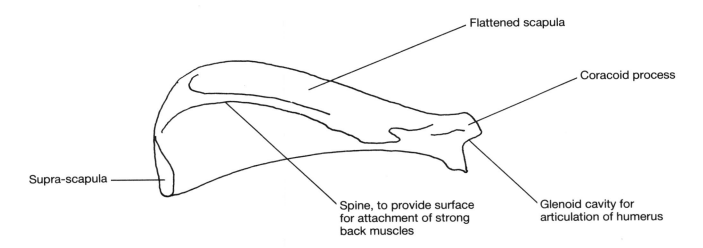

Flattened scapula

Coracoid process

Supra-scapula

Spine, to provide surface for attachment of strong back muscles

Glenoid cavity for articulation of humerus

PELVIC GIRDLE (× 2)

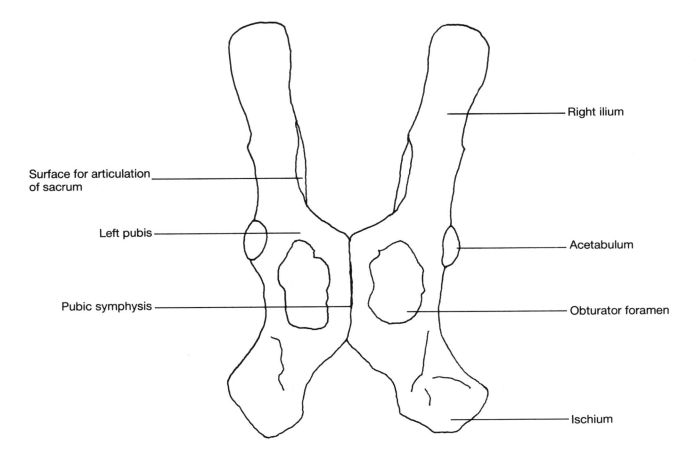

Right ilium

Surface for articulation of sacrum

Left pubis

Acetabulum

Pubic symphysis

Obturator foramen

Ischium

MAMMALIAN LIMBS, e.g. RABBIT

FORE LIMB (× 1)

May have fused radius and ulna to absorb shock of
landing, or for strength in digging. Olecranon process
present — long in running mammals, with phalanges
reduced. In digging types, e.g. the mole, the carpals
and metacarpals may be fused.

HIND LIMB (× 1)

May be long and thick in jumping types; longer and
thinner in running mammals.

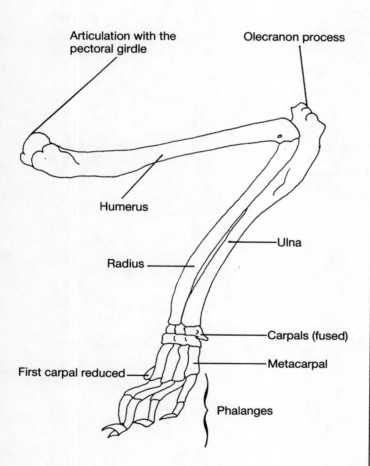

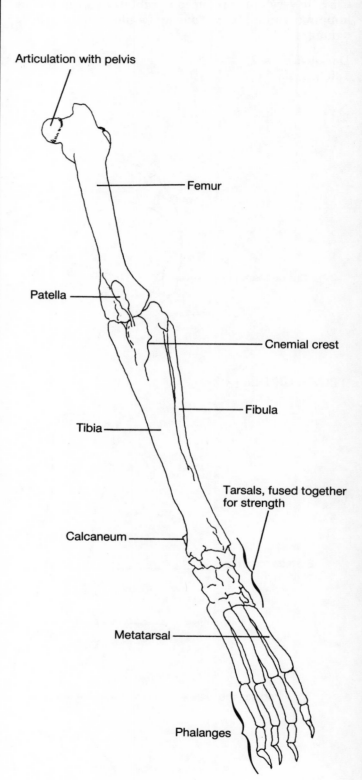

TISSUES

A **tissue** is a collection of similar cells, all specialised for one particular purpose.

EPITHELIAL TISSUES

These are cells lining a surface, usually only one cell thick, except where protection is needed. Easily replaced. Rest usually on a basement membrane.

PAVEMENT EPITHELIUM (× 400), e.g. CHEEK LINING

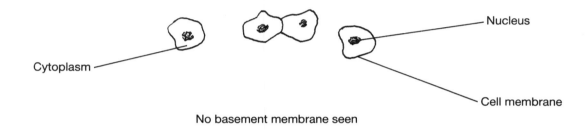

Cytoplasm

Nucleus

Cell membrane

No basement membrane seen

STRATIFIED EPITHELIUM (× 400), e.g. OESOPHAGUS

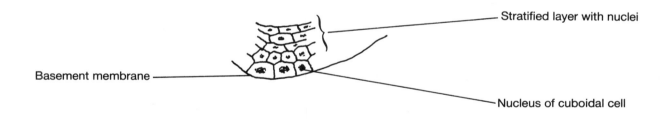

Basement membrane

Stratified layer with nuclei

Nucleus of cuboidal cell

COLUMNAR EPITHELIUM (× 400), e.g. LINING OF GALL BLADDER

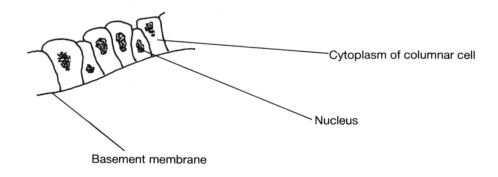

Cytoplasm of columnar cell

Nucleus

Basement membrane

CONNECTIVE TISSUES

These have a large amount of intercellular substance, secreted usually by the cells themselves. Some tissues have fibres in them.

BLOOD, e.g. HUMAN (× 400)

Fluid matrix, not secreted by blood cells. Contains disc-shaped corpuscles; red ones with no nuclei, white with various types of nuclei. (N.B. Frog and bird red cells have nuclei.)

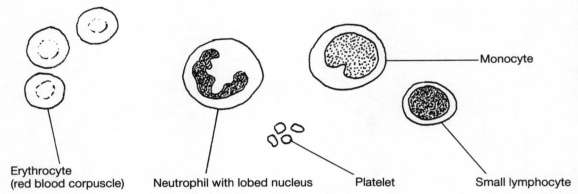

Erythrocyte (red blood corpuscle)

Neutrophil with lobed nucleus

Platelet

Monocyte

Small lymphocyte

BONE

Solid, rigid matrix with calcium salts, mainly phosphates. Haversian systems can be seen — lacunae, originally containing osteoblasts arranged in lamellae, connected by canaliculi (protoplasmic connections).

Not every type of white cell is seen; often platelets are barely distinguishable at this magnification

TS GD (× 60)

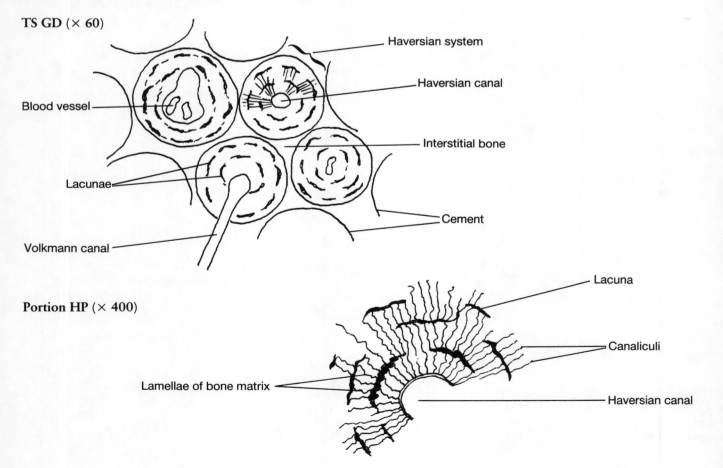

Haversian system

Haversian canal

Interstitial bone

Blood vessel

Lacunae

Cement

Volkmann canal

Portion HP (× 400)

Lacuna

Canaliculi

Lamellae of bone matrix

Haversian canal

MUSCLE

Consists of elongated cells, or coenocytic (with many nuclei) fibres. Each muscle fibre is made up of fine myofibrils consisting of a bundle of filaments lying among sarcoplasm.

SKELETAL, STRIATED OR VOLUNTARY MUSCLE

TS bundle (× 40)

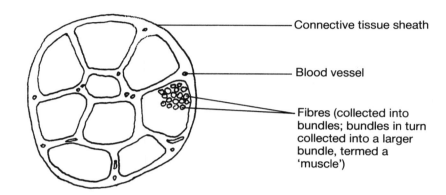

HP portion (× 900)

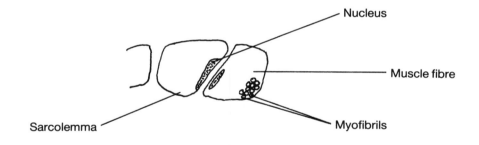

HP (× 400) LS teased muscle fibre

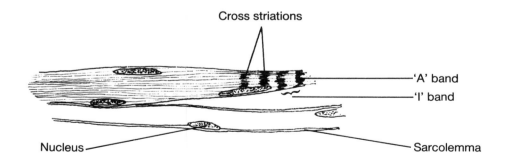

Striated muscle consists of two types of filament within the myofibrils — thicker myosin, showing as dark 'A' bands when overlapping with the thinner actin filaments. These alone give the light 'I' bands.

SMOOTH, UNSTRIATED OR INVOLUNTARY MUSCLE

LS HP (× 400), e.g. stomach

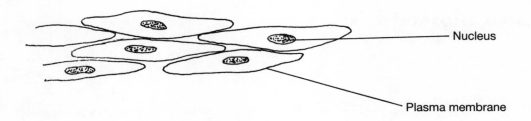

CARDIAC (HEART) MUSCLE

LS HP (× 400)

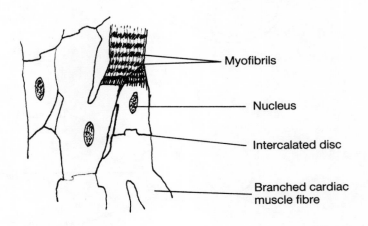

Sarcolemma not seen

Comparison of muscle types

Skeletal	Smooth	Cardiac
Sarcolemma present	No sarcolemma	Sarcolemma present
Myofibrils with cross-striations clearly seen	No myofibrils seen; no cross-striations	Faint myofibrils with cross-striations seen
Very long unbranched fibres	Short, unbranched fibres	Fairly short, branched fibres
Multinucleate	Single nucleus in cell	Singly nucleate cells with intercalary discs
Innervated by the central nervous system	Usually controlled by autonomic nervous system	Myogenic; also under control of autonomic nervous sytem

NERVOUS TISSUE

Neurones (nerve cells) — single cells with processes extending from the cell body. White matter is made up of nerve fibres with a medullary sheath. Nerve cell bodies are not so covered, and occur in ganglia and grey matter.

TS nerve bundle LP (× 40)

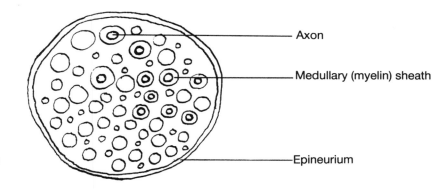

Schwann cells not seen

— Axon

— Medullary (myelin) sheath

— Epineurium

LS nerve HP (× 600)
(To show small portion of nerve fibre only.)

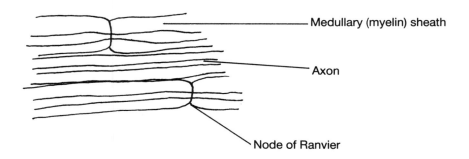

— Medullary (myelin) sheath

— Axon

Node of Ranvier

MOTOR END-PLATE; SYNAPSE ENDING IN MUSCLE FIBRE (× 600)

(Prepared by silver impregnation — structure of motor end-plates difficult to distinguish.)

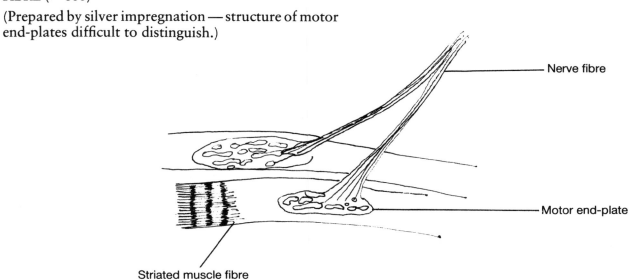

— Nerve fibre

— Motor end-plate

Striated muscle fibre

ORGANS

An **organ** is a group of tissues. Each of these tissues has
an individual role to fulfil. As a group, they co-operate
to carry out a major function.

SMALL INTESTINE

DUODENUM
TS GD (× 30)

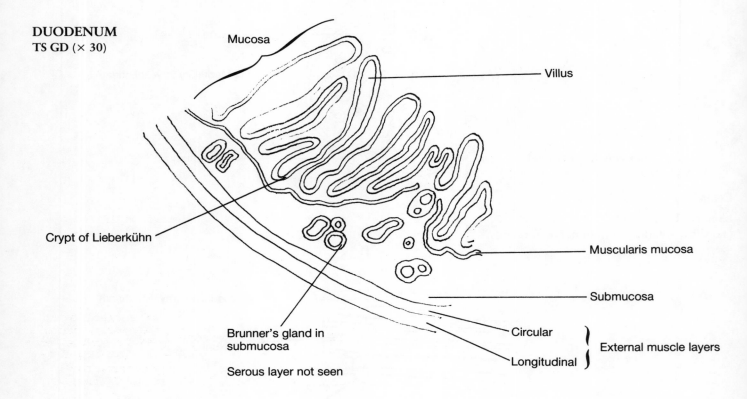

Mucosa

Villus

Crypt of Lieberkühn

Muscularis mucosa

Submucosa

Brunner's gland in
submucosa

Circular
Longitudinal   } External muscle layers

Serous layer not seen

ILEUM
TS GD (× 30)

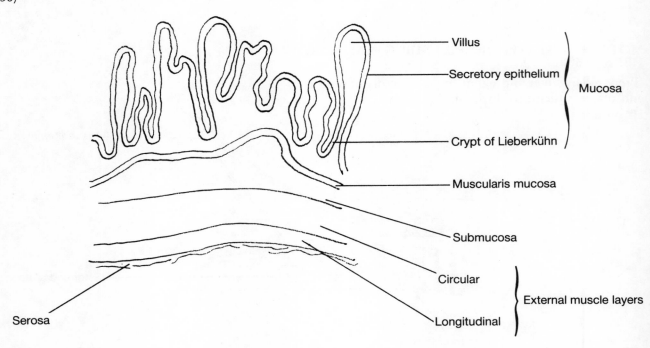

Villus

Secretory epithelium   } Mucosa

Crypt of Lieberkühn

Muscularis mucosa

Submucosa

Circular
Longitudinal   } External muscle layers

Serosa

LIVER

Very difficult to interpret. Recognised as liver because a generally hexagonal-shaped series of lobules can usually be seen, together with central veins and sinusoids. Regular-shaped cord cells with glycogen granules are also visible.

e.g. Pig GD (× 30)

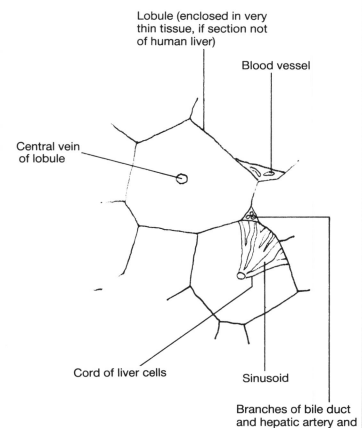

Lobule (enclosed in very thin tissue, if section not of human liver)

Blood vessel

Central vein of lobule

Cord of liver cells

Sinusoid

Branches of bile duct and hepatic artery and vein

HP portion (× 400)

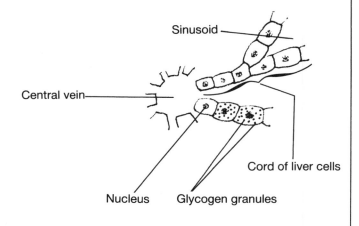

Sinusoid

Central vein

Cord of liver cells

Nucleus   Glycogen granules

OVARY

GD of section to show stages in follicle formation (× 10)

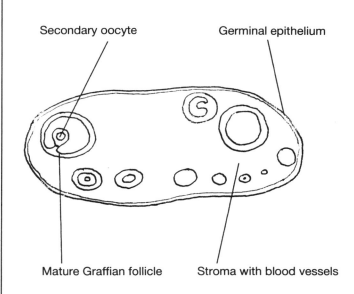

Secondary oocyte

Germinal epithelium

Mature Graffian follicle

Stroma with blood vessels

HP (× 200) GD of portion

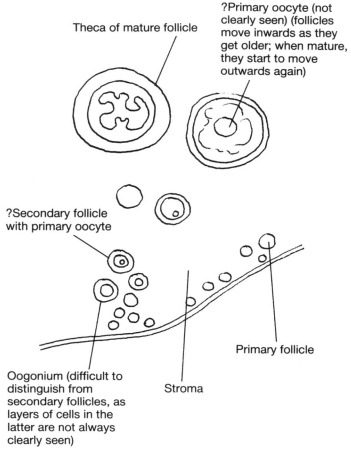

Theca of mature follicle

?Primary oocyte (not clearly seen) (follicles move inwards as they get older; when mature, they start to move outwards again)

?Secondary follicle with primary oocyte

Primary follicle

Oogonium (difficult to distinguish from secondary follicles, as layers of cells in the latter are not always clearly seen)

Stroma

TESTIS

HP (× 400), but GD only

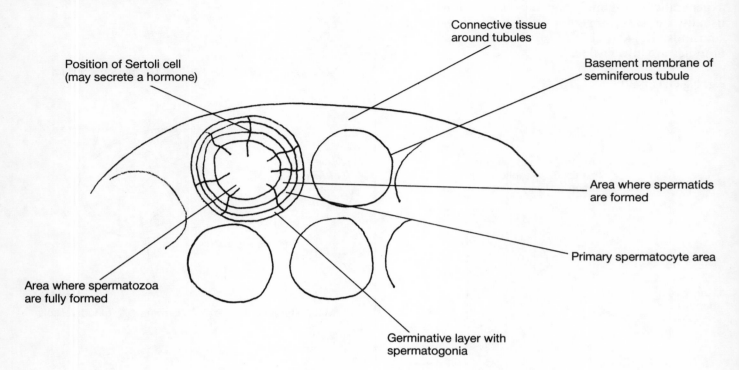

Connective tissue
around tubules

Position of Sertoli cell
(may secrete a hormone)

Basement membrane of
seminiferous tubule

Area where spermatids
are formed

Primary spermatocyte area

Area where spermatozoa
are fully formed

Germinative layer with
spermatogonia

SPINAL CORD

TS GD (× 10)

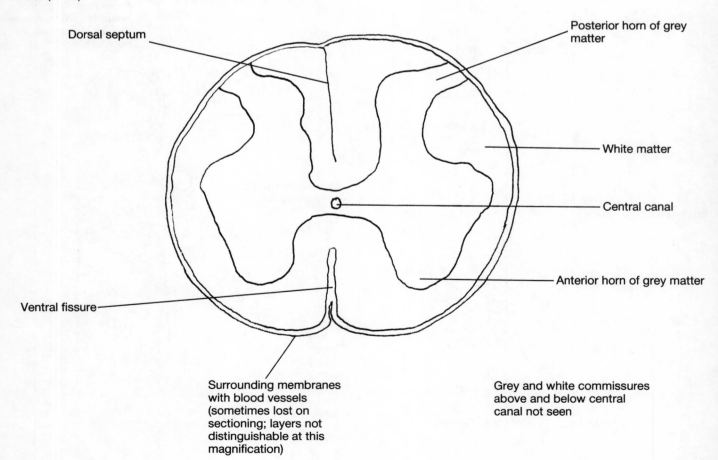

Dorsal septum

Posterior horn of grey
matter

White matter

Central canal

Anterior horn of grey matter

Ventral fissure

Surrounding membranes
with blood vessels
(sometimes lost on
sectioning; layers not
distinguishable at this
magnification)

Grey and white commissures
above and below central
canal not seen

KIDNEY

(For gross structure see dissection drawings.)

TS Medulla GD HP (× 400)

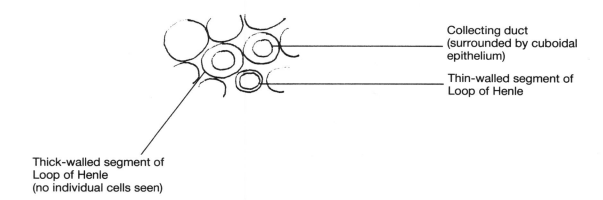

Collecting duct
(surrounded by cuboidal
epithelium)

Thin-walled segment of
Loop of Henle

Thick-walled segment of
Loop of Henle
(no individual cells seen)

TS Cortex GD HP (× 400)

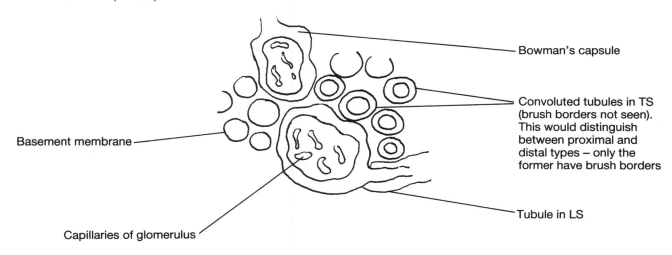

Bowman's capsule

Convoluted tubules in TS
(brush borders not seen).
This would distinguish
between proximal and
distal types – only the
former have brush borders

Basement membrane

Capillaries of glomerulus

Tubule in LS

ARTERY AND VEIN
TS GD (× 60)

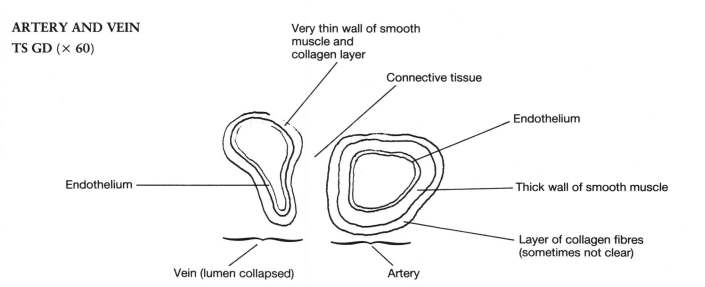

Very thin wall of smooth
muscle and
collagen layer

Connective tissue

Endothelium

Thick wall of smooth muscle

Endothelium

Layer of collagen fibres
(sometimes not clear)

Vein (lumen collapsed)

Artery

6 PLANT TAXONOMY

Living organisms may be divided into two main groups:

1 Prokaryotes
   a Bacteria
   b Blue-green algae
2 Eukaryotes
   a Fungi
   b Plantae
   c Animalia

A possible classification of the Fungi is shown below.
It is an example of a traditional scheme.

	Phycomycetes, e.g. *Phytophthora.*
Class	**Pythium, *Mucor*
Eumycophyta	Ascomycetes, e.g. *Yeast, Penicillium*
	Basidiomycetes, e.g. **Agaricus,*
	Psalliota
	Fungi Imperfecti, e.g. 'Athletes foot'
	fungus

A *possible* classification for the Kingdom Plantae:

Phylum (Division)	Subgroup (usually Class)	Examples
Algae	Chlorophyta (Chlorophyceae)	*Chlamydomonas, *Spirogyra*
	Phaeophyta (Phaeophyceae)	**Fucus*
	(Euglenophyta) (Euglenophyceae)	*(Euglena)*
Bryophyta	Hepaticeae	*Pellia*
	Musci	**Funaria*
Pteridophyta	Lycopsida	*Selaginella*
	Sphenopsida	*Equisetum*
	Pteropsida (Filicales)	**Dryopteris*
Spermatophyta	Gymnospermae	**Pinus*
	Angiospermae	
	● Monocotyledonae	**Zea, Lilium*
	● Dicotyledonae	**Ranunculus, *Helianthus*

SCHIZOMYCOPHYTA: THE BACTERIA

Unicells with rigid walls of bacterial cellulose. Reproduction by binary fission.
Prokaryotic — genetic material not in a discrete nucleus.
May have flagella.

BACTERIA
HP (× 1400)

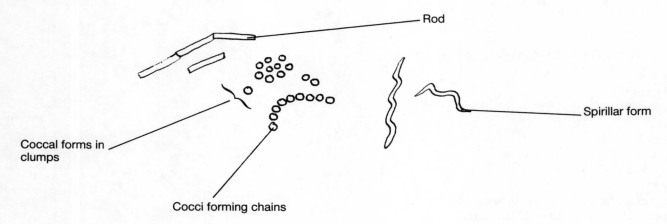

BACILLUS ANTHRACIS
HP (× 1400)

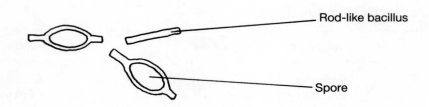

LS root nodule of legume
GD (× 60)

Portion HP (× 450)

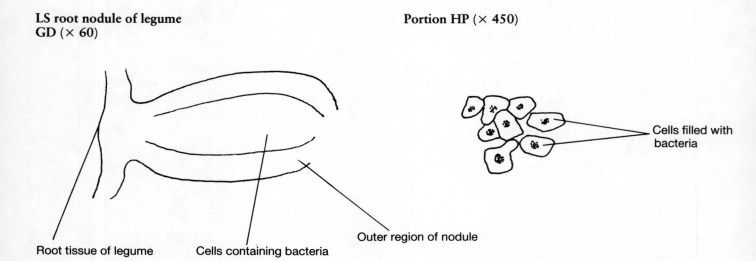

EUMYCOPHYTA: THE FUNGI

Fungal body (mycelium) made up of filaments (hyphae). Lack chlorophyll. May be parasitic or saprophytic. Reproduction by spores, produced sexually or asexually. Exoenzymes secreted. Cell walls of fungal cellulose.

SUB-CLASS: PHYCOMYCETES

Haploid mycelium, of non-septate, multinucleate hyphae. Produce asexual spores in sporangia.

MUCOR SP. HP (× 120)

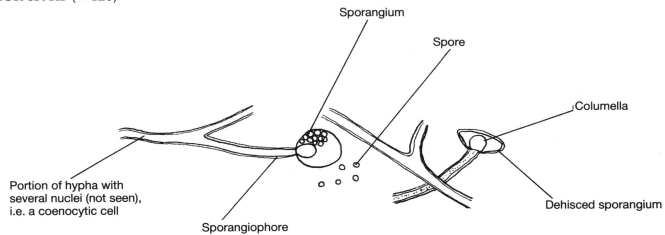

Zygote production HP (× 100)

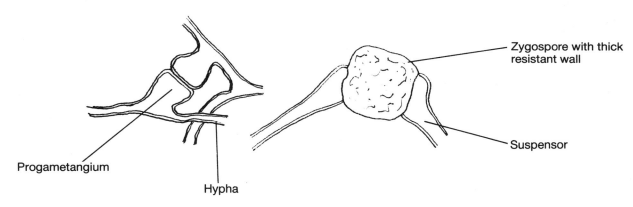

Life history

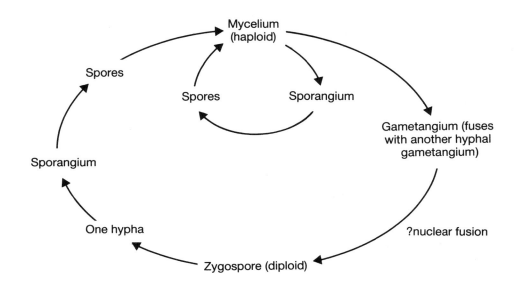

PHYCOMYCETES

PYTHIUM SP.

May reproduce by airborne conidia, which may be replaced by biflagellate zoospores in wet conditions.

HP (× 200)   **Young stage — asexual**   HP (× 200)   **Old stage — sexual**

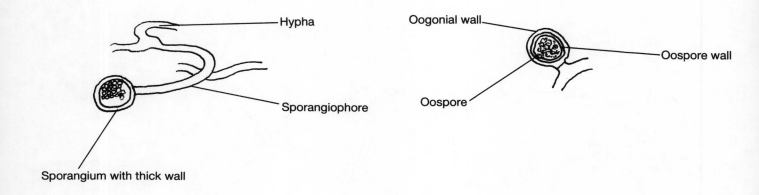

Hypha

Sporangiophore

Sporangium with thick wall

Oogonial wall

Oospore wall

Oospore

Life history

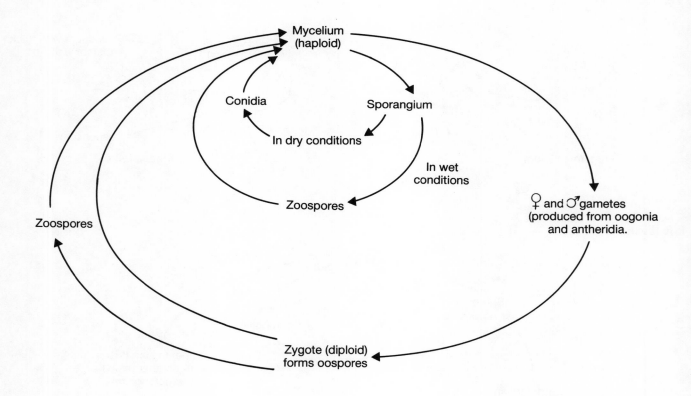

Mycelium
(haploid)

Conidia

Sporangium

In dry conditions

In wet
conditions

Zoospores

Zoospores

♀ and ♂ gametes
(produced from oogonia
and antheridia.

Zygote (diploid)
forms oospores

BASIDIOMYCETES

Septate mycelium. Fructifications above ground — mushrooms or toadstools. Basidia borne on a fertile layer, the hymenium, produce four basidiospores each.

AGARICUS SP.: COMMON MUSHROOM

($\times$ ½)

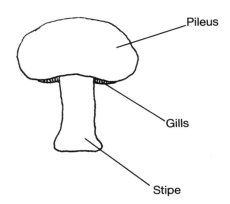

Young fruiting body (sporophore)

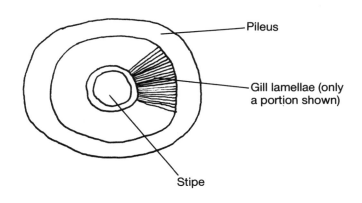

From below

Portion of pileus VS GD ($\times$ 40)

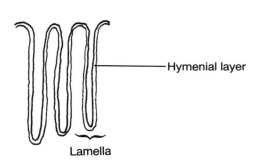

Portion of gill HP ($\times$ 400)

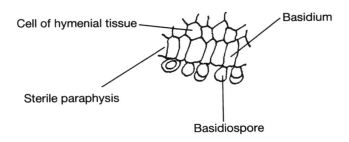

Life history

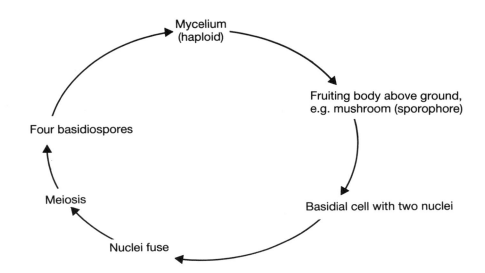

KINGDOM: PLANTAE

Contain chlorophyll. Usually cellulose cell walls.

PHYLUM (DIVISION): ALGAE

Usually aquatic, with photosynthetic pigments (which are used for classification). Sexual reproduction well defined. Asexual reproduction by vegetative cell division, by fragmentation, and sometimes by zoospores.

CLASS: CHLOROPHYTA

Pigments are green chlorophylls a, and b, carotene and xanthophyll. Zoospores are asexual reproductive cells. Sexual gametes are motile.

CHLAMYDOMONAS SP. HP (× 400)

Cup-shaped chloroplast. Two flagella. Unicellular.

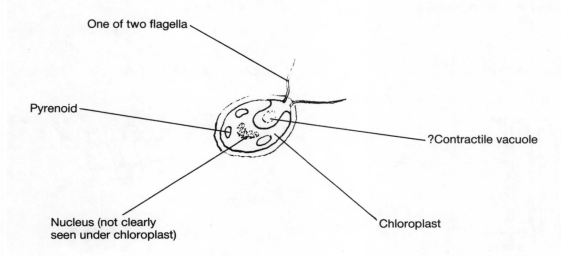

Life history

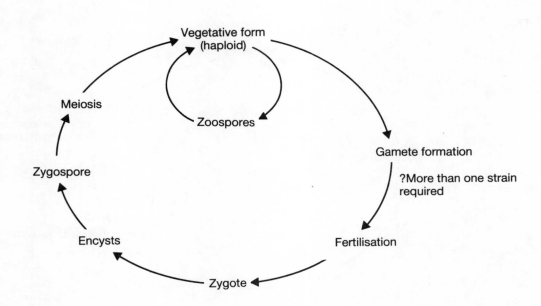

PHYLUM (DIVISION): ALGAE

CLASS: CHLOROPHYTA

SPIROGYRA SP.

Unbranched filamentous alga with spiral chloroplast. Cell cylindrical. Large vacuoles. Nucleus suspended near the centre of the cell. Sexual reproduction by conjugation, forming zygospores. Asexual reproduction by fragmentation.

Vegetative form HP ($\times$ 400)

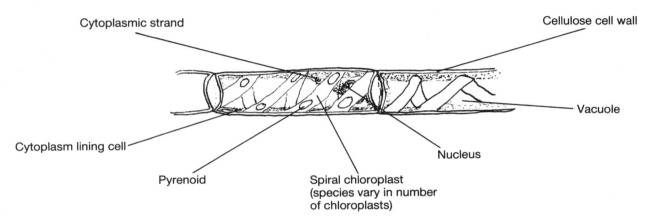

Cytoplasmic strand

Cellulose cell wall

Vacuole

Cytoplasm lining cell

Nucleus

Pyrenoid

Spiral chloroplast
(species vary in number
of chloroplasts)

Stages in conjugation and zygote formation HP ($\times$ 400)

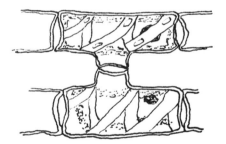

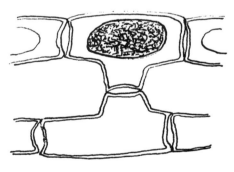

Conjugation tube formed.
Cell contents rounding off
in 'male' gamete

Cell contents passing
through conjugation tube

Zygote formed

Life history

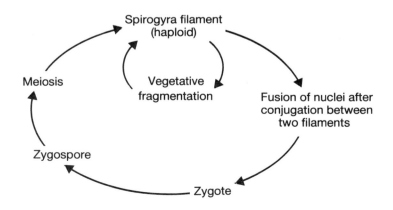

Spirogyra filament
(haploid)

Meiosis

Vegetative
fragmentation

Fusion of nuclei after
conjugation between
two filaments

Zygospore

Zygote

PHYLUM (DIVISION): ALGAE

CLASS: PHAEOPHYTA – THE BROWN ALGAE

Mainly marine. Chlorophylls, xanthophylls and fucoxanthin present in chloroplasts. Monoecious (both male and female gametes present in the same conceptacles) or dioecious (separate conceptacles for male and female).

FUCUS SP.

(This species is 'serratus' — each one varies in form.) Flat thallus attached to substrate by a holdfast. Thallus branches dichotomously. Some species have air bladders for buoyancy. Gametophyte plant is diploid, unlike Chlorophyta.

Life history

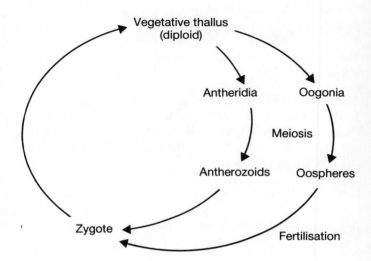

Vegetative form (× 1)

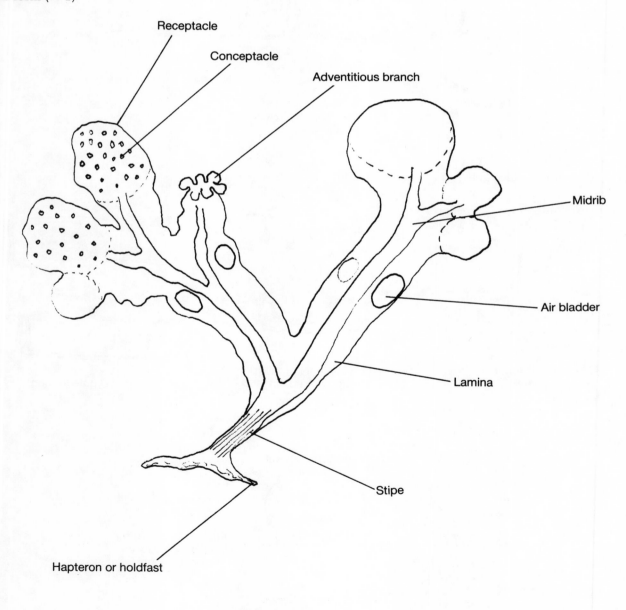

PHYLUM (DIVISION): BRYOPHYTA

Vegetative body composed of dichotomously branched thallus, and rhizoids. Photosynthetic pigments present. Female archegonia and male antheridia well developed. Main persisting thallus is the haploid gametophyte. Diploid sporophyte is usually dependent on the gametophyte.

CLASS: MUSCI — THE MOSSES

Gametophyte erect — axis with leaf-like structures. Rhizoids multicellular. Capsules dehisce by teeth. Spores germinate into protonemata.

FUNARIA SP. (× 2)

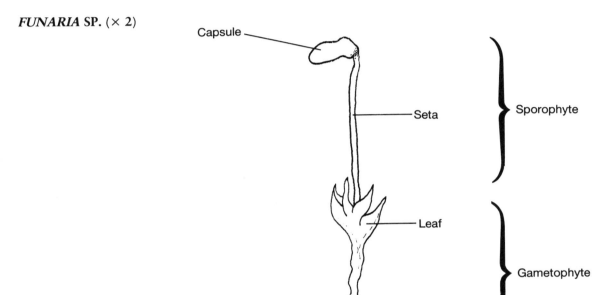

Life history

Note alternation of generations

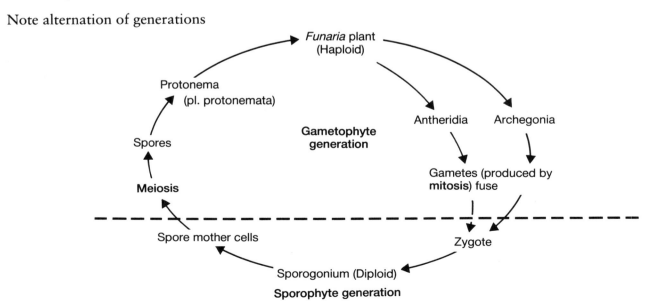

PHYLUM (DIVISION): PTERIDOPHYTA

Vegetative body of stem, rhizome and leaf systems. Xylem and phloem present. Antheridia and archegonia formed. Alternation of generations, but persisting plant is the diploid sporophyte. Haploid gametophyte is independent. Spores may be of one type (homosporous) or of two types (heterosporous).

CLASS: FILICALES — THE FERNS

Leaves large and spirally arranged. Homosporous. Sporangia in clusters or sori.

DRYOPTERIS SP. (× 1)

Life history

Note alternation of generations

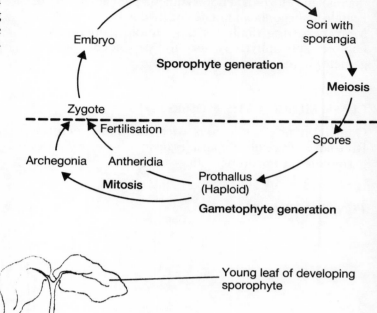

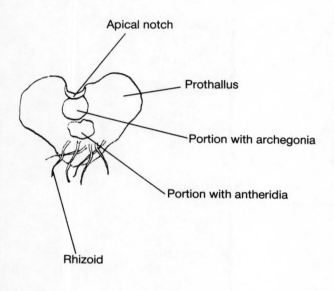

Portion of pinna (× 5)

Undersurface

Sketch of entire plant to show arrangement of parts

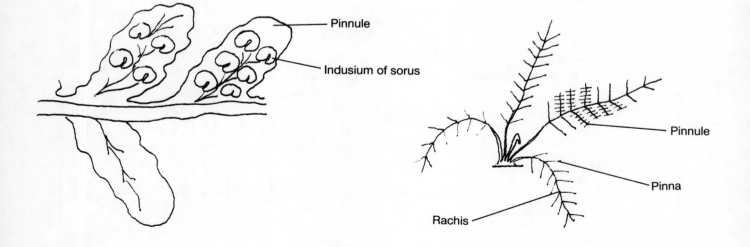

PHYLUM (DIVISION): SPERMATOPHYTA

Clear division of plant body into stems, roots and leaves. Highly developed internal cellular differentiation. Secondary thickening common. Male gametophyte is pollen grain. Fertilizes female in the sporophyte. Gametophytes much reduced. Seeds formed either naked or enclosed.

CLASS: GYMNOSPERMAE

Xylem elements always tracheids. Flowers of cone type; bear naked seeds.

SUB-CLASS: CONIFERALES

Large trees with needle-shaped leaves.

PINUS SP. (× 1)

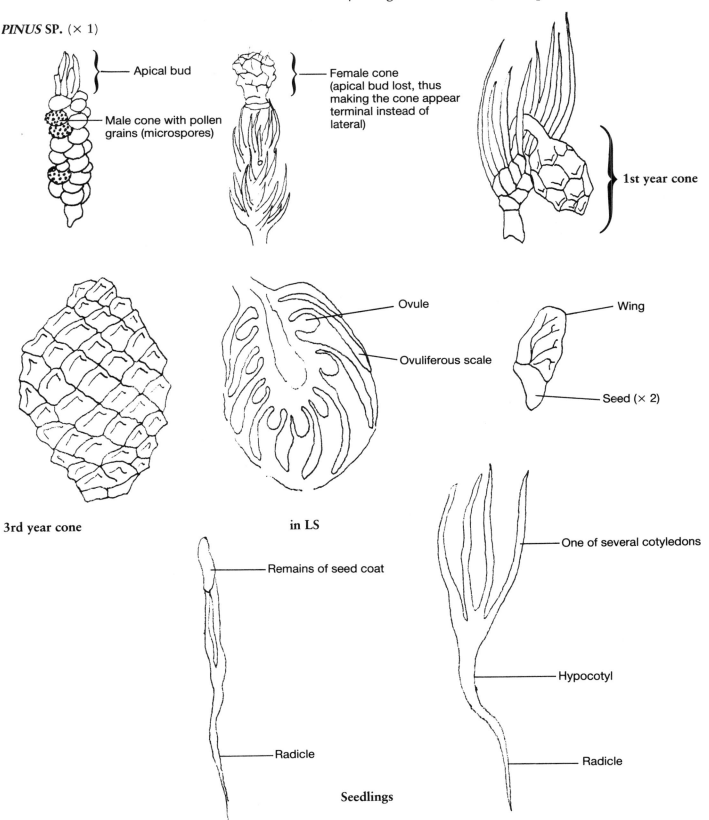

- Apical bud
- Male cone with pollen grains (microspores)
- Female cone (apical bud lost, thus making the cone appear terminal instead of lateral)
- 1st year cone
- Ovule
- Ovuliferous scale
- Wing
- Seed (× 2)

3rd year cone   in LS

- Remains of seed coat
- One of several cotyledons
- Hypocotyl
- Radicle
- Radicle

Seedlings

PINUS LEAF

Note xerophytic characteristics.
TS GD (× 100)

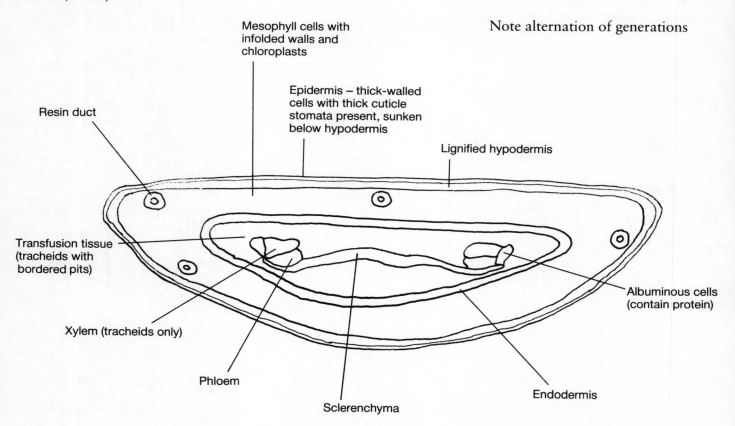

Mesophyll cells with infolded walls and chloroplasts

Epidermis – thick-walled cells with thick cuticle stomata present, sunken below hypodermis

Note alternation of generations

Lignified hypodermis

Resin duct

Transfusion tissue (tracheids with bordered pits)

Xylem (tracheids only)

Phloem

Sclerenchyma

Endodermis

Albuminous cells (contain protein)

Life history

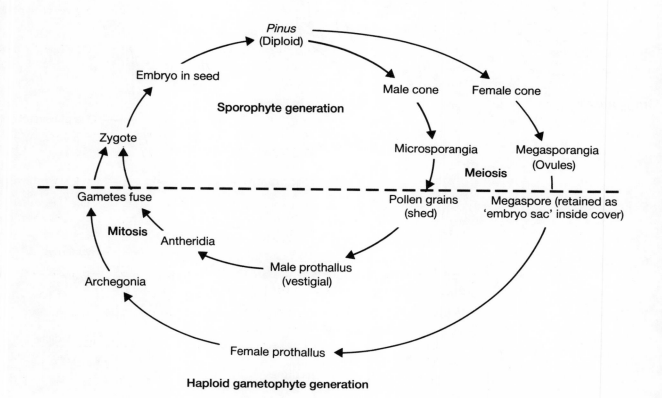

Pinus (Diploid)

Embryo in seed

Sporophyte generation

Male cone

Female cone

Zygote

Microsporangia

Megasporangia (Ovules)

Meiosis

Gametes fuse

Pollen grains (shed)

Megaspore (retained as 'embryo sac' inside cover)

Mitosis

Antheridia

Male prothallus (vestigial)

Archegonia

Female prothallus

Haploid gametophyte generation

7 ANGIOSPERM ANATOMY AND HISTOLOGY

TYPES OF PLANT TISSUE

A **tissue** is a group of cells specialised in structure for a particular function

Type	Structure and function	Examples of locations
1 Meristematic	A region of actively dividing cells; unspecialised, with dense cell contents and thin cell walls. In vascular tissue known as cambium.	e.g. *Helianthus* stem; stem or root apex
2 Parenchyma	The least specialised tissue. Confers rigidity due to the turgor of the cells. May be close-packed or with air spaces. May be modified for further functions.	
a With small air spaces	For rigidity; sometimes also storage.	e.g. *Helianthus* stem or root
b Chlorenchyma	(i) Modified for photosynthesis. Cells elongated with long axis at right-angles to surface. Numerous chloroplasts, peripheral in position along anticlinal walls	e.g. *Helianthus* leaf
	(ii) Arm palisade parenchyma — provides extra surface area for positioning chloroplasts, and for gas exchange.	e.g. *Pinus* leaf
c Aerenchyma	Numerous large air spaces to allow circulation of gases.	
	(i) Spongy mesophyll.	e.g. *Helianthus* leaf
	(ii) Strands of cells forming lacunae in aquatic plants for buoyancy and gas storage	e.g. Hydrophyte stem
3 Collenchyma	Cells with irregular cellulose thickening. Provide mechanical support but are still capable of further growth. Found in angles of ridged stems.	e.g. *Lamium* stem (Dead nettle)
4 Sclerenchyma	Lignin thickening – no further growth possible. Give mechanical support.	
	(i) Fibres and tracheids	e.g. *Zea* stem
	(ii) I-shaped sclereids support xerophytic leaves and prevent wilting.	e.g. *Hakea* leaf
	(iii) Astrosclereids – support aquatic leaves	e.g. *Nymphaea* leaf
5 Epidermal cells	Protective layer with cuticle of various types. May bear hairs. No chloroplasts, except in guard cells of stomata. These stomata allow gas exchange.	e.g. *Helianthus* leaf, *Psamma* leaf
6 Xylem	Conducting vessels. Lignified thickening, spiral or reticulate with pits. Cross walls break down in advanced vessels, allowing conduction of water and mineral salts.	e.g. Stem
7 Phloem	Sieve tubes for conduction – no contents. Companion cells carry out metabolism for sieve tubes.	e.g. Stem

VEGETATIVE MORPHOLOGY OF HERBACEOUS PLANTS

DICOTYLEDON, e.g. *RANUNCULUS* SP. (× 1)

MONOCOTYLEDON, e.g. A GRASS (× 1)

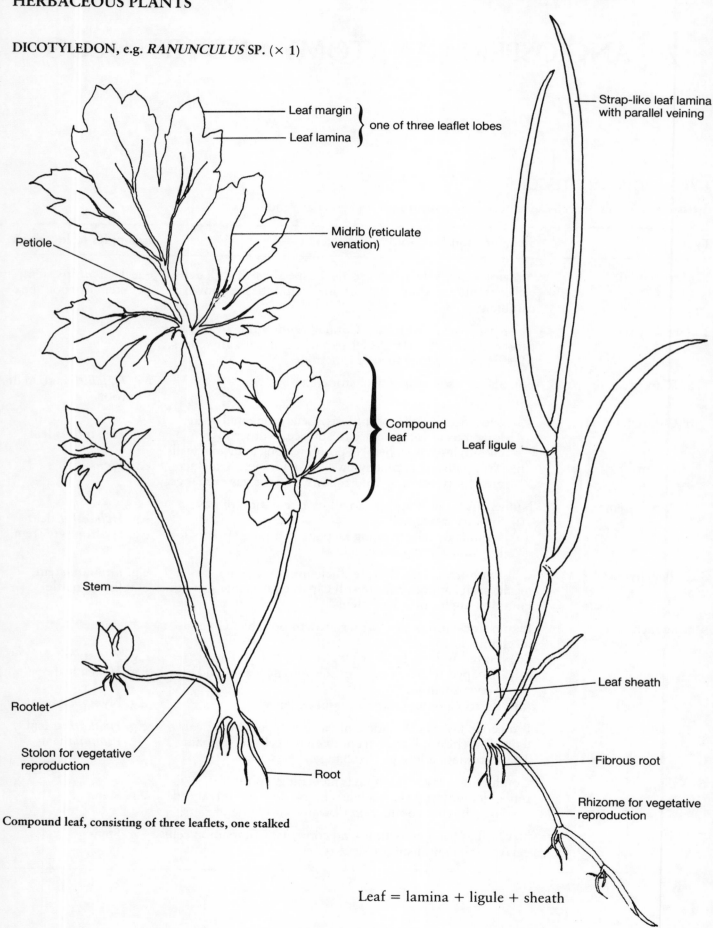

Leaf margin
Leaf lamina
} one of three leaflet lobes

Midrib (reticulate venation)

Petiole

Compound leaf

Stem

Rootlet

Stolon for vegetative reproduction

Root

Strap-like leaf lamina with parallel veining

Leaf ligule

Leaf sheath

Fibrous root

Rhizome for vegetative reproduction

Compound leaf, consisting of three leaflets, one stalked

Leaf = lamina + ligule + sheath

MICROSCOPIC STRUCTURE OF HERBACEOUS PLANTS: STEMS

Herbaceous or non-woody plants generally have no secondary thickening, if annuals. Biennial or perennial herbs overwinter underground, and have no persistent aerial parts during the winter, in general. Stems of *dicotyledonous* plants have their vascular tissue arranged in a peripheral ring, to allow bending of the stem without breaking. The central parenchyma may be lost, giving a pith cavity. There are only a limited number of vascular bundles. *Monocotyledon* stems have numerous vascular bundles arranged throughout the stem, and often no central cavity. *Mesophytes* show no special adaptations to water preservation, nor to living in an aquatic environment.

MONOCOTYLEDON STEM

ZEA MAIS

GD LP (× 30)

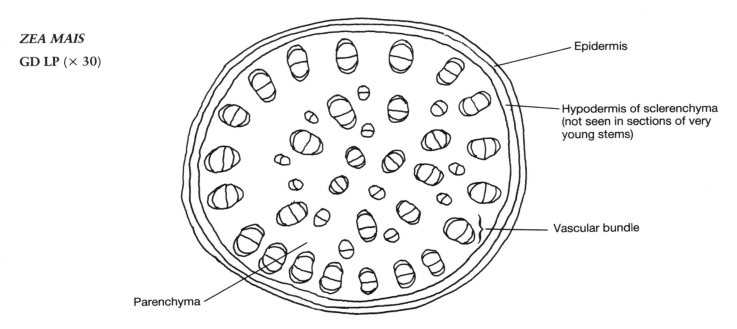

HP portion of vascular bundle near epidermis (× 600)

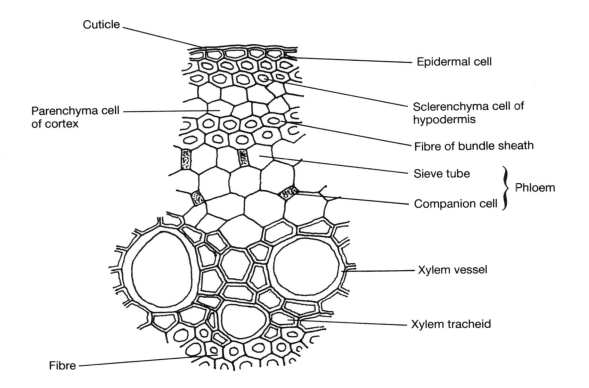

ANGIOSPERMAE; DICOTYLEDONAE

HELIANTHUS SP.
TS stem GD LP (× 30)

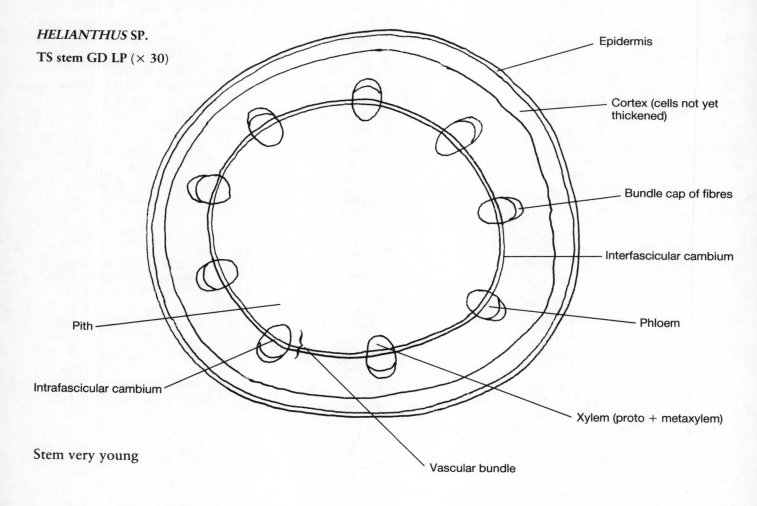

- Epidermis
- Cortex (cells not yet thickened)
- Bundle cap of fibres
- Interfascicular cambium
- Phloem
- Xylem (proto + metaxylem)
- Vascular bundle
- Intrafascicular cambium
- Pith

Stem very young

Portion of vascular bundle HP (× 600)

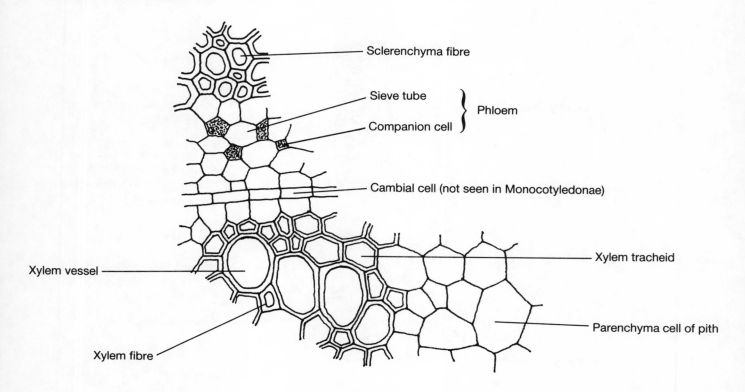

- Sclerenchyma fibre
- Sieve tube ⎫ Phloem
- Companion cell ⎬
- Cambial cell (not seen in Monocotyledonae)
- Xylem tracheid
- Xylem vessel
- Parenchyma cell of pith
- Xylem fibre

LAMIUM SP.: DEAD NETTLE

TS stem GD (× 30)

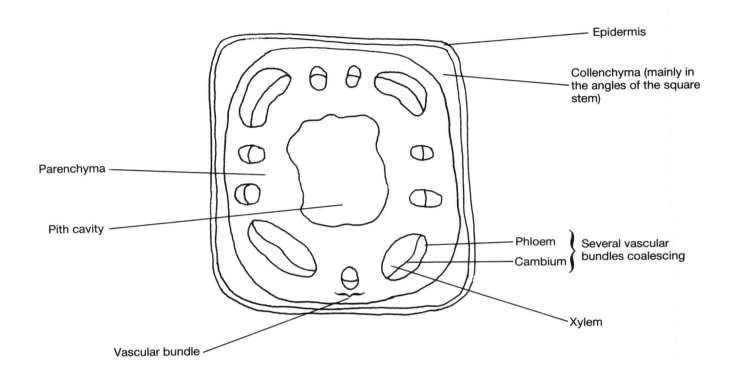

Epidermis

Collenchyma (mainly in the angles of the square stem)

Parenchyma

Pith cavity

Phloem ⎱ Several vascular
Cambium ⎰ bundles coalescing

Xylem

Vascular bundle

HP portion of stem to show collenchyma (× 600)

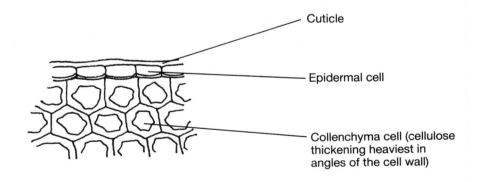

Cuticle

Epidermal cell

Collenchyma cell (cellulose thickening heaviest in angles of the cell wall)

HYDROPHYTE STEM, e.g. *HIPPURIS* STEM

GD (× 30)

Hydrophyte stems have reduced lignin, as support is not needed. Thin cuticle as waterproofing is not needed. Cortex of parenchyma cells with large air spaces for support in water, and for gas storage. Xylem not well developed, as water transport is not essential.

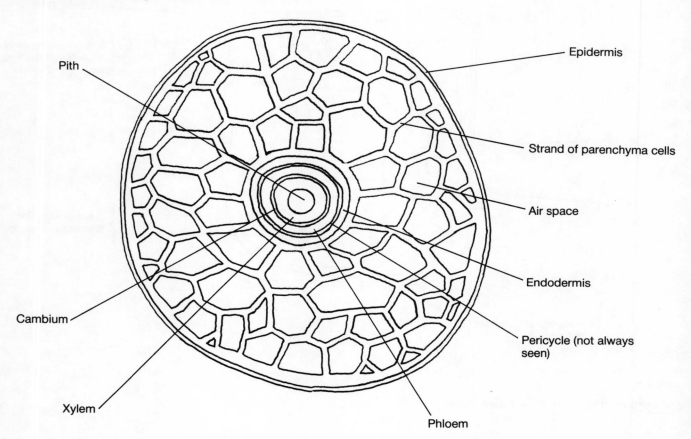

HP portion aerenchyma (× 600)

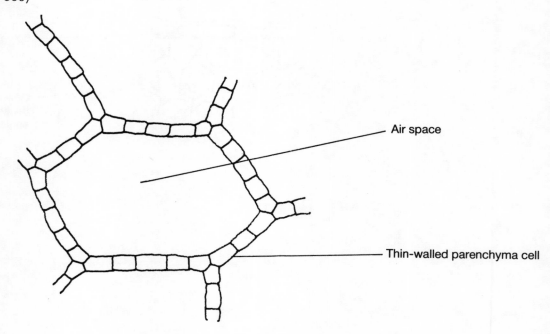

HYDROPHYTIC MODIFICATIONS: *JUNCUS* STEM

TS GD (× 30)

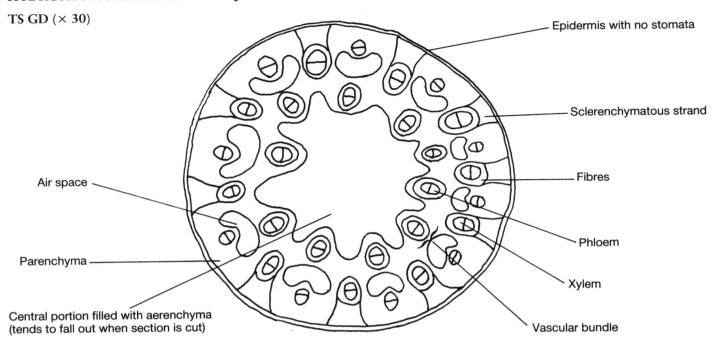

Epidermis with no stomata

Sclerenchymatous strand

Fibres

Phloem

Xylem

Vascular bundle

Air space

Parenchyma

Central portion filled with aerenchyma
(tends to fall out when section is cut)

HP portion to show aerenchyma (× 600)

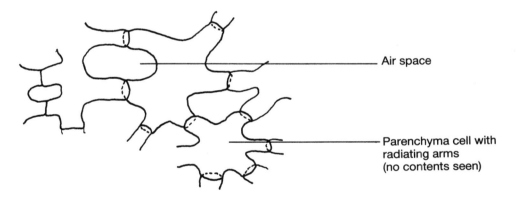

Air space

Parenchyma cell with
radiating arms
(no contents seen)

HP portion of *Nymphaea* stem: to show supporting sclereid (× 600) (Hydrophyte)

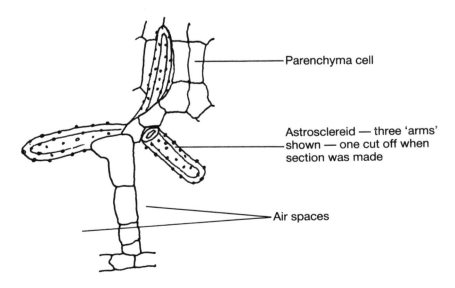

Parenchyma cell

Astrosclereid — three 'arms'
shown — one cut off when
section was made

Air spaces

CUSCUTA SP.: DODDER: AN OBLIGATE PARASITE

Stem not connected to the ground. No root system developed. Twining stem connected with host stem by haustoria.
(× 1)

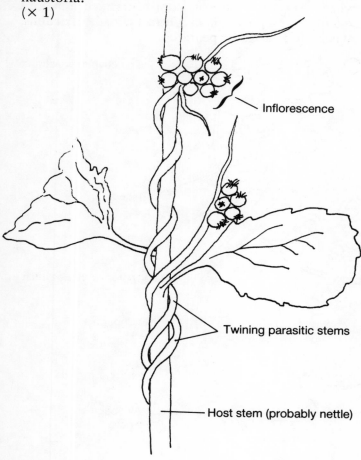

Inflorescence

Twining parasitic stems

Host stem (probably nettle)

TS stem GD (× 30)

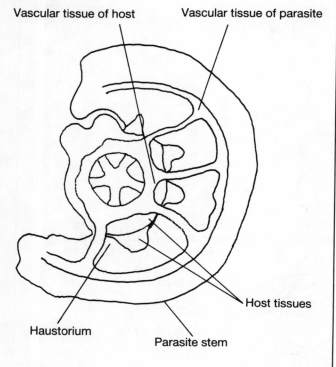

Vascular tissue of host

Vascular tissue of parasite

Host tissues

Haustorium

Parasite stem

GENERAL DIAGRAM OF STEM APEX, e.g. *VICIA FABA*: BEAN

GD LD (× 30)

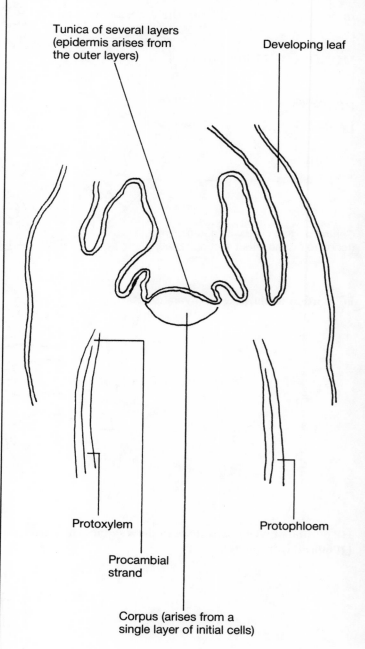

Tunica of several layers (epidermis arises from the outer layers)

Developing leaf

Protoxylem

Protophloem

Procambial strand

Corpus (arises from a single layer of initial cells)

MICROSCOPIC STRUCTURE OF HERBACEOUS PLANTS: ROOTS

Vascular tissue organised as a central stele gives strength and resistance to pulling strains. Cortex without chloroplasts. Endodermis with suberised Casparian strip, which acts as a control over water and mineral ions. Formed from the innermost layer of the cortex. Xylem alternates with phloem; the xylem elements occupy also the innermost central portion of the stele. The outermost layer of cambium forms the pericycle, able to divide and produce lateral roots when necessary. Monocotyledon roots have numerous xylem groups, polyarch, in contrast with dicotyledons, which are tetrarch or pentarch.

MONOCOTYLEDON ROOTS

ZEA MAIS

LP plan (× 30)

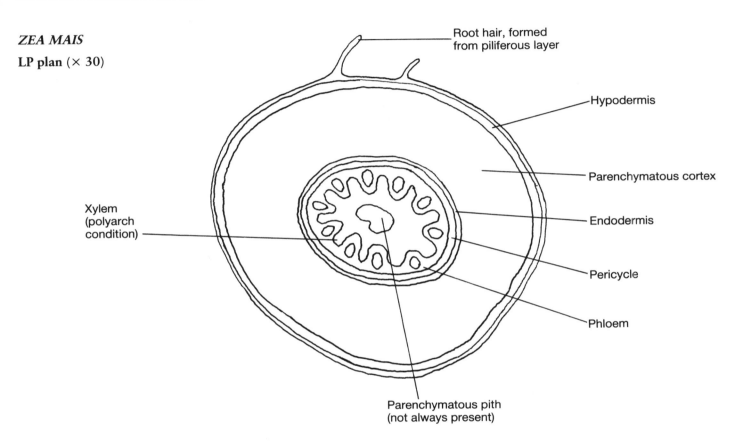

Root hair, formed from piliferous layer

Hypodermis

Parenchymatous cortex

Endodermis

Pericycle

Phloem

Xylem (polyarch condition)

Parenchymatous pith (not always present)

HP portion (× 600)

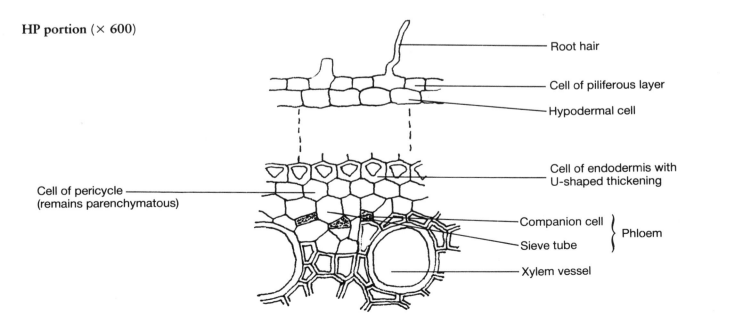

Root hair

Cell of piliferous layer

Hypodermal cell

Cell of endodermis with U-shaped thickening

Companion cell ⎫
                          ⎬ Phloem
Sieve tube   ⎭

Xylem vessel

Cell of pericycle (remains parenchymatous)

DICOTYLEDON ROOTS

These are usualy tetrarch or pentarch, i.e. four or five
bundles of phloem alternating with the xylem. Vascular
tissue still central (c.f. stems).

RANUNCULUS ROOT

LP plan (× 30)

Piliferous layer often rubbed off

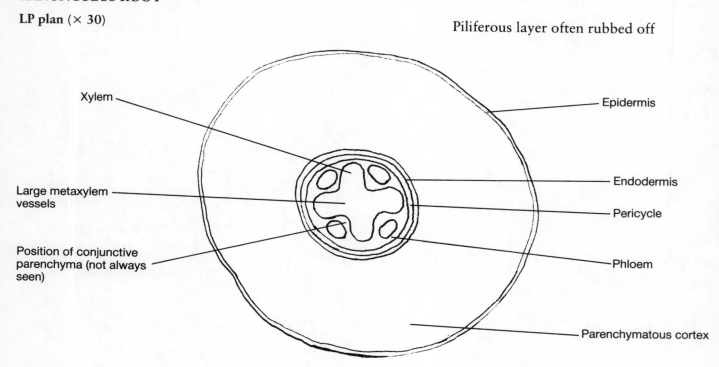

Xylem

Large metaxylem
vessels

Position of conjunctive
parenchyma (not always
seen)

Epidermis

Endodermis

Pericycle

Phloem

Parenchymatous cortex

Metaxylem vessels easily distinguishable in this root.
Usually very difficult to distinguish proto- from metaxylem by position (labelled xylem only in most cases)

HP portion of central stele
(× 600)

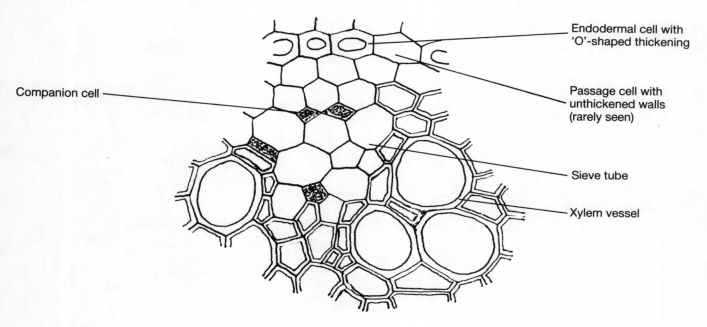

Companion cell

Endodermal cell with
'O'-shaped thickening

Passage cell with
unthickened walls
(rarely seen)

Sieve tube

Xylem vessel

TS *DAUCUS* ROOT: CARROT

LP plan (× 20)

Modified for storage

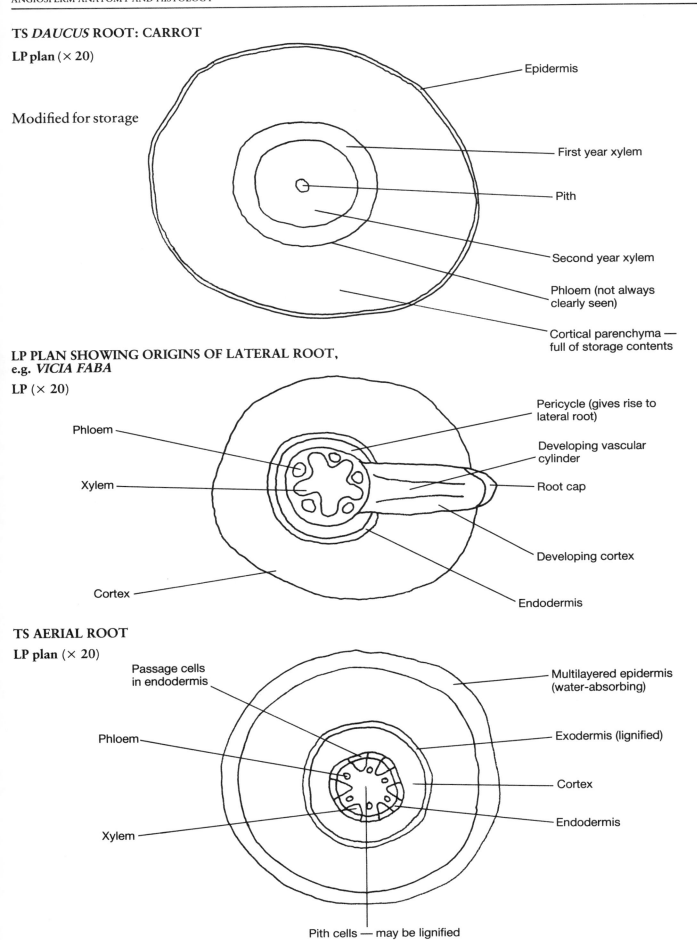

- Epidermis
- First year xylem
- Pith
- Second year xylem
- Phloem (not always clearly seen)
- Cortical parenchyma — full of storage contents

LP PLAN SHOWING ORIGINS OF LATERAL ROOT, e.g. *VICIA FABA*

LP (× 20)

- Phloem
- Xylem
- Cortex
- Pericycle (gives rise to lateral root)
- Developing vascular cylinder
- Root cap
- Developing cortex
- Endodermis

TS AERIAL ROOT

LP plan (× 20)

- Passage cells in endodermis
- Phloem
- Xylem
- Multilayered epidermis (water-absorbing)
- Exodermis (lignified)
- Cortex
- Endodermis
- Pith cells — may be lignified

LP PLAN OF ROOT APEX LS, e.g *VICIA FABA*: BROAD BEAN

LP plan (× 30)

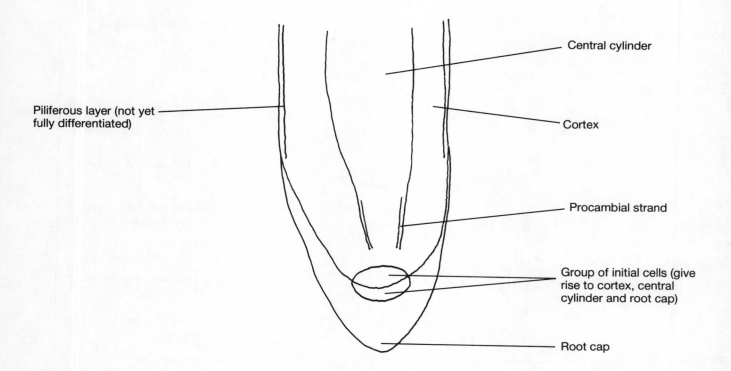

Central cylinder

Piliferous layer (not yet fully differentiated)

Cortex

Procambial strand

Group of initial cells (give rise to cortex, central cylinder and root cap)

Root cap

MICROSTRUCTURE OF HERBACEOUS PLANTS: LEAVES

Leaves are thin and flat. The epidermis has no chloroplasts but a cuticle for waterproofing. Palisade layer with numerous chloroplasts and spongy mesophyll with air spaces. Stomata usually on lower surface only.

MONOCOTYLEDON LEAVES

These have parallel venation and stomata on both surfaces. Leaves take up an upright, vertical position. Palisade layer not so elongated.

IRIS SP.

LP leaf plan

TS leafblade from higher up

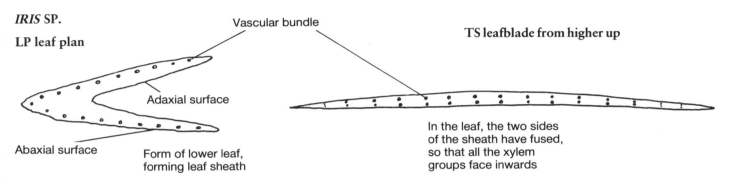

In the leaf, the two sides of the sheath have fused, so that all the xylem groups face inwards

TS leaf, LP plan (× 30)

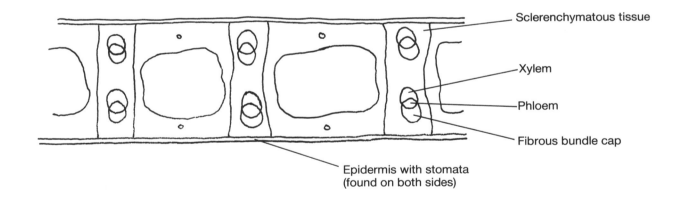

HP portion of lamina (× 600)

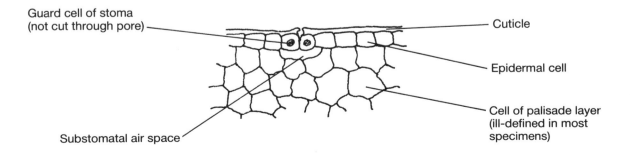

ANGIOSPERMAE; DICOTYLEDONAE

HELIANTHUS SP.

TS leaf, LP plan (× 30)

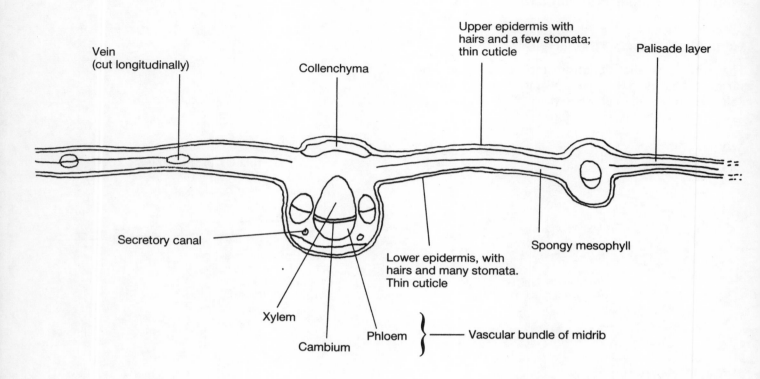

Vein
(cut longitudinally)

Collenchyma

Upper epidermis with
hairs and a few stomata;
thin cuticle

Palisade layer

Secretory canal

Lower epidermis, with
hairs and many stomata.
Thin cuticle

Spongy mesophyll

Xylem

Cambium

Phloem

Vascular bundle of midrib

HP portion of lower leaf surface (abaxial) (× 600)

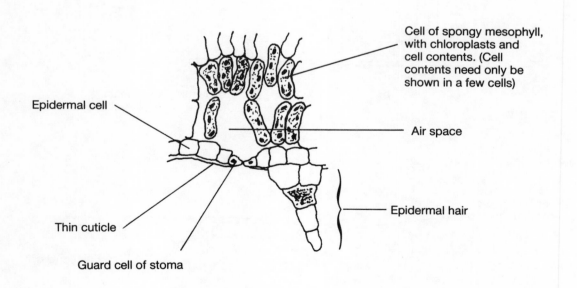

Cell of spongy mesophyll,
with chloroplasts and
cell contents. (Cell
contents need only be
shown in a few cells)

Epidermal cell

Air space

Thin cuticle

Epidermal hair

Guard cell of stoma

DICOTYLEDONOUS LEAVES have reticulate venation, stomata usually on lower surface only. Take up a horizontal position. Palisade tissue under the upper surface much more elongated and well-defined than in monocotyledons. Xylem faces towards the adaxial surface, and phloem to the abaxial.

HP portion adaxial surface (× 600)

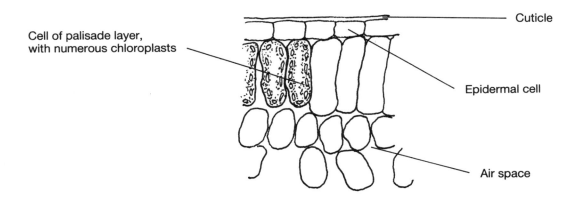

Cell of palisade layer, with numerous chloroplasts

Cuticle

Epidermal cell

Air space

Surface view of stomata

Monocotyledon epidermis (× 140)   **Dicotyledon epidermis (× 280)**

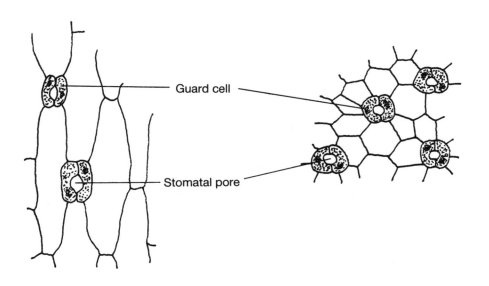

Guard cell

Stomatal pore

HYDROPHYTE LEAVES are of two types — surface and submerged. The former have stomata only on the upper surfaces. In submerged leaves the stomata are never fully functional. Compact parenchyma surrounds the vascular bundles in surface leaves, sclerenchyma in submerged leaves. Air spaces for buoyancy and gas storage. Lignin reduced — support and water transport largely unnecessary.

TS *POTAMOGETON NATANS*

Surface leaf LP plan (× 30). Central portion only

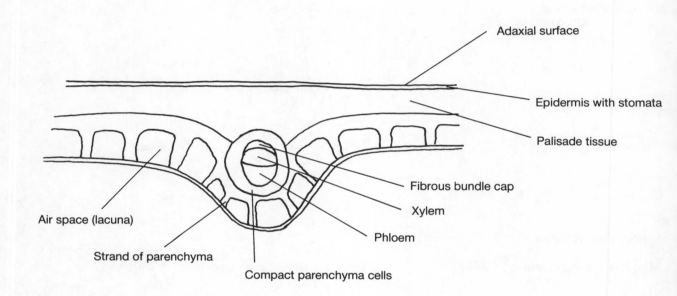

TS SUBMERGED LEAF

LP plan (× 30)

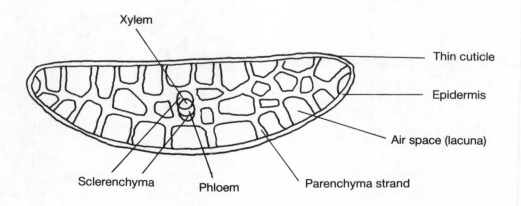

XEROPHYTE LEAVES are often rolled, or needle-like, in order to reduce the leaf surface. Rolled leaves also protect stomata which are usually sunken, and surrounded with hairs to reduce transpiration. Very thick, waxy, outer cuticle. Reduction of air spaces. Succulent tissue for water storage. Sclereids and lignified tissue help to prevent collapse of leaf when water is lost.

TS LEAF OF *PSAMMA* SP.: MARRAM GRASS

GD LP (× 30)

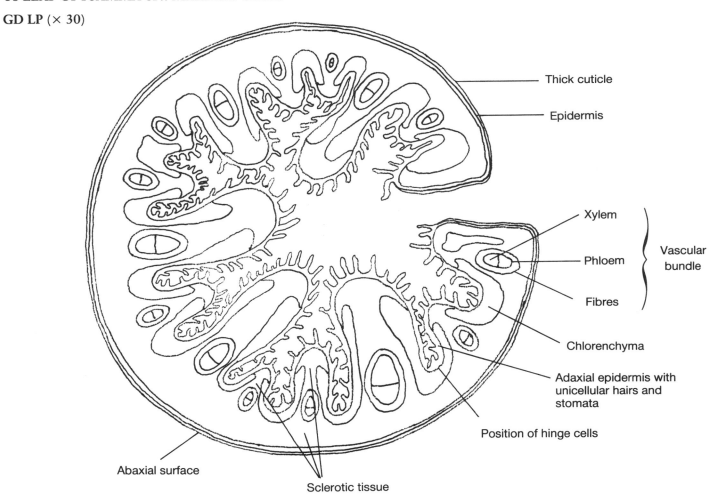

HP portion of inner surface of leaf to show hinge cells (× 600)

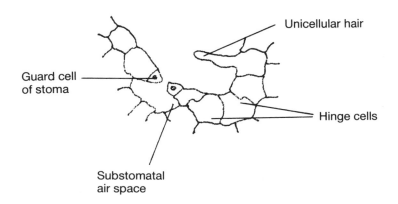

TS *HAKEA* LEAF

GD LP (× 30)
(Centric type)

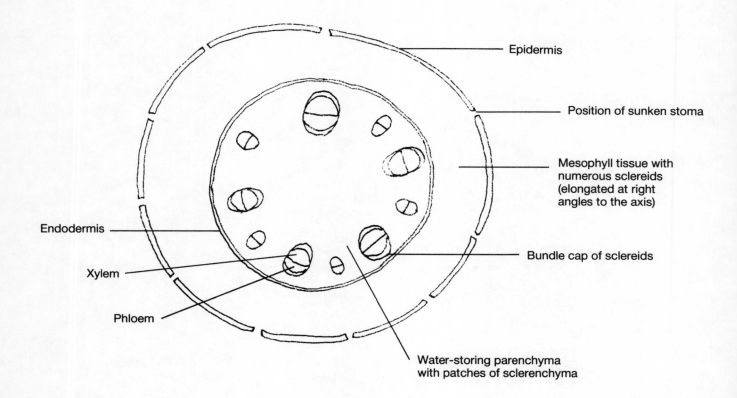

Epidermis

Position of sunken stoma

Mesophyll tissue with
numerous sclereids
(elongated at right
angles to the axis)

Endodermis

Bundle cap of sclereids

Xylem

Phloem

Water-storing parenchyma
with patches of sclerenchyma

Note xerophytic characteristics

HP portion to show sunken stoma (× 600)

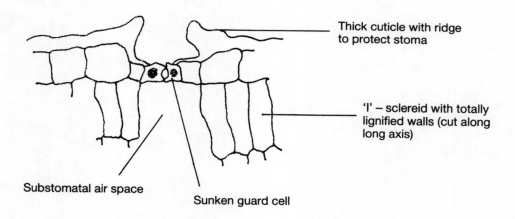

Thick cuticle with ridge
to protect stoma

'I' – sclereid with totally
lignified walls (cut along
long axis)

Substomatal air space

Sunken guard cell

HP portion to show sclerenchyma (× 600)

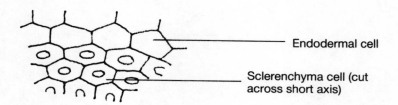

Endodermal cell

Sclerenchyma cell (cut
across short axis)

WOODY PLANTS

Usually dicotyledons; very few monocotyledons are secondarily thickened — they usually perennate and overwinter as bulbs, corms or rhizomes.

WINTER TWIG, e.g. HORSE CHESTNUT (× 1)

Apical portion only shown

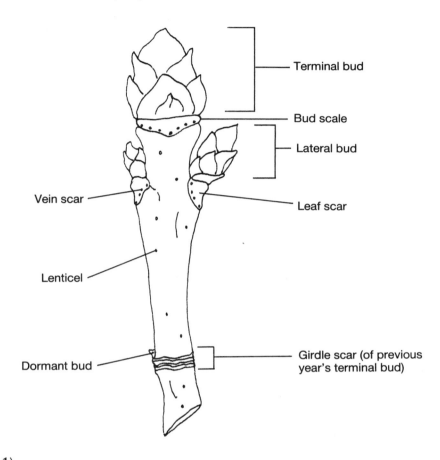

Terminal bud

Bud scale

Lateral bud

Vein scar

Leaf scar

Lenticel

Dormant bud

Girdle scar (of previous year's terminal bud)

FRUIT: A CAPSULE (× 1)

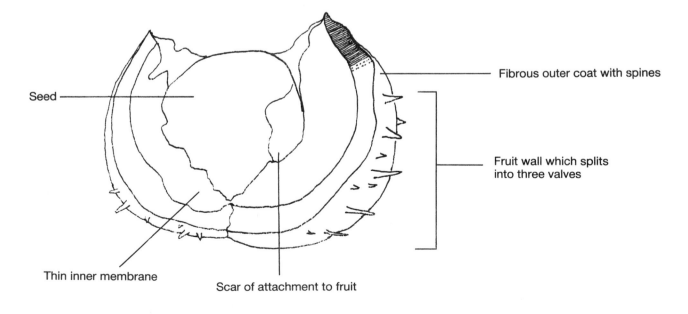

Fibrous outer coat with spines

Seed

Fruit wall which splits into three valves

Thin inner membrane

Scar of attachment to fruit

LEAF OF WOODY PLANT, e.g. HORSE CHESTNUT
($\times$ 1)

Dicotyledon — venation is reticulate

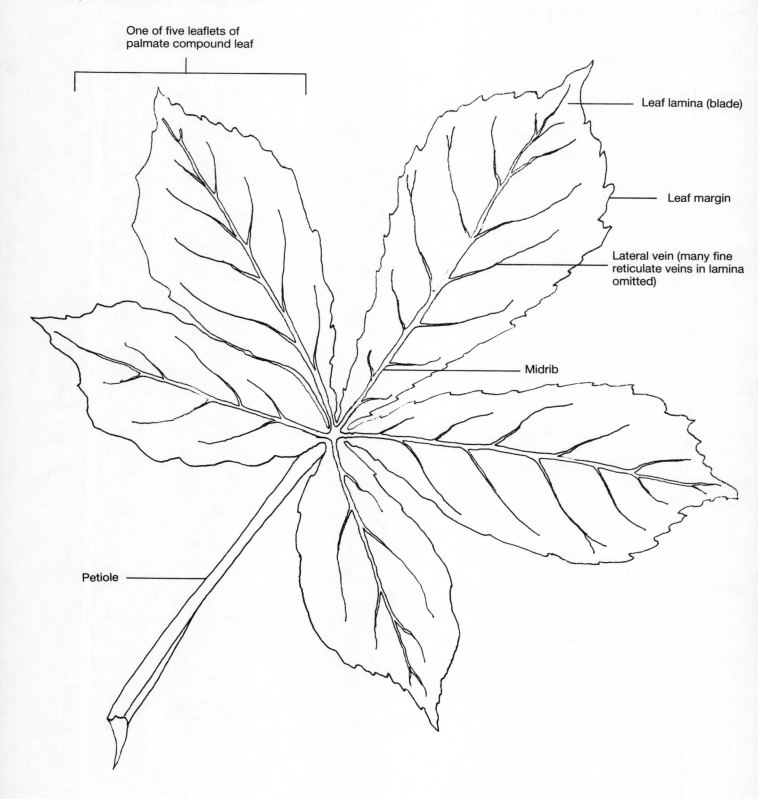

One of five leaflets of
palmate compound leaf

Leaf lamina (blade)

Leaf margin

Lateral vein (many fine
reticulate veins in lamina
omitted)

Midrib

Petiole

LP PLAN TO SHOW ABSCISSION LAYER, e.g. OF *ACER* SP.: ASH

LS stem (× 20)

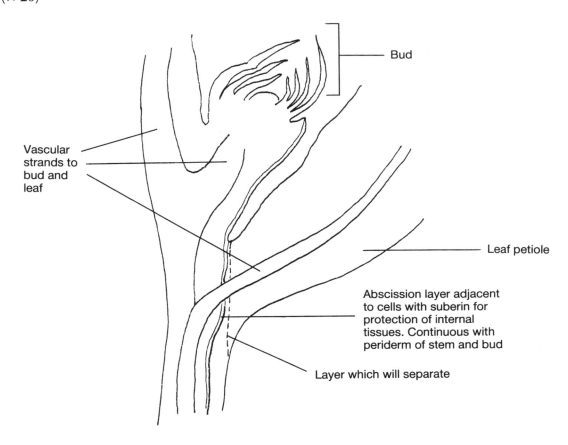

Bud

Vascular strands to bud and leaf

Leaf petiole

Abscission layer adjacent to cells with suberin for protection of internal tissues. Continuous with periderm of stem and bud

Layer which will separate

TS LENTICEL OF *SAMBUCUS* SP.: ELDER

LP plan (× 20)

Developing cork

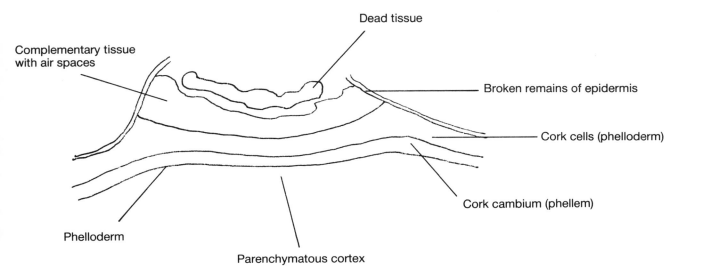

Dead tissue

Complementary tissue with air spaces

Broken remains of epidermis

Cork cells (phelloderm)

Cork cambium (phellem)

Phelloderm

Parenchymatous cortex

FLOWER STRUCTURE

NOTES ON MAKING HALF-FLOWER DIAGRAMS

A half-flower diagram is a drawing of the cut surfaces of the flower, when sectioned vertically through that exact centre, plus the background structures in that half. The outlines of the petals in the background may be sketched in, but for clarity are often omitted. Such a drawing is then an 'LS flower'. The surfaces actually cut, e.g. where a petal is cut in two, are always shown as double lines, but where the section has passed *between* two petals a single line is used. The arrangement of the parts on the receptacle must be *clearly* shown, and also the arrangement of the ovules on the gynaecium.

FLORAL DIAGRAMS

The various whorls of parts are shown as rings, and the overlapping of various members, e.g. of the sepals with each other, must be correctly shown. If, for example, petals are fused, they are shown as joined by '⌒' in the diagram. The position of the axis of the plant in relation to the flower is indicated by a small circle 'O'.

FLORAL FORMULAE

Each type of part is denoted by a letter:

K – calyx ⎫
C – corolla ⎬ or P if perianth is undifferentiated
A – androecium
G – gynaecium
·|· – zygomorphic flower (bilaterally symmetrical)
⊕ – actinomorphic flower (radially symmetrical)

The numbers of each part are shown in figures, one for each whorl, e.g. A5 + 5 indicates two whorls of five stamens each. If the stamens are numerous, ∞ is used, but does not imply that all the stamens are in one whorl. Fusion of parts is indicated by brackets: K(5) is 'K five joined', i.e. five sepals joined together in a tube. Usually there will be points or teeth to the sepals to indicate the number. {C(5)A4} or sometimes $\overline{C(5)}$A4 indicates a corolla of five joined petals, with the filaments of the stamens arising from the corolla tube. The receptacle may be below, or around the ovary. The former gives a **superior ovary**, shown as, e.g. G(2); the latter is termed an **inferior ovary**, e.g. G(5). The line denotes the level at which the stamens are attached.

MONOCOTYLEDONAE — FAMILY: IRIDACEAE

The floral parts are arranged in threes in a monocotyledon.

IRIS SP.

Half-flower

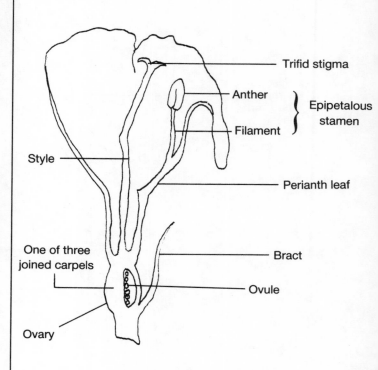

Floral diagram

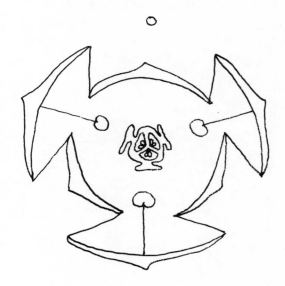

Floral formula: ⊕ {P(3+3)A3}G($\bar{3}$)

DICOTYLEDONAE — FAMILY: RANUNCULACEAE

RANUNCULUS SP.: BUTTERCUP

Actinomorphic flower

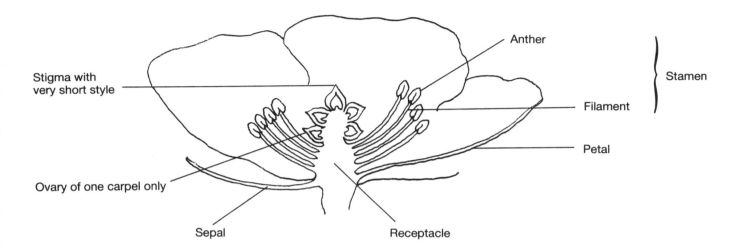

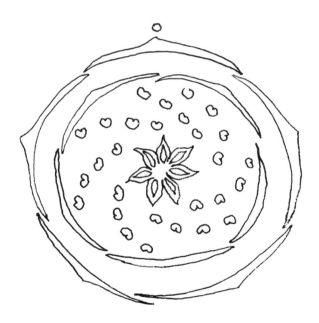

Floral formula: ⊕ K5C5A∞G∞

DICOTYLEDONAE — FAMILY: PAPILIONACEA (LEGUMINOSAE)

LATHYRUS SP.: SWEET PEA

Zygomorphic flower. This is a flower symmetrical about one plane only.

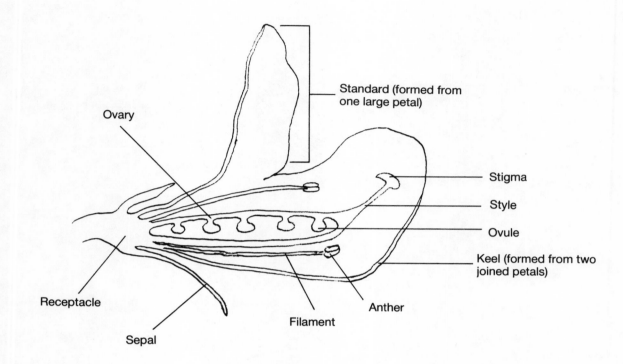

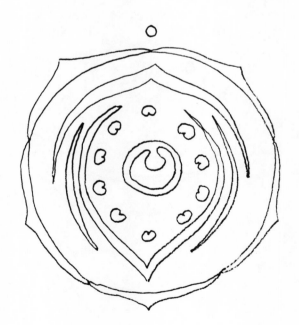

Floral formula: ·|· K(5)C5A(9)+1 G <u>1</u>

DICOTYLEDONAE — FAMILY: COMPOSITAE

In **composite flowers** the inflorescence is a capitulum — numerous florets arise on a flattened axis surrounded by an involucre of bracts that is calyx like. The florets are dimorphic — of two types:

- a ligulate floret with the corolla tube expanded into a strap-like structure
- tubular florets — the corolla remains tubular and symmetrical.

BELLIS PERENNIS: THE DAISY

Two types of florets occur together on the capitulum

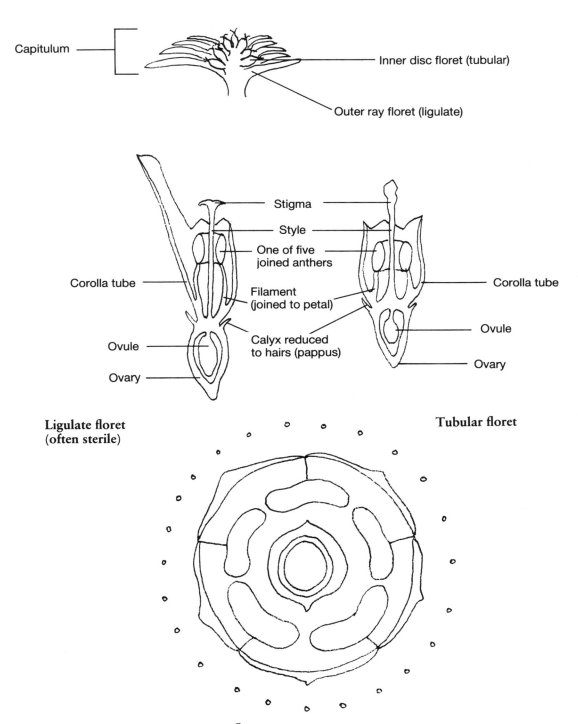

Floral formula: $\oplus$ K(pappus){C(5)A(5)}G($\bar{2}$)

STAGES IN THE DEVELOPMENT OF AN ANTHER, e.g. IN *LILIUM* SP.: THE LILY

HP portion of lumen of developing pollen sac (× 600)

GD LP (×30)

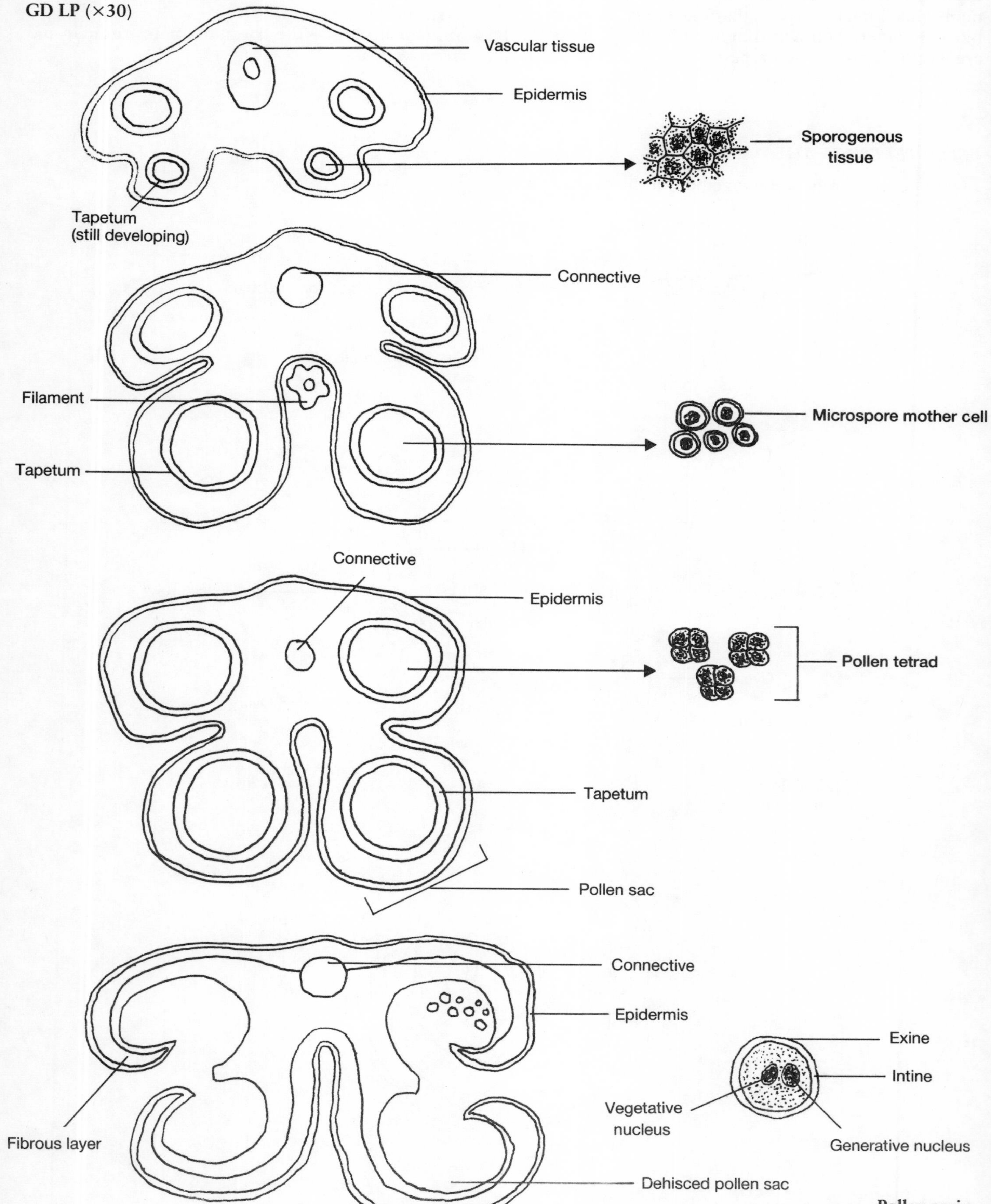

Vascular tissue

Epidermis

Sporogenous tissue

Tapetum (still developing)

Connective

Filament

Tapetum

Microspore mother cell

Connective

Epidermis

Pollen tetrad

Tapetum

Pollen sac

Connective

Epidermis

Exine

Intine

Vegetative nucleus

Generative nucleus

Fibrous layer

Dehisced pollen sac

Pollen grain

STAGES IN THE DEVELOPMENT OF AN OVULE, e.g. *LILIUM* SP.

LS Developing ovule GD LP (× 100)

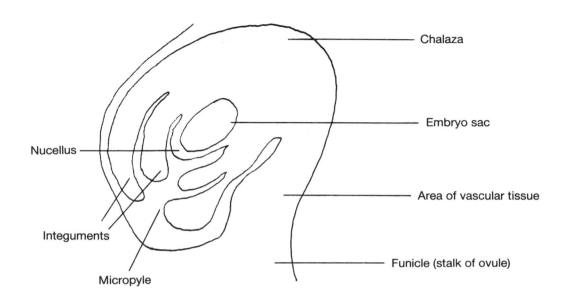

STAGES IN THE DEVELOPMENT OF AN EMBRYO SAC
HP (× 600)

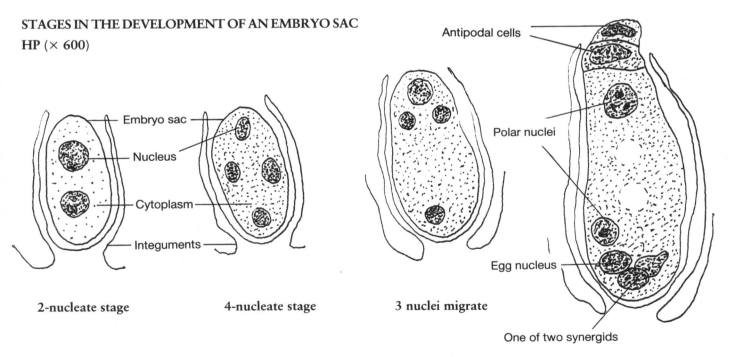

2-nucleate stage   4-nucleate stage   3 nuclei migrate

Mature megaspore stage

Polar nuclei will fuse to form the endosperm nucleus

DEVELOPMENT OF THE EMBRYO OF *CAPSELLA BURSA-PASTORIS*: SHEPHERD'S PURSE

HP (× 600)

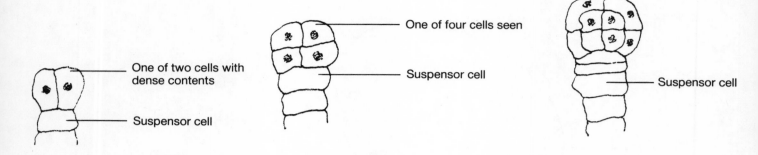

One of two cells with dense contents

Suspensor cell

One of four cells seen

Suspensor cell

Suspensor cell

2-celled stage

Octet stage

Later stage

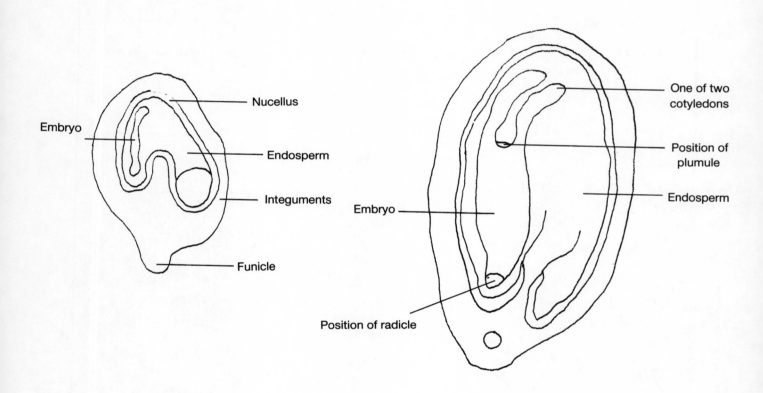

Nucellus

Embryo

Endosperm

Integuments

Funicle

One of two cotyledons

Position of plumule

Endosperm

Embryo

Position of radicle

LS ovule GD
LP (× 30)

LS ovule – later stage
GD LP (× 30)

MITOSIS

Stages from root squash preparation of *Allium* sp.
Some stages not clearly distinguishable

HP (× 600)

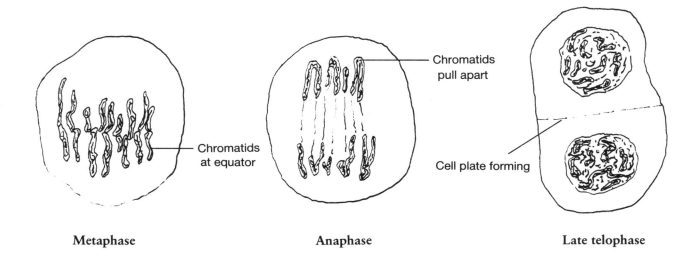

Chromatids pull apart

Chromatids at equator

Cell plate forming

Metaphase   **Anaphase**   **Late telophase**

MEIOSIS

Stages from pollen sacs of *Lilium*

HP (× 1400)

Chromatid pairs should be present in Anaphase I and not in Anaphase II. Difficult to see in either case.

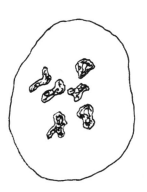

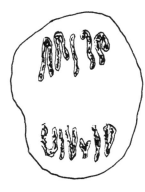

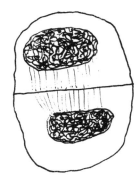

Metaphase I   **Anaphase I**   **Late telophase I**

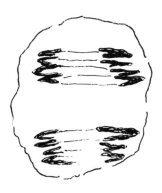

Cell membrane barely visible

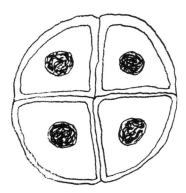

Late anaphase II   **Pollen tetrad**

METHODS OF ENSURING CROSS POLLINATION

STRUCTURAL DIFFERENCES, e.g. PRIMROSE (FAMILY: PRIMULACEAE)

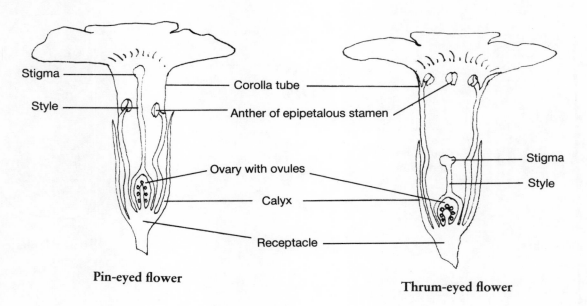

Pin-eyed flower

Thrum-eyed flower

Dimorphic flower. The pollen is usually only compatible *between* the two types. The thrum-eyed flower produces large pollen grains which stick to the base of the proboscis of a visiting insect, and are thus in a position to reach the stigma of a pin-eyed flower. Small pollen grains stick to the middle of the proboscis and thus can be easily deposited onto the stigma of a thrum-eyed flower. This condition is known as heterostyly.

DIOECISM, e.g. *SALIX* SP.: WILLOW (FAMILY: SALICACEAE)

Male and female flowers are on separate plants. (Separate male and female flowers on the same plant — monoecism.) Both male and female flowers are borne on long pendulous catkins.

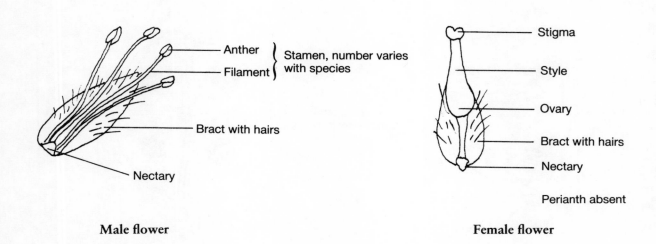

Male flower

Female flower

OTHER METHODS OF POLLINATION

(× 5)

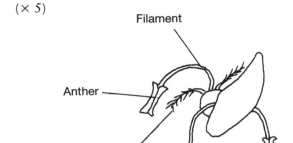

WIND (ANEMOPHILY), e.g. GRASSES

Small, inconspicuous flowers. Petals often reduced or absent. Flowers mature before the foliage leaves. No scent or nectar. Large quantities of pollen produced, often from pendulous catkins. Stamens pendulous; stigmas large, feathery and sticky; often hang outside the flower. Pollen grains small, light and smooth, some with air bladders. Trees, or plants with flowers high above surrounding foliage — no interference with pollen transfer.

(× 5)

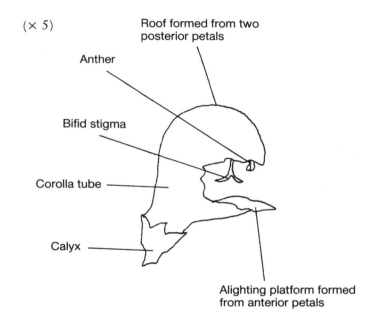

INSECTS (ENTOMOPHILY), e.g. *LAMIUM* SP.: DEAD NETTLE

Brightly coloured flowers with large petals or, if small, aggregated into clusters. Scented; nectaries present. Pollen grains large and sticky, sometimes spiny. Flowers often zygomorphic, with parts arranged so that only heavy insects, e.g. bees, can enter or arranged with deep nectar for butterflies and moths. May trap insects for a while to ensure pollination.

As the insect alights on the platform it brings down the ripe stamens onto its back. On visiting other flowers in a later stage of development, the ripe open stigma touches the insect's back, and the stamens bend away.

TYPES OF FRUIT

APPLE: A FALSE FRUIT (PSEUDOCARP)

Succulent fruit formed from fleshy receptacle surrounding true fruit (core). 'Pips' are seeds.
(× ¼)

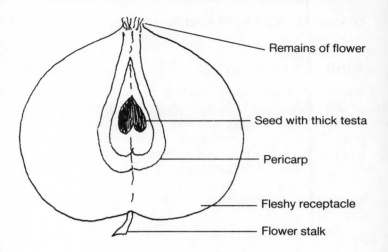

Remains of flower

Seed with thick testa

Pericarp

Fleshy receptacle

Flower stalk

PEA: A LEGUME

A dehiscent fruit formed from a single carpel, splitting dorsally and ventrally.
(× 1)

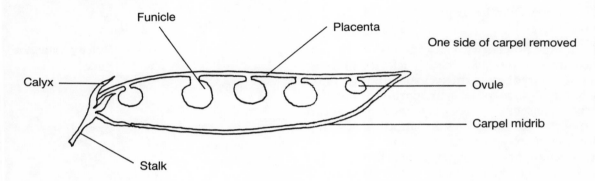

Funicle

Placenta

One side of carpel removed

Calyx

Ovule

Carpel midrib

Stalk

TOMATO: A BERRY

A fleshy fruit formed from a syncarpous ovary, containing several seeds, which are surrounded at dispersal only by a seed coat.

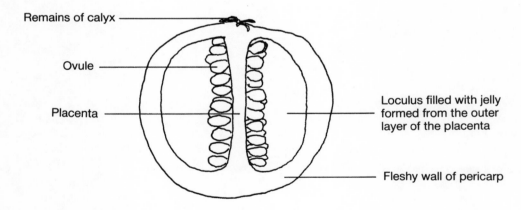

Remains of calyx

Ovule

Placenta

Loculus filled with jelly formed from the outer layer of the placenta

Fleshy wall of pericarp

STRAWBERRY: A FALSE FRUIT

True fruits are achenes on the surface. Achenes are indehiscent with a single seed.

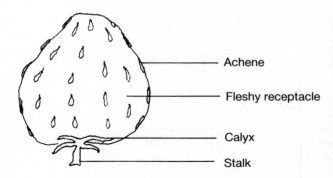

Achene

Fleshy receptacle

Calyx

Stalk

DISPERSAL OF FRUITS AND SEEDS

WIND

Dandelion: a pappus of hairs
(× 5)

Sycamore: a winged extension of the pericarp
(× 2)

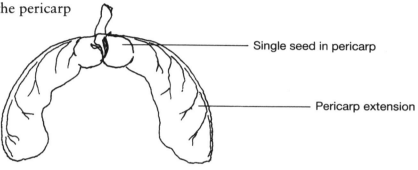

Single seed in pericarp

Pericarp extension

Poppy: a censer mechanism
(× 2)

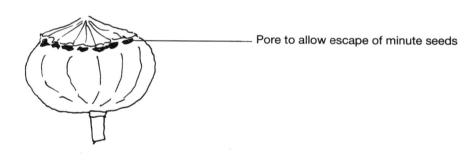

Pore to allow escape of minute seeds

ANIMALS

Geum: hooked achenes for sticking to mammal coats. Some animals, e.g. birds, eat fleshy fruit and egest the seeds.
(× 5)

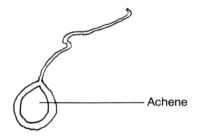

Achene

EXPLOSION

Gorse: drying of pod causes twisting, shooting out seeds.
(× 1)

SEED STRUCTURE AND GERMINATION

MONOCOTYLEDON, e.g. *ZEA MAIS*
(× 6)

**Stages in germination
Hypogeal (× 1)**

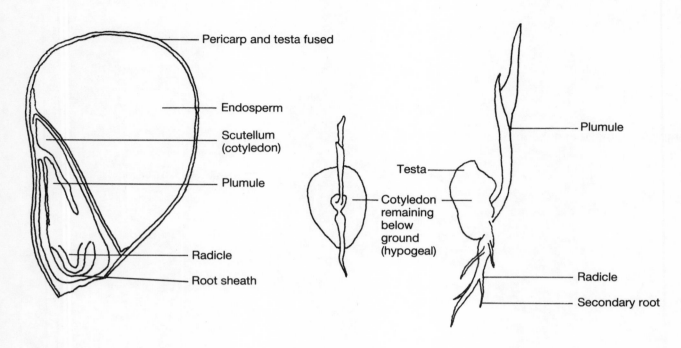

Pericarp and testa fused

Endosperm

Scutellum (cotyledon)

Plumule

Radicle

Root sheath

Plumule

Testa

Cotyledon remaining below ground (hypogeal)

Radicle

Secondary root

DICOTYLEDON, e.g. *HELIANTHUS*: SUNFLOWER
(× 5)

**Stages in germination
Epigeal (× 1)**

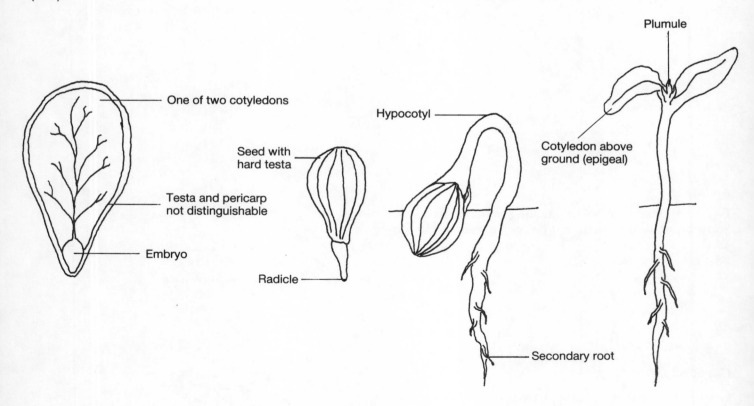

One of two cotyledons

Testa and pericarp not distinguishable

Embryo

Seed with hard testa

Radicle

Hypocotyl

Plumule

Cotyledon above ground (epigeal)

Secondary root

Other dicots may be hypogeal

VEGETATIVE PROPAGATION

RUNNER, e.g. STRAWBERRY

A prostrate stem, bearing scale leaves, from which foliage leaves may arise. Adventitious roots arise, and eventually on decay of the parent runner, a new plant is produced.
(× ½)

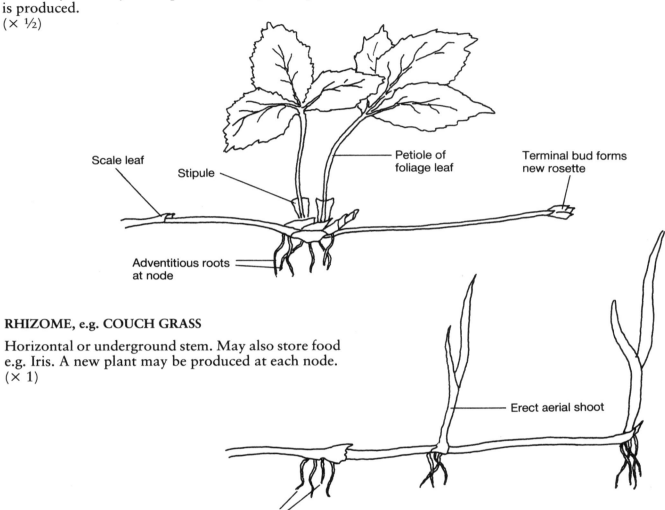

RHIZOME, e.g. COUCH GRASS

Horizontal or underground stem. May also store food e.g. Iris. A new plant may be produced at each node.
(× 1)

TUBER, e.g. POTATO

An underground stem. The potato also stores starch. Each piece of tuber with an axillary bud is capable of producing a new plant.
(× ¼)

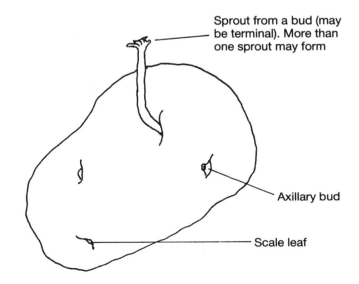

BULB, e.g. ONION

Fleshy storage leaves borne on a compressed stem.
LS (× 1)

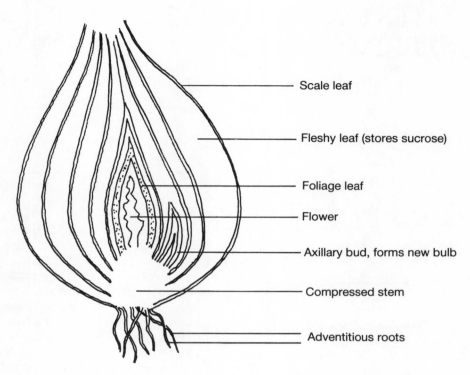

Scale leaf

Fleshy leaf (stores sucrose)

Foliage leaf

Flower

Axillary bud, forms new bulb

Compressed stem

Adventitious roots

CORM, e.g. CROCUS

Underground stem. Bears lateral buds, nodes, and internodes under scale leaves.
(× 2)

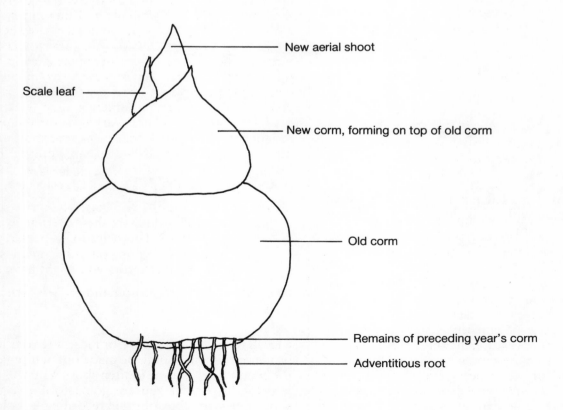

New aerial shoot

Scale leaf

New corm, forming on top of old corm

Old corm

Remains of preceding year's corm

Adventitious root

8 NOTES ON WRITING UP YOUR EXPERIMENTS

As a general rule your written accounts, at least of the experiments performed in class, should follow this type of format.

AIM Express as clearly as possible the effect of *one* variable that the experiment is designed to investigate. Never try to do too much in one experiment; this leads to difficulties in including controls. In an examination your aim will, of course, be dictated by the examiner's instructions.

APPARATUS This might be just a list, or a diagram if a particular piece of apparatus was used. A diagram would be necessary to show a unique arrangement designed for a particular experiment. Remember that one of the points of writing up an experiment is to enable another worker to repeat your experiment exactly and get similar results.

In an examination, you could probably omit the apparatus section since quite often the instructions are to 'use the apparatus provided'. If a complicated set-up is required, you are usually supplied with a printed diagram from which to work. It is obviously unnecessary to repeat this in the written account.

METHOD A very important section. In assessment schemes, particular note is taken of the way in which the method has been set out. Bear in mind again the requirement to be able to repeat work from a written account. In class you may be given detailed instructions, possibly as a handout. Assessment of practicals requires the method to be your account, and specifies that handouts (i.e. your teacher's method) will do if your own annotations are added. However, in exams you are frequently asked to devise your *own* experiment, and in this case your method requires careful planning before you begin.

First, look for and list any variables which might occur other than the one you are asked to investigate and see how you can control them. Examples might be

- **temperature:** use a water bath or carry out the experiment at room temperature, making careful readings at intervals with a thermometer
- **concentration of substances:** take care to check volumes; e.g. if in an enzyme experiment you perhaps omit a substance, be careful to replace it with an equal volume of water so as not to vary the total volume

Examples like this must be looked for in every experiment, and you must use your own judgement as to how to control them. A control that is only too often omitted when testing the effect of a living organism or a substance such as an enzyme is to repeat the procedure using dead or denatured material. An enzyme may be denatured by boiling; this control ensures that any changes which take place in the experiment are brought about only by the enzyme. For example, if germinating pea seeds are being used, seeds killed by boiling are used as a control. It is often customary when using animals, e.g. small arthropods, to omit the dead animal and to use a control with no organism. Sometimes glass beads of similar total volume to the animals are used. It is well to make a note of this in your account as a possible, though remote, source of error.

Having decided what controls you need to use, list the components of your experiment and decide what quantities of substances to use, how to set the experiment up and so on. Quite often a table can be constructed showing various components and quantities. This is also the stage at which you should decide what type of readings or measurements you are going to make, how often and how many. These, of course, are dictated by the time available for the class or the examination. As you go along, make a note of any sources of error that you come across, e.g. insufficient time for as many readings as you would like, varying room temperature resulting from your desk being near a radiator, solutions not having been stirred and so on. You will have to bring these out in your discussion on how valid you consider your results to be.

In an examination it is better to write up your method before you start the experiment, so that you can refer to it. This helps to keep what you are trying to achieve clear in your mind, and also helps you to pick up any errors you might have made.

Always use the third person and the past tense when writing your account.

RESULTS A suitable chart for recording your readings or measurements should be made out before you start the experiment, as time is often short. You will already have decided what you are going to do, so arrange some means suitable for rapid recording — a chart or a table including the timing of the measurements, if this is relevant, and which tube etc. is being measured. You can do this in rough and make a fair copy later, but in examinations it is better to set this chart out neatly in your written account before you start. Readings can then be entered quickly and neatly, thus saving time. Remember that your account of the results must be absolutely honest — do not leave out a reading if it appears to be odd, or even completely wrong. Discuss it later, and then decide whether or not to leave it out of your conclusions as aberrant.

In class you will have a clear idea of what your experiment should be doing. Quite often the results from the whole class will be pooled, so as to get a more valid conclusion; any odd results will probably then be averaged out.

> In an examination, however, you must record exactly what you see. Remember that you do not need to get excellent experimental results to pass the question; indeed, quite often the examiners warn that results might be unpredictable. Much more weight is given to your account of the method, why you have taken those particular readings, and your discussion of the validity of those readings. You may be required to present your results as a graph or a histogram from which to draw your conclusions.

CONCLUSIONS   Be very careful to conclude only what your readings can tell you, not what you think they should tell you. In extreme circumstances you may find that you can draw none at all! In this case, say so, and discuss why not.

DISCUSSION   This is the most important part of your write-up. It should fall into three sections. The first section should give the theory behind the experiment. It is impossible to say what your results may mean without giving a brief account of the physiological processes involved. (There are some examination questions where you are asked simply to *record* what you see. Be careful always to follow instructions.)

In the second section you should assess how far your results accord with this theory, and what they might prove or disprove. This is the place where you should discuss any variable factors that were difficult or impossible to control, factors (e.g. too few measurements) that might lead to inaccurate results, and clear sources of error. Discuss what you would do about these, whether or not they could have been avoided and how you might redesign or modify the experiment to exclude them. You are then in a position to say whether or not your experiment succeeded in proving what it set out to prove.

The third part of your write-up should consist of suggestions for further work that might clarify some of the points ignored, improve the experiment, or take the investigation a step further. It could also include the types of experiment that you would like to have carried out had you had more time, equipment and so forth.

All this will show the examiner whether or not you have fully understood the purpose of the experiment and how it relates to the background theory. Some experiments are much more 'open ended' than others and leave you free to devise with as much originality as you can, but some give very precise details as to how to proceed, what measurements to take and how to record them. Follow the examiners' instructions *in every detail*. This means that you must read the examination questions very carefully indeed. Most errors are made by students who did what they *thought* the questions asked, instead of what was really asked.

STATISTICS   You are required to have some idea of the mathematical processes involved in checking the validity of your results, although actual calculations are not set by the majority of examiners. Such calculations are also used in genetics experiments and in ecological surveys. Both types of investigation require some statistical idea of the probability of results occurring by chance. Decisions are made to accept or reject a theory on the basis of whether factor X could have produced result Y purely by chance.

Curve of normal distribution   A set of readings in biology is often distributed as a 'curve of normal distribution':

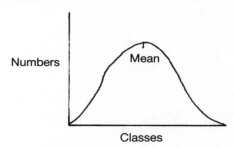

Frequency diagram   This is used to plot the numbers of individuals having a particular measurement, e.g. 10 insects with five bristles on a leg, 20 insects with six bristles etc. These must be expressed as a histogram, since categories are involved:

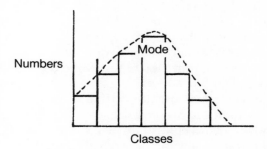

A curve drawn through the tops of the bars of the histogram may approximate to the curve of normal distribution, or it may not. It depends on whether the mode and the mean are similar.

Mode This is the most frequent class, e.g. of a set of readings of size from 24 to 28 cm, 26.5 occurred most often. Such a value is not necessarily the same as the mean.

Median This is the middle observation, e.g. the 10th of 19 readings.

Mean This is the average value.

Standard deviation This describes the amount by which values vary around the average value.

$$SD = \sqrt{\frac{\Sigma d^2}{n}}$$

where Σ refers to the sum of all d values, d is the individual value minus the average value (d is squared so as to eliminate negative figures) and n is the number of individual measurements.

For example, suppose you are investigating the population of wandering snails in a particular pond. You take samples at different places and record them:

Sample number	Numbers counted	Mean	d	d^2	Σd^2
1	294		4.3	18.49	
2	306		16.3	265.69	
3	285	289.7	9.0	81.0	706.2
4	279		15.0	225.0	
5	284		10.0	100.0	
6	290		4.0	16.0	

The standard deviation is then given by

$$SD = \sqrt{\frac{706.2}{6}} = 10.8$$

Standard error This gives a guide to the statistical significance of two sets of figures, each of which may give a different mean value. If the phenomenon under investigation is very variable, then n must be high to give good accuracy:

$$SD = \sqrt{\frac{SD^2}{n}}$$

The mean is then expressed as mean $\pm$ SE, e.g. 8 ± 0.4 indicates that any mean value determined for this particular phenomenon will fall between 7.6 and 8.4.

For two sets of measurements

$$SE = \sqrt{\frac{(SD_1)^2 + (SD_2)^2}{n_1 + n_2}}$$

If $mean_1 - mean_2 = 2 \times SE$ or more, then there is a significant difference between the two sets of figures,

and the difference is due to factors other than chance.

Suppose that you now investigate a second population of wandering snails in another pond:

Sample number	Numbers counted	Mean	d	d^2	Σd^2
1	200		1.7	2.9	
2	198		0.3	0.1	
3	204	198.3	5.7	32.5	123.4
4	196		2.3	5.3	
5	190		8.3	68.9	
6	202		3.7	13.7	

Similarly $SD = \sqrt{\dfrac{123.34}{6}} = 4.5$

To compare the two sets of measurements:

$$SE = \sqrt{\frac{(10.8)^2}{6} + \frac{(4.5)^2}{6}} = 4.8$$

$mean_1 - mean_2 = 289.7 - 198.7 = 91$

This is much greater than 2×4.8, i.e. 9.6; thus the difference is not only due to chance.

The χ^2 (chi-squared) test This is used to measure the difference between an expected and an observed result, and tells us if such a difference is of any significance:

$$\chi^2 = \Sigma \frac{d^2}{x}$$

where d is the observed result minus the expected result and x is the expected result.

For example, pure-breeding red-flowered plants are crossed with pure-breeding white-flowered plants, giving an F_1 generation with red flowers. Interbreeding in this generation gave the following results in the F_2 generation:

Total number of offspring	Red flowered	White flowered	
1624	1224	400	i.e. observed result
Expected result for 1624 plants	1218	406	i.e. *expected* result a 3:1 ratio

For red-flowered plants

d (observed result $-$ expected result) $= 6$

x (expected result) $= 1218$

Therefore

$$\frac{d^2}{x} = \frac{36}{1218} = 0.029$$

For white-flowered plants

$$d = 6 \qquad \frac{d^2}{x} = \frac{36}{406} = 0.088$$
$$x = 406$$

$$\sum \frac{d^2}{x} = 0.088 + 0.029 = 0.117 = \chi^2$$

Values of χ^2 are looked up in tables relating to the number of classes (e.g. red and white flowers = two classes) and the degrees of freedom (the number of classes minus 1). These tables supply the **probability** of the deviation being due to chance for the figures given. If the probability factor arrived at is 0.05 (5%) or greater, then chance is operating and the deviation is not considered significant. However, if the probability factor is less than 0.05, then factors other than chance are operating since the deviation is significant.

This test may be used for ratios, e.g. in genetics

$$\frac{d_a^2}{x_a} + \frac{d_b^2}{x_b} = \chi^2$$

where the ratio is $d_a : d_b$.

DRAWING GRAPHS   Use a fine-pointed pencil — a point has position but no magnitude, so if you make points very large

your graph will be difficult to read and not very accurate. It is advisable to use a cross $\times$ where the point to be plotted is at the junction of the two lines since this can be much more accurate than a point:

The horizontal (bottom) axis of your graph should be the 'fixed' measurements, e.g. the time in hours. The vertical axis should be the 'variable' measurement, e.g. the rate of enzyme activity. Choose the length of your axes carefully — neither should be greatly magnified with respect to the other, or the graph will give an unbalanced picture. Axes should fit neatly into the space available, but need not use it all. Label the axes carefully, using units accurately. (Be careful not to omit units!) Give the graph a suitable title. This is the item most often omitted — it will lose you marks.

In biological graphs, it is not always necessary to try to fit the points onto a smooth curve. Growth curves, for example, do follow such a pattern but some curves, e.g. the height of plants, may have no particular pattern. In such a case you can use

which gives an indication of trends without obscuring the points. Trying to fit points onto a curve without a

sufficient number of points may give a curve where none exists, and hence inaccurate readings will be obtained at points A and B:

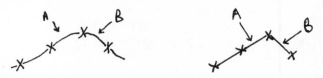

Graphs are normally plotted using a great number of readings at each particular measurement. Plotting many points results in some areas, where there are a lot of similar measurements, having a greater density of points than other areas. Thus aberrant readings can more easily be distinguished from the average. Curves are then run through the areas of greatest density, giving a more accurate representation of what is actually happening during an experiment. The more readings there are, the more the result is statistically valid. However, in a physiology practical class, or during an examination, there is not usually time for more than one reading at each variable. This inevitably means less accurate results. The validity of your results must be clearly discussed in your summing up of the experiment with regard to both the number of measurements made and the number of specimens, for example, that are measured. Class results may, of course, be pooled for greater accuracy.

Histograms or bar graphs are used when variations cannot be expressed by single points. For example, readings may be taken of oxygen evolution over successive periods of 3 minutes:

Time period	Reading
0–3 min	10 cm^3
3–6 min	15 cm^3
6–9 min	12 cm^3

Dividing the results by three and plotting them per minute would be inaccurate since we cannot assume that the oxygen is evolved at a constant rate. In such a case a histogram gives a better picture.

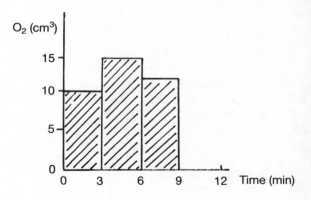

Bar charts are often used in ecological surveys, e.g. to plot the extent of vegetation. Readings might be taken of the percentage cover of water plants A and B at various distances from the shore of a pond:

Distance from shore (metres)	% cover (plant A)
10	0
15	40
20	40
25	100
30	100
35	60
40	0

This would give a bar chart as shown below. Values are marked in at each distance, half above and half below the axis for plant A. Where no plant A occurs, e.g. at 10 m and at 40 m, the bar is brought to zero *halfway* between 40 m and the previous reading at 35 m, i.e. at 37.5 m. Similarly, it would be brought to zero at 12.5 m. This particular type of chart is called a kite histogram or diagram.

Charts and tables, which you will often use for recording methods or results, must be carefully planned beforehand. Decide which variable you are going to put along the top. If you are recording a method, e.g. the contents of various test-tubes, it is best to use contents along the top, and the number of individual tubes vertically:

	Ingredient		
	X	Y	Z
Tube 1			
Tube 2			
etc.			

Spaces may then be filled in with the volumes of ingredients used; this will save a lot of time.

For results, a similar format could be used. Individual experiments could be entered vertically with results, e.g. of food tests, along the top. Results could be indicated by + or −, or by a colour change, for example. Always provide a key to identify the symbols used.

Many of the marks for writing up an experiment are awarded for the clarity and the logic of the way in which tables such as these are constructed.

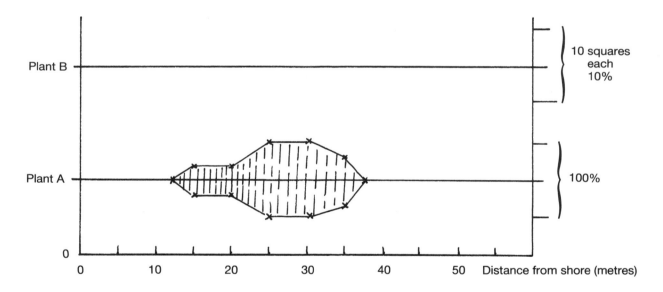

9 EXPERIMENTAL WORK

1 To investigate the effects of temperature on the heart rate of *Daphnia* species

APPARATUS   Cavity slides and coverslips
Cotton wool
Three 250 cm³ beakers
Ice
Water baths at 25 °C, 30 °C and 35 °C
Test-tubes of culture medium,
e.g. 'Instant pond', about 10 cm³ in
each (see Appendix 1 for recipe)
Daphnia species
Thermometers
Stop-clock
Tally counter

METHOD   Place about 12 *Daphnia* in each of the test-tubes. These should be sufficient for the entire class, as it is easier if students work in pairs. Put one test-tube of *Daphnia* in each of the water baths, and one in a beaker of water at room temperature. By adding various amounts of ice to two further beakers of water you should be able to achieve temperatures of about 5 °C, and 10–15 °C. The precise interval between the temperatures is not so important — it is difficult to achieve accurate 5° intervals in practice. Allow the test-tubes to equilibrate in their water baths for at least 10 minutes. Using a teat pipette with a fairly wide mouth to avoid damaging the organism, gently remove a *Daphnia* from one of the test-tubes. Place it in a cavity slide in a drop of the medium. Place a few strands of cotton wool in the drop. This will immobilise the animal without harming it, and will enable you to count the heart beats. Place a coverslip over the cavity.

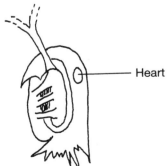

Check carefully that you can recognise the heart amidst all the other moving parts of the organism. One of the pair of students should now operate the stop-clock, timing intervals of 30 seconds each. The other student should count the heart beats, viewing the animal through the low power of the microscope. Tally counters are easy to use and quite accurate. If a tally counter is not available, make a dot on a piece of paper for every heart beat. You can count quite rapid beats in this way.

Be very careful not to get the microscope lamp too close to the slide. The temperature will alter slightly throughout the time interval in any case, but the bench light may heat the slide quite considerably if you do not take care. Ideally, you need to make at least three counts on each organism, and preferably you should count several organisms at each temperature. However, in a class situation, results can be pooled to achieve this effect.

RESULTS   Record your readings at each temperature in the form of a chart. Then record the class results, and finally produce a chart of average heart rate for each temperature. Plot these figures as a graph of the number of beats per minute against temperature.

$$\text{temperature coefficient } Q_{10} = \frac{\text{rate at } (T + 10)\,°C}{\text{rate at } T\,°C}$$

Calculate Q_{10} for 5–15 °C, 15–25 °C, 20–30 °C and 25–35 °C taking the readings from your graph. A Q_{10} of 2 indicates a doubling of the rate for a 10 °C rise in temperature and is typical of biological systems.

CONCLUSIONS   You should word your conclusion to express *only* what your graph shows you about the relationship between heart rate and temperature.

DISCUSSION   The heart rate in this experiment is taken as a measure of the metabolic rate, i.e. the amount of enzyme activity. Therefore you might expect to find the typical relationship between temperature and enzyme action, that is a graph of this shape:

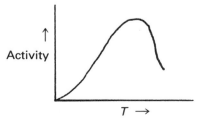

Your Q_{10} calculations might show a value of approximately 2 for temperatures between 10°C and 30°C, i.e. 10°C above and below the optimum temperature for the animal. Bear in mind that the Q_{10} will be high, as the temperature increases from 5°C, since activity at 5°C may be nearly zero, whereas at 15°C there might be appreciable activity. You might also expect enzyme activity to fall off as a higher temperature is reached, if the enzymes do not denature completely. Discuss this in terms of enzyme structure.

Look for your sources of error. In this experiment it is notable that it is very difficult to keep a constant temperature. Numbers of readings on each animal, and numbers of animals tested, must be large in order to give any accuracy. Different *Daphnia* have differing heart rates. Calculation of the standard error could be used to measure the validity of your results.

Think of ways in which you might be able to improve the experimental technique, perhaps with regard to counting procedures, or temperature control. Suggest any other experiments that you might do to explore this area further.

A modification of this experiment, in the light of recent examination questions, would be to place the cavity slide in a petri dish of water at the required temperature. Alternatively, a small watch glass could be used. Either of these systems would delay temperature changes for a while. The waterflea could also be held in position by pressing it gently onto a spot of vaseline on the glass or watch slide. It is difficult to tell if this would cause more or less stress to the *Daphnia* than the cotton fibres.

2   To determine the osmotic potential of epidermal cells from an onion bulb scale

APPARATUS   Slides and coverslips
Scalpel, forceps
Eight stoppered test-tubes with labels
Distilled water
Sucrose solutions of the following concentrations (see Appendix 1 for recipes): 0.2 M; 0.3 M; 0.35 M; 0.4 M; 0.45 M; 0.5 M; 1.0 M
10 cm³ pipette or measuring cylinder
Fresh onion bulb
Tally counter
Thermometer

METHOD   Take a scale leaf from the onion and gently peel away the thin inner epidermis. Cut into squares of as nearly equal size as possible, about 10 mm square. Keep them in the tube with the distilled water until you have cut all the squares you need. Then place 10 cm³ of sucrose solution of each molarity in the appropriately labelled test-tube. Put in one square of onion epidermal tissue, and leave for a minimum of 30 minutes. Make sure that the tissue does not float on

the surface, causing some of the cells to dry up.

Examine each square in turn under the microscope by mounting it in a drop of its sucrose solution on a slide and covering it with a coverslip.

RESULTS   Using a tally, count all the cells that you can see under the LP field of view. Count also those which show the slightest degree of plasmolysis (i.e. have the cytoplasm detached from the cell wall). Record these two figures for each tissue square. Work out the percentage of plasmolysed cells for each. Plot a graph of percentage plasmolysis against the molarity of the sucrose solution. From your graph, read off the molar concentration at which 50% of the cells are plasmolysed. This gives you the concentration at which the osmotic potentials on either side of the cell wall are equal ($OP_{int} = OP_{ext}$). You are now in a position to work out this potential.

1 molar sucrose at 273 K creates an osmotic pressure of 22.4 atmospheres. Thus x molar sucrose at $273 + y$ K (room temperature) will create an osmotic pressure (in atmospheres) of

$$\frac{22.4 \times x \times (273 + y)}{1 \times 273}$$

Nowadays Pascals (Pa) are used (1 atmosphere = 101.32 kPa).

DISCUSSION   50% of cells plasmolysed is taken to indicate the condition of 'incipient plasmolysis' of the tissue (which is very difficult to recognise under the microscope).

Incipient plasmolysis indicates that when the osmotic potential of the cell sap, i.e. OP(cell), equals that of the surrounding medium, i.e. OP(soln), no inward pressure is exerted by the cell wall (WP or wall pressure) and there is no outward pressure of the protoplast against the cell wall (TP or turgor pressure). The two pressures are equal and opposite. The term water potential ψ (equivalent to negative diffusion pressure deficit, a term still used in some texts) measures the tendency of the cell to take up water:

ψ(cell) = TP(cell) − OP(cell)
ψ(soln) = − OP(soln)

The amount of water that can be taken into the cell depends on the difference between the osmotic potential, drawing water in, and the turgor pressure, opposing the intake of water.* When the turgor pressure is zero, the water potential equals the osmotic potential. This osmotic potential reflects the difference between the internal and external concentrations. Thus, when there is no difference, the osmotic potential is zero and

---

* Some texts use the term pressure potential (PP) to indicate the forces of turgor pressure and wall pressure influencing the movement of water in or out of the cell

ψ = OP(cell) + PP

ψ(cell) = ψ(soln). Then by measuring the external concentration (i.e. ψ(soln)), you measure ψ(cell.).

Take into account in your discussion the possible errors inherent in determining visible plasmolysis, the number of cells counted for the percentage calculations and the difficulties in keeping the onion tissue properly submerged in the sucrose solutions. How could you set about overcoming these sources of error?

3 To investigate the effect of differing external osmotic potential on potato 'chips'

A variation of the experiment to examine the effect of osmotic pressure on plant cells is to use 'chips' of potato. Chips about 5 cm × 2 cm × 1 cm are cut out of fresh, firm potatoes, and placed in suitable containers of distilled water. Make sure that there is sufficient liquid to cover the chips. Each chip is carefully blotted dry, and measured accurately in all three dimensions. The measurements are recorded, together with some means of identifying each piece of potato. Two or three are then placed in each of several sucrose solutions of varying molarity. After 30 minutes the chips are remeasured. The total volume for each is calculated in cubic centimetres, i.e. width × length × thickness. This is then expressed as a percentage increase over the original volume. A graph can be plotted of percentage increase or decrease against the molarity of the sucrose solution.

The reasons for the change in volume are discussed in terms of water potential. Record also, and discuss, any changes in texture that you observe.

4 To observe the effect of varying osmotic potentials on red blood cells

APPARATUS Distilled water
0.05% saline solution
0.09% saline solution
2.5% saline solution
Pasteur pipettes and tests
Counting chamber (see Experiment 32)
Test-tubes and rack
Labels
Oxalated blood sample (oxalate prevents clotting). This is obtainable from biological suppliers — regulations no longer permit you to take blood samples from yourself

METHOD Place a few drops of blood in each of four test-tubes. Add an equal quantity of distilled water to tube 1, and to tubes 2, 3 and 4 the same quantity of a saline solution (see Appendix 1 for recipes). Label each tube with its saline percentage.

Prepare a counting chamber with a drop of liquid from the tube containing blood and 0.09% saline. This saline is iso-osmotic to body fluids, so that the blood cells should be intact. Count a suitable proportion of squares, recording the numbers of squares and the numbers of cells in each. Calculate the number of cells per cm^3.

In the tubes containing distilled water and 0.05% saline, the cells should have taken up water as $OP_{int} > P_{ext}$. Some or all of them will have burst, i.e. haemolysed, as there is no opposing wall pressure, as in plant cells. Perform similar counts on these solutions. Subtracting the counts that you get here from the numbers found in the iso-osmotic sample, i.e. a normal blood count, will give you the numbers of cells haemolysed. Observe the cells in the 2.5% saline. They should have become plasmolysed since $OP_{int} < OP_{ext}$. Count again the numbers plasmolysed and the numbers entire.

Discuss these results in terms of the properties of the cell membrane, osmotic potentials and in terms of observations on the colours of the solution in the original tubes where haemolysed cells have liberated haemoglobin into the saline solution.

5 To determine the rate of oxygen consumption of an organism, using a respirometer

APPARATUS Suitable organisms such as locusts, woodlice or germinating pea seeds
2 M KOH solution (see Appendix 1 for recipe)
Filter paper
Water bath at room temperature, with thermometer
Clock

METHOD N.B. If the experiment is carried out as described, then the apparatus is functioning as a Dixon–Barcroft constant-pressure manometer. Alternatively, if the greased syringe is left undisturbed and the manometer reading is recorded, then the apparatus is a Barcroft differential respirometer.

Pipette 5 cm^3 of 2 M KOH into both respirometer tubes, making sure that the solution does not touch the sides of the tubes. Place a small roll of filter paper in each tube to act as a wick and increase the surface area for absorption.

Support the mesh on a glass rod if necessary to keep it clear of the filter paper. Ideally a dead locust of similar size should be used as a control in tube A. If you do not want to do this, add about 5 cm^3 of water to the KOH solution. This is about the volume of the locust, and will ensure that you have the same volume of air in both tubes. If you are using pea seeds, equal quantities of boiled pea seeds are used for a control.

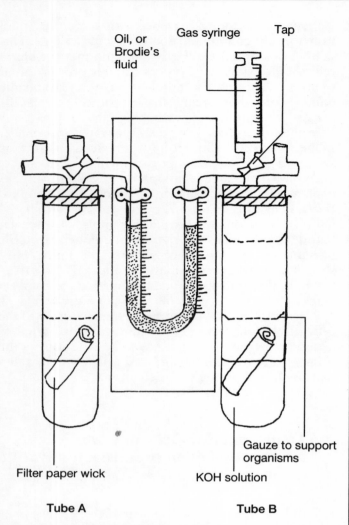

Oil, or Brodie's fluid

Gas syringe

Tap

Filter paper wick

KOH solution

Gauze to support organisms

Tube A **Tube B**

Draw coloured oil, or Brodie's fluid (see Appendix 1 for recipe), into the manometer tube so that there are no air bubbles, and it comes about halfway up the scale on each side. Open the screw clip, remove the syringe and connect up the manometer tube. Place both tubes of the apparatus in a water bath at about 20 °C and leave to equilibrate with the taps open. After about 5 minutes, set the well-greased piston of the syringe at the 0.5 cm³ mark and put in its place as shown in the diagram. By means of the syringe, adjust the manometer so that the fluid levels are equal on both sides. Close the tap. The syringe plunger should stay in position. If it falls slowly, you have a leak. Check that all the connections are well-greased and airtight. Record the time and the exact position of the piston and the manometer menisci. Record readings at suitable intervals, perhaps every minute for 5 minutes. Adjust if the rate seems to be very quick or very slow.

To take a reading, restore the levels of the menisci in the manometer tube to their original values by raising or lowering the syringe. Read the new level of the piston — in this experiment you are measuring net gas uptake by the organism as the CO_2 given out is absorbed by the KOH. Your syringe piston should register a decreasing reading. If your organism has a high metabolic rate, you may find that you need to set your initial syringe at more than 0.5 cm³.

Record a chart of syringe readings against time. Plot these readings as a graph. The slope of your graph will provide you with the rate of oxygen uptake in $cm^3 \ min^{-1}$. You must then take the weight of the organisms you used, and express the result as $cm^3 \ min^{-1} \ g^{-1}$.

Tube A is the control tube, and any changes in temperature or pressure affecting the volume of air in tube B should be mirrored in tube A. This is the reason for using a water bath, even at room temperature, to ensure an even and constant temperature. Other sources of error might be leaking of the joints or the syringe giving incorrect readings. A check of your results with the rest of the class should show if yours are wildly inaccurate — the main type of result in the case of a leak is to find no change at all over a period of 5 minutes.

6 To find the change in rate of oxygen uptake with temperature

APPARATUS As for Experiment 5, but placing the apparatus in water baths at 10 °C, 15 °C, 25 °C and 30 °C

METHOD Carry out the experiment as before. Record your results as a chart, then plot graphs to show the rate at each temperature. Look for Q_{10}, the temperature coefficient

$$Q_{10} = \frac{\text{rate at } (T + 10) \,°C}{\text{rate at } T \,°C}$$

Over a limited range of temperature, the temperature coefficient may be 2, which is typical of biological systems:

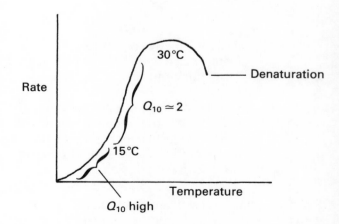

i.e. zero activity at, for example, 5 °C and good activity at 15 °C.

7 To determine the respiratory quotient (RQ)

APPARATUS Respirometer as for Experiment 5 in a water bath at 20 °C (the KOH is omitted from the tubes)

METHOD No KOH is used in the tubes since in this experiment the ratio of CO_2 given off to oxygen taken up is measured

$$RQ = \frac{\text{volume of } CO_2 \text{ given off}}{\text{volume of } O_2 \text{ absorbed}}$$

The initial reading of the syringe is recorded. If the RQ is 1, i.e. the amounts of gas given off and absorbed are the same, then the final reading should be identical. If the final reading is higher or lower, then this indicates that the amounts of gas given off are greater or less than the amounts absorbed, and this gives some idea of the substance used as a respiratory substrate.

An RQ of 1 indicates a carbohydrate source, i.e.

$$C_6H_{12}O_6 + \underline{6O_2} \rightarrow \underline{6CO_2} + 6H_2O$$

A fat may give an RQ of 0.7, i.e.

$$2C_{51}H_{98}O_6 + \underline{145O_2} \rightarrow \underline{102CO_2} + 98H_2O$$

Proteins are difficult to measure as they are of variable composition. Values have been measured between 0.5 and 1.5. In contrast, anaerobic respiration gives a very high value:

$$C_6H_{12}O_6 \rightarrow 2C_2H_5OH + 2CO_2$$

$$RQ = \frac{2}{0} = \infty$$

Different types of respiring seeds may be used, but conclusions are not easy to draw, as more than one type of substrate may be used at any one time.

8 To investigate the fermentation of sucrose by yeast

APPARATUS A respirometer set up in a 25 °C water bath
Dried yeast
0.5 M sucrose solution
Measuring cylinder
Clock
Test-tube of lime-water
Iodine (solid)
10% KOH solution
Bunsen burner
Distilled water
KOH pellets

METHOD Add a weighed quantity of dried yeast to 30 cm³ of sucrose solution, and stir gently until a smooth suspension is obtained. Pour into the experimental tube of the respirometer, and add an equal quantity of water to the control tube. Connect the manometer and set the syringe piston to 0.5 cm³. Record the position of this, and the menisci of the fluid in the manometer. Start the clock.

Take readings at suitable intervals (perhaps every minute) of the piston position when the manometer readings are brought back to their original values. Plot your readings as a graph to obtain the rate of gas production at 25 °C. Knowing the quantity of *dry* yeast that you took, you can express the rate as cm³ gas min⁻¹ g⁻¹ for 0.5 M sucrose. Carefully remove the syringe from the apparatus, making sure that the piston position does not change. Insert the nozzle into the lime-water and push the plunger home. This should give you the customary milky reaction for CO_2. An increase in the manometer readings shows that gas is being produced, but you cannot prove that oxygen is *not* taken up without repeating the experiment using KOH to absorb the CO_2. This is not easy; you could set up the respirometer tube as shown in the diagram, and show that no change in volume occurs.

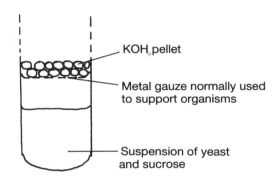

- KOH pellet
- Metal gauze normally used to support organisms
- Suspension of yeast and sucrose

Perform the iodoform test (see Appendix 1) by heating a sample of the yeast suspension at the end of the experiment with iodine and KOH solution. This should give you the characteristic smell of iodoform, showing that it is likely that ethanol has been produced. (What other substances give the iodoform test?) Perform a similar experiment and leave it until all the CO_2 has been produced and there is no further change in gas volume in the syringe. Convert this volume to standard temperature and pressure, and calculate the fraction of a mole of CO_2 present (1 mole of gas at STP occupies 22 400 cm³). Calculate the fraction of a mole of sucrose present in the volume of solution taken. You should be able to arrive at an equation for the reaction.

9 To compare the ventilation movements of a locust under differing carbon dioxide conditions

APPARATUS   5 cm^3 of 1 M HCl
             5 cm^3 of 1 M NaHCO$_3$
             Stop-clock

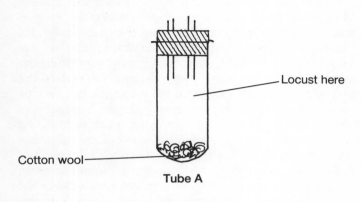

Tube A

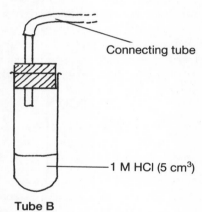

Tube B

METHOD   Observe the ventilation movements of the locust by watching the movement of the abdomen drawing air into the spiracles. Having allowed the locust to settle, count the ventilation movements over a minute. Repeat this for 5 minutes, record your results as a table and calculate the average number of movements per minute.

Add the sodium hydrogen carbonate (NaHCO$_3$) to the acid in tube B and shake gently. Attach the connecting tube of B to tube A for about 1 minute. Remove the connecting tube, and take another set of readings as before. Record your results and calculate the average. Pool the class results to obtain a more accurate average. Discuss carefully the reasons why an increased level of carbon dioxide in inspired air would cause the breathing rate to change.

10 To demonstrate the evolution of carbon dioxide by living organisms, using a bicarbonate indicator

Bicarbonate indicator consists of 0.001 M sodium hydrogen carbonate, and the indicators cresol red and thymol blue (see Appendix 1 for recipe). The solution is an orange-red colour. On equilibration with ordinary air the colour does not change appreciably, since the concentration of carbon dioxide in the solution is about the same as air with 0.03% carbon dioxide:

$$CO_2 + H_2O \rightarrow H_2CO_3 \rightleftharpoons H^+ + HCO_3^-$$

Carbon dioxide given out into the solution can thus be seen to give more acid ions, thus decreasing the pH, or negative logarithm, of the hydrogen ion content.

APPARATUS   Boiling tubes fitted with rubber bungs
             Test-tube racks
             Dilute sodium hyroxide (1 M)
             Dilute hydrochloric acid (1 M)
             Bicarbonate indicator
             Small water snails
             Germinating pea seeds (soaked in
             water for at least 24 hours)
             Similar pea seeds killed by boiling

METHOD   Set up the following test-tubes with their contents:

Tube 1   5 cm^3 bicarbonate indicator and five snails.
Tube 2   5 cm^3 indicator and five living pea seeds.
Tube 3   5 cm^3 indicator and five dead seeds.
Tube 4   5 cm^3 indicator into which you have exhaled several times (stopper quickly).
Tube 5   5 cm^3 indicator — unaltered.
Tube 6   5 cm^3 indicator and 1 cm^3 dilute acid.
Tube 7   5 cm^3 indicator and 1 cm^3 dilute alkali.

Observe the colour changes at 5 minute intervals for 30 minutes. This regime may be altered if you find a very rapid rate of carbon dioxide evolution. The indicator in tube 6 will turn bright yellow with the acid. That in tube 7 will go bright purple with the alkali. These two tubes will show you the extremes of colour changes possible with this indicator.

This is not an experiment to measure the amount or rate of carbon dioxide evolution, it merely shows whether or not the organism gives out carbon dioxide, and whether one organism does so more rapidly than the other.

Discuss the effect of temperature changes on the bicarbonate indicator. How would you attempt to discover what they are? Should the experiment be carried out in a beaker of water at room temperature, rather than in air? What would be the best way of presenting your results?

11 To investigate the compensation point of a plant such as *Elodea* species using bicarbonate indicator

APPARATUS Boiling tubes with well-fitting rubber bungs.
Bicarbonate indicator (see Experiment 10)
Several sprigs of *Elodea* species
Light source, e.g. bench lamp
Beakers of water to act as water baths
Thermometers
Measuring tape
Light meter, if available
Light-proof box, large enough to take a beaker of water containing a boiling tube and thermometer

METHOD Place a sprig of *Elodea* in a boiling tube, and add sufficient bicarbonate indicator to cover the plant. Stopper firmly. Place the tube, together with a thermometer, in a beaker of water, and place this in the light-proof box. Set up further tubes of *Elodea* in the same way, but place these at various measured distances from the light source, e.g. 10, 25, 50, 100, 200 and 300 cm. Seal some bicarbonate indicator in each of two further test-tubes as a record of the original indicator colour. Put one of these in the beaker nearest the light, and the other in the box in the dark. Darken the laboratory. Leave the experiment for 6 hours, if this is convenient; otherwise, the experiment can be examined after 3 hours. If necessary, it may be left until the next day. The indicator in the tube kept in the dark should show the acid colour — respiration alone has been occurring. The indicator in the tubes furthest from the light may also still be yellow, but at some nearer distance you should find the indicator returning to normal and eventually, nearest the light, showing the alkaline colour, i.e. recording carbon dioxide uptake. This may take quite a long time, since the indicator itself is a source of bicarbonate ions. Note the temperature of each beaker.

The distance and measured light intensity at which the indicator returns to its normal colour indicate the compensation point, i.e. the point at which respiration and photosynthesis are occurring at equal rates. This may well be at a lower intensity for *Elodea* than for terrestrial plants accustomed to brighter light. Terrestrial shade plants would be expected to have a lower compensation point. However, *Elodea* only can be satisfactorily used with bicarbonate indicator.

Discuss also the effect of temperature on respiration and photosynthesis, and any 'limiting factors' that may be operating.

How would you attempt to improve this experiment? Make careful note of temperature changes in the beakers of water — these are probably due to the proximity of the light source. A mercury vapour lamp gives light without heat, but this may not be available. Find out how the rate of respiration changes with temperature. It actually increases faster than does the rate of photosynthesis. Is this difference big enough to affect your results?

12 To investigate various aspects of photosynthesis

Many of the studies connected with this process may conveniently be carried out by using the photosynthetic apparatus shown below, obtainable from biological suppliers.

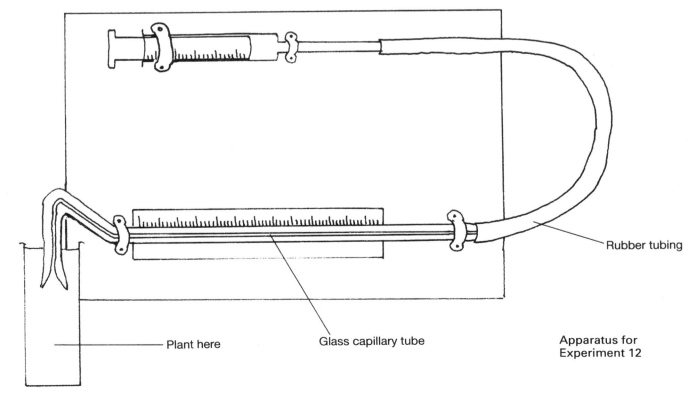

Plant here   Glass capillary tube   Rubber tubing

Apparatus for Experiment 12

The plant most convenient to use is *Elodea*, an aquatic water weed. A sample that is actively photosynthesising in an aquarium or pond is placed in a boiling tube, together with the pond or aquarium water. The tube is supported inside a beaker of water at room temperature containing a thermometer. This arrangement helps to keep the temperature constant as you conduct light intensity experiments.

Remove the plunger from the syringe and gently fill the part of the apparatus connected to the baseboard with water from the tap. Clamp the baseboard in position so that the flared end of the capillary tube is over the cut end of the *Elodea* in its tube.

12A To record the rate of oxygen evolution at different temperatures

APPARATUS   Set up the apparatus as shown
Beakers of ice-water at 5 °C and 15 °C
Thermostatic water bath with variable setting
Light source

METHOD   Illuminate the specimen but not so brightly that the temperature is affected. Collect the oxygen evolved, e.g. over a period of 5 minutes. Draw the bubble evolved into the capillary tube over the scale by manipulating the syringe plunger. Record the length of the bubble. Knowing the bore of the capillary tube (probably 0.5 mm), you can calculate the volume of the bubble:

length $\times \pi r^2$ = volume
where $r = \dfrac{\text{bore of tube}}{2}$

Repeat this procedure several times to give several consecutive 5 minute values. Then replace one temperature with another and take further readings. Set out your results as a table and draw histograms of cm³ of oxygen evolved against time for each temperature, e.g. 5 °C, 15 °C, 25 °C, 30 °C and 35 °C. The gas evolved in each case is unlikely to be pure oxygen — other gases dissolve into the bubble from the water, e.g. nitrogen. The extent to which this happens may not be the same at different temperatures.

The concept of limiting factors will also come into your discussion both here and in subsequent photosynthesis experiments. Here you are measuring the effect of temperature, but the concentrations of carbon dioxide, and the light intensity, are limiting factors. These may, for example, inhibit the appearance of $Q_{10} = 2$ in certain temperature ranges, as the enzymes may not be able to work at their optimum rate. Increasing the CO_2 concentration of the light intensity will solve this problem, and the effects of these factors will be investigated in following experiments.

12B To investigate the effect of light intensity on the rate of oxygen evolution

APPARATUS   A bright light source
Meter rule
Otherwise as before

METHOD   Darken the room and use a small bright source of light such as a slide projector. A bench lamp with a 40 watt bulb will do if a projector bulb is not available. A mercury vapour lamp, if available, is best because it produces no heat to change the temperature during the course of the experiment. A light meter could be used to measure the intensity of the light, but meters vary in their response. They should function adequately for comparative readings. However, the fact that the plant is in water is a further source of error.

Place the light source 1 cm from the plant. Make several 5 minute readings as before. Then repeat, moving the light source various distances from the plant, e.g. from 5–100 cm.

Record your results as a table, and plot a graph or histogram of the volume of O_2 evolved per minute against light intensity. The intensity of light varies inversely as the square of the distance, i.e.

intensity $= \dfrac{1}{d^2}$

where d is the distance of the light source from the plant.

13 To investigate the effect of carbon dioxide concentration on the rate of oxygen evolution

APPARATUS   Audus apparatus as supplied commercially
Elodea species
Stop-clock
$KHCO_3$ solutions (see below)
Beaker of water with thermometer

The reservoir is used to contain a solution of potassium hydrogen carbonate. This is less toxic than the sodium salt and a solution of it gives off 22% by weight of CO_2 on dissociation (at room temperature). Take the temperature of the water in the beaker — remember that the amount of dissolved gases varies inversely as the temperature. Make up solutions containing 0.25%, 0.5%, 0.75%, 1%, 1.5% and 2% of $KHCO_3$ by weight (see Appendix 1 for recipes), and work out the amounts of CO_2 supplied by each. Make a chart of these concentrations, and enter the results of oxygen evolution in cm³ min⁻¹ at the given temperature.

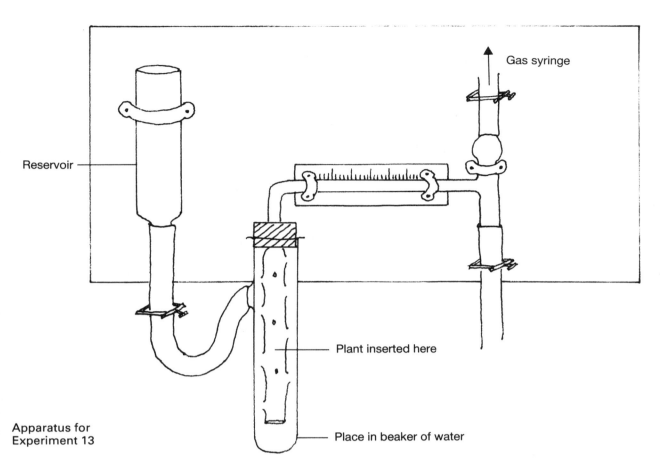

Reservoir

Gas syringe

Plant inserted here

Apparatus for
Experiment 13

Place in beaker of water

14 Separation of chlorophyll pigments by chromatography

14A Extraction of chlorophyll pigments from plant material

APPARATUS   Acetone (**inflammable!**)
Boiling tubes
Glass rod
Filter funnel, filter paper
Nettle powder (can be bought dry from biological suppliers; you cannot use the fresh leaves)

METHOD   5 cm^3 of acetone is placed in a boiling tube, with 2 g of the nettle powder. The mixture is stirred well and allowed to stand. The solution is then filtered into a fresh boiling tube. A further 3 cm^3 of acetone is placed in another boiling tube, together with the material from the filter paper. This is stirred again, allowed to stand and refiltered. The combined filtrates (8 cm^3) are allowed to evaporate down to a total volume of about 3 cm^3 to concentrate the pigments. (Use a water bath to do this, or allow it to stand in the laboratory overnight. Do *not* use any naked flames in the laboratory while this extraction is being carried out.) The extract is now ready for running on the chromatogram.

14B Running the chromatogram

APPARATUS   Large sheets of Whatman No. 1 filter paper
Gas jars with glass lids
Vaseline
Heavy cotton
Solvent — 1 part acetone : 9 parts petroleum ether (80–100 °C fraction)
Paper clips
Pasteur pipettes and teats
Concentrated extract of nettle powder

METHOD   Be careful to handle the filter paper so as to avoid finger-marks on the part that you are going to use. Cut strips of filter paper 5 cm wide and about 5 cm longer than the height of the jar. Rule a pencil line 3 cm from the bottom end of the paper. Using a fine Pasteur pipette, gently place a tiny drop of extract in the centre of the ruled line:

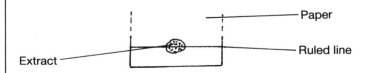

Paper

Extract

Ruled line

Allow to dry. This process can be hastened by using a hairdryer if one is available. Further tiny spots of extract are placed on the same area and dried until a considerable concentration of dried pigment has been built up. Keep the total area of the spot as small as possible, and certainly no larger than 5 mm.

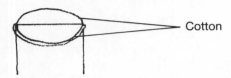

Cotton

Tie cotton around the jar and across the top so as to give a support for the paper. Handling it carefully, hang the strip of paper over the cotton so that the base of the paper is just touching the bottom of the jar. Secure it to the cotton with a small paper clip. Carefully pour solvent down the side of the jar, without touching the paper, until the level is about 1 cm below that of the pigment spot. Place the lid on the jar — the edges only may be carefully greased to make an airtight seal, but do not get the paper greasy. The jar must be saturated with solvent vapour for a good result. Leave the jar undisturbed until the solvent front has reached about 0.5 cm from the lid. Remove and allow to dry. Rapidly outline in pencil the areas covered by each coloured spot; they tend to fade rapidly when dry. Mark with a pencil line the extent of the solvent front. Calculate for each spot an Rf value:

$$Rf = \frac{\text{distance moved by substance}}{\text{distance moved by solvent}}$$

Measure from the baseline to the centre of each spot. You can see now that it is important to get discrete spots with as little spreading as possible. Possible pigment Rf values for this solvent at 20 °C are

- Carotene, 0.95
- Phaeophytin, 0.85
- Xanthophyll, 0.71
- Chlorophyll a, 0.65
- Chlorophyll b, 0.45

Using this information, identify your spots. These spots may not all be a single pigment.

For further identification, each spot may be cut from the chromatogram, eluted (allowed to dissolve from the paper into a small quantity of fresh solvent) and re-run on a further chromatogram, choosing suitable solvents, to see if other constituents are present.

Such a method as outlined here can give only approximate results. Much depends on getting a small, concentrated spot at the starting point. The chromatogram must run as slowly as possible, at an even temperature, and the jar must be saturated with solvent fumes. Pigments tend to break down on exposure to light — you may be seeing the breakdown products rather than the actual pigments. Run a similar chromatogram in the dark, and compare.

15 To investigate water uptake rate using a potometer

APPARATUS   Plant shoot
Clock
(N.B. For most practical purposes water uptake equals transpiration, but they are not in fact identical.)

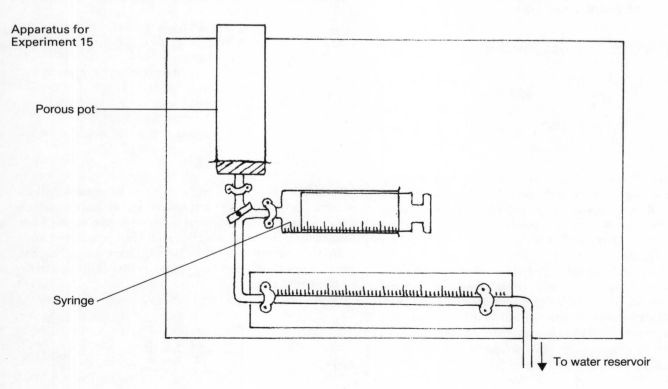

Apparatus for Experiment 15

Porous pot

Syringe

To water reservoir

METHOD Fill the apparatus with water by immersing it in a water-filled sink. Check carefully for air bubbles. Cut a fresh plant shoot under water and, still under water, insert it into the vertical arm, connecting the two together by means of a short length of plastic tubing. Remove from water and seal the junctions of the tubing with the plant and with the side arm with vaseline. This procedure should ensure that no air gets into the vascular tissue of the plant to interfere with the passage of water, and that there are no leaks to the outside atmosphere.

Allow an air bubble to enter the apparatus from below the seal by using the syringe plunger, and adjust the bubble to the zero mark on the scale. This is achieved by withdrawing the plunger of the syringe while the end of the tube is open to the air, and then continuing to withdraw the plunger with the end of the tube under water. Set up the apparatus vertically in a clamp and place a beaker full of water under the open end of the tube. Time the passage of the air bubble along the graduated capillary tube. Use either the anterior or the posterior end of the bubble to indicate your readings, but be consistent throughout.

$$\text{length moved} \times \pi r^2 = \text{volume of water taken up in that time}$$

where $r = \dfrac{\text{diameter of tube}}{2}$

Replace the plant with the porous pot. Repeat your readings. This is a control to measure the losses due to natural evaporation into the environment. Subtracting the control reading from the first reading will give a measure of the water transpired in that time. This assumes that the rate of transpiration and water uptake are equal. This may not necessarily be so. Another control including a shoot without leaves might clarify this.

This experiment should ideally be repeated in varying conditions, i.e. varying light intensity, temperature, humidity and wind speed, all of which affect transpiration. One control should be carried out at the same time and under the same conditions as the experiment so as to try and duplicate exactly. However, this is very difficult to do, since it is hard to measure variations such as wind speed and humidity. These may also vary unevenly throughout the experiment. Light meters and humidity meters, if available, could monitor these factors. Thermometers to measure air temperature do not present such a problem. All these factors together affect the transpiration rate and water uptake under natural conditions (acting as limiting factors) so that for accurate results three out of the four conditions must be kept constant. Artificial conditions can be created by putting a hairdryer, running on 'cold', at varying distances from the apparatus, or by repeating the experiment in dim light, in bright light and in the dark, and repeating all these at different temperatures. This is, of course, extremely time consuming — you will probably have to content yourself with putting the apparatus in warm, cold, light, dark, windy and still situations, and drawing only limited conclusions.

16 Estimation of stomatal numbers

APPARATUS Leafy plant, e.g. *Impatiens* species (Balsam)
Clear nail varnish or polystyrene cement
Brush or mounted needle for spreading
Slide
Filter paper
Petri dish of water
Forceps

METHOD Spread a thin layer of varnish or cement over the particular surface of the leaf that you wish to investigate. Allow it to dry for about 5 minutes. Cut off the leaf and immerse it in water. Peel off the cement or varnish layer with forceps and place it 'leaf side' uppermost on a slide. Doing this in a drop of water will make it easier to spread out the fine layer of varnish. Blot dry with filter paper.

Examine the layer under the microscope and count the number of stomata in an LP field of view. The numbers of stomata open or shut may also be counted.

This method may be used to compare numbers of stomata on the upper and lower surfaces of leaves on the same plant, numbers of stomata on leaves of different species, or numbers of open or shut stomata on the same plant in differing environmental conditions.

Unfortunately, with this relatively simple method you cannot make repeat measurements on the same leaf. A possible way round this problem would be to make a replica of the leaf using a rubber latex preparation. A varnish impression could then be made from this replica. This would enable several replicas to be made of the same leaf over a period of time and under varying conditions.

17 Using a colorimeter

Colorimetry is based on the principle that a coloured solution will absorb light of particular wavelengths only, and that the denser the colour, the more the light is absorbed. Thus the essential features would be as shown in the diagram overleaf.

The photocell contains a meter to measure the current passing through, which is directly proportional to the intensity of the light allowed through the sample. The filter must be the one which allows light of the correct wavelength for maximum absorption in the sample. For example, a blue solution will allow blue light to pass through unimpeded but will absorb principally red light. Therefore a red filter would be used. For red solutions a green filter is used, and for yellow solutions,

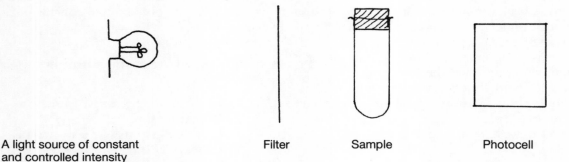

A light source of constant   Filter   Sample   Photocell
and controlled intensity

a blue filter. The machine must be set so as to allow maximum transmission of light when the reagents only are present. For most purposes, distilled water is sufficient but if the reagents are not totally colourless, you must use a sample tube containing a mixture of the reagents as they would be used in the test before the reaction is induced. Such a tube is known as a 'blank'. The machine is set so as to allow 100% transmission through the blank tube. The sample tubes that you use should also be checked while filled with distilled water to make sure that they too allow 100% transmission, regardless of which way round they are placed in the sample holder. Reject any that have imperfections. This also means that your glassware must be scrupulously clean, and that you should be careful to handle the tubes only by the rims so as to avoid finger-marks on the glass. A solution that is at all turbid will give incorrect results.

If you are not certain which filter to use, take two sample tubes, one filled with distilled water and the other with the coloured reaction mixture. Set the machine using the blank. Insert one of the filters and record the percentage transmission through the reaction tube. Repeat with other filters. The filter giving the highest transmission (otherwise known as OD or optical density) is the one that you should use. In most cases, however, you will be told which filter to use.

Before you carry out the experiment, a calibration curve should be prepared. This can be kept in the laboratory and used for subsequent experiments using the same reagents. The only time when a calibration curve need not be used is when you are comparing two reactions, and need only to know which one is quicker.

The calibration curve is prepared using standard solutions of known concentrations within the range measurable by the colorimeter. For example, if you are carrying out an experiment involving the measurement of the starch–iodine complex, your calibration curve would be made using starch solutions of known concentration to which standard amounts of iodine indicator had been added.

If your experimental solutions are too strong for the range of the colorimeter, they must be diluted until the meter registers a reading. The dilution should be noted, and a calculation made to compensate for this when assessing the concentration of your unknown solution.

Your calibration curve will be one of two types:

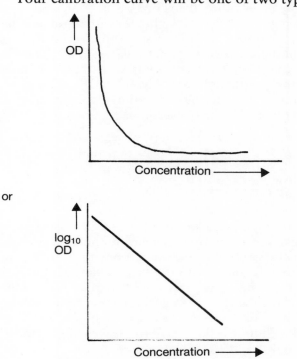

or

Usually the first type will be quite satisfactory. The calibration curve is then used to convert the readings of your unknown solutions to actual concentrations. N.B. Those readings will apply to the particular volume of solution in your sample tube, e.g. perhaps 20 or 25 cm^3.

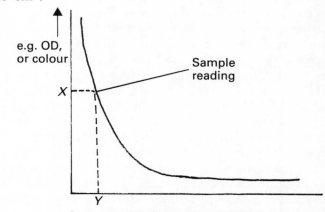

Concentration (e.g. units of dehydrogenase activity, or mg of starch per 20 cm^3 solution)

18 Food tests

Before starting experiments on food stores or on enzyme reactions, it is wise to familiarise yourself with the following tests for the commoner substances that you will come across. (Recipes for reagents are found in Appendix 1.)

1 MONOSACCHARIDES

a Fehling's test: This is a test for reducing sugars, i.e. those containing the —CHO group, e.g. glucose, fructose. Fehling's solution A contains dilute copper(II) sulphate. Fehling's solution B contains sodium ammonium tartrate and sodium hydroxide. Mix equal volumes (1–2 cm^3) of solutions A and B. Add an equal volume of the solution to be tested. Boil by placing in a beaker of boiling water. A red precipitate of copper(I) oxide is produced in the presence of a reducing sugar.

b Benedict's test: this is also a test for reducing sugars, but it is more sensitive than Fehling's test. Benedict's solution contains sodium citrate, sodium carbonate and copper(II) sulphate. Add 1–2 cm^3 of the solution to a test-tube and add an equal volume of the solution under test. Boil as for Fehling's test. The colour and density of the precipitate give an indication of the amount of reducing sugar present. A first sign is a very slight greenish coloration, later a slight yellowish precipitate develops, which becomes brown and finally brick-red with increasing concentration. The red precipitate is again copper(I) oxide.

2 DISACCHARIDES

a Reducing sugars, e.g. maltose, lactose. Tests with Fehling's or Benedict's solution give a positive result.

b Non-reducing sugars, e.g. sucrose:
- Fehling's test is negative.
- Boil some fresh solution with dilute HCl for 10–15 minutes. This hydrolyses the disaccharide to monosaccharides. Neutralise the solution with dilute NaOH. The test with Fehling's or Benedict's solution will now give a positive result.

3 POLYSACCHARIDES

a Starch:
- Add iodine in a solution of potassium iodide. A blue-black colour is produced.
- Fehling's test is negative. Repeat the hydrolysis with acid on a fresh sample; neutralise, and test again with Fehling's. A positive result is seen.

b Cellulose (cotton wool can be used as a demonstration substance):
- Add iodine in potassium iodide solution — no blue colour is produced. Add a few drops of concentrated sulphuric acid to the tested area — a blue colour is produced, i.e. the acid has dissolved the cellulose molecule which then reacts.
- Schultze's solution — chlor-zinc iodine (**poisonous**). Stains cellulose purple.

c Inulin: use a section, e.g. of *Dahlia* or dandelion root. Mount in alcoholic orcin. Add concentrated sulphuric acid (H_2SO_4). An orange colour is produced where inulin is present.

d Lignin (carbohydrate and protein) — see section on staining. Sections of stem or root tissue immersed in acidified phloroglucinol have the lignified areas stained red. Using aniline sulphate (**poisonous**) the lignified tissues are stained yellow.

4 PROTEINS

Egg albumen, bought commercially in the dry state, can be used as a test substance.

a Biuret test: to a solution of albumen add excess dilute NaOH then one or two drops of 1% copper(II) sulphate. A violet colour is produced.

b Xanthoproteic test: add three drops of concentrated nitric acid (with care) to about 1 cm^3 of albumen solution. Boil in a boiling water bath. A yellow precipitate is produced. Cool, and add dilute ammonium hydroxide solution. The precipitate turns orange.

c Millon's test (**take care** — Millon's reagent contains mercury salts and is poisonous. Wash your hands after use). To a solution of albumen add three drops of Millon's reagent. A white precipitate is formed. On boiling in a water bath, this precipitate turns brick-red.

5 LIPIDS

Cooking oil may be used as a test substance.

a Ethanol emulsion test: to a few cm^3 of oil in a test-tube add 5 cm^3 of absolute alcohol. Shake well. Add 5 cm^3 of water. A cloudy white emulsion is formed.

b Sudan III: shake up equal quantities of oil and water. Add three drops of Sudan III stain and shake again. As the layers separate out, the fat layer is seen to be stained red.

19 To investigate the food reserves in various plant substances

APPARATUS   Benedict's or Fehling's solutions
Solutions of dilute HCl and NaOH
Litmus papers
Iodine in potassium iodide solution
Concentrated sulphuric acid
Concentrated nitric acid
1% copper(II) sulphate solution for
Biuret test
Ethanol
Sudan III solution
Glass slides
Pestle and mortar
A variety of plant materials and soaked
seeds, e.g. slices of carrot, potato, turnip,
Dahlia tuber
Portions of grape, apple, orange (test
the components, i.e. skin, pips and flesh,
separately)
Seeds, e.g. castor oil, pea, bean or maize,
soaked beforehand for 24 hours

METHOD   Thin slices of the materials may be tested for starch by irrigating with the iodine solution on a slide while watching the slice under the microscope. The other tests are carried out on material ground up with a pestle in a mortar containing a little water. Test as instructed.

Present your results as a chart, listing the plant organs and indicating which tests were found to be positive. Are there any correlations, e.g. soluble food reserves being found in the flesh of the fruits and storage organs, and insoluble reserves being found in the cotyledons or endosperm or testa of the seeds? Are soluble storage products found in other organs?

Polysaccharides, e.g. starch, are long chains of six-carbon-atom units, often glucose and fructose, joined by covalent bonds and oxygen bonds. The following is a portion of a starch molecule:

A starch granule consists of amylopectin surrounding a core of amylose (it is the amylose which forms the blue colour with iodine in the starch test). On hydrolysis with HCl the following reaction occurs:

i.e. the long-chain polysaccharide is broken up into six-carbon-atom units and these will react with Fehling's solution. Reducing sugars are so-called from their ability to reduce copper(II) ions to copper(I) ions. You can distinguish between monosaccharide and disaccharide sugars only by using Barfoed's reagent. This is a similar reaction to that with Fehling's or Benedict's solution but it relies on the fact that a monosaccharide will reduce copper ions more quickly than a disaccharide which will only do so on longer boiling. A reducing disaccharide, e.g. maltose, retains an aldehyde –CHO or ketone C=O group but is not as effective at reducing as monosaccharides. A non-reducing disaccharide, e.g. sucrose, contains no free reducing groups and hence will only give a positive result after hydrolysis. Not all proteins respond to Millon's reagent — a mixture of mercury(II) nitrate and nitrite. A phenolic group is required on the amino acid. The Biuret test requires only the presence of a peptide link –NH–CO–.

Storage products in seeds and fruits and so on are either insoluble, and thus unable to move out of the organ, or very large molecules which become colloidal and are still unable to move away. Insoluble substances do not contribute to the total osmotic potential of the cell sap and so do not upset homeostasis if present in very large quantities.

Why do you think some soluble substances were found? Are they storage products or maybe substances in the process of being utilised? Are the substances that you found energy supplying?

20 To investigate the effect of temperature on an enzyme-catalysed reaction

APPARATUS   White tile
Glass rod
Iodine in potassium iodide solution
10% starch solution (pre-tested to
show that no reducing sugars are
present)
1% amylase solution (bacterial amylase
is free from reducing sugars)
Benedict's solution
Water baths at 30 °C, 40 °C and 50 °C
Boiling water bath (or water beaker)
Beaker of water at room temperature
with thermometer
Beaker of ice-water and thermometer
(10–12 °C)
Beaker of water in refrigerator (5 °C)
(check temperature with thermometer)
Test-tubes and racks
Labels
Stop-clock
10 cm³ graduated pipettes
Dropping pipettes and teats

METHOD Set up the various water baths and beakers, either controlled thermostatically or with thermo- meters, and allow them to come to a steady temperature. The actual temperatures do not need to be exactly those stated, but must be measured and remain con- stant throughout the test.

Set out a series of drops of iodine solution on the white tile. Draw up a chart ready to put in the results as you get them. A table showing time in 5 minute intervals against tube numbers will do. Into each of eight test-tubes place 5 cm³ of starch solution. Label them 1–8 and place one into each of the seven water baths or beakers. The eighth serves as a control and is placed also in the beaker at room temperature. Allow to equilibrate for 10 minutes. Place 0.1 cm³ of enzyme solution into each of tubes 1–7. In tube 8 place 0.1 cm³ of water. Stir each with a cleaned glass rod to ensure maximum exposure of active sites on enzyme to sub- strate. Strictly speaking, this control of the starch solution should be repeated at each of the temperatures to make sure that no change occurs in the starch solution itself during incubation, but these may be omitted if time is short. At 5 minute intervals, withdraw a drop of the mixture from each test-tube and add to a drop of iodine solution on your white tile. A dark blue colour produced indicates that starch is still present, whereas no colour change indicates that starch is absent. Record your findings. Continue to test at 5 minute intervals for 30 minutes. At the end of the period, test a sample from each tube with Benedict's solution to find out if reducing sugars are present.

Enzyme activity increases with temperature. The kinetic energy increases and therefore the number of collisions between enzyme molecules and substrate group also increases, resulting in an increased rate of reaction. Do you find any evidence of a 10°C rise in temperature doubling the rate of reaction? (Did the time taken for the starch to disappear halve, for example, for the reactions at 15°C and 25°C?)

After a certain temperature (probably 40°C and upwards) the enzyme activity would have slowed down and ceased; there should have been no activity in the tube in the boiling water bath. Enzymes are proteins, and hence dependent on hydrogen bonds, electrostatic attraction and some –S–H– or –S–S– bonds to hold the molecule in its shape, often globular. Vibrations due to increased kinetic energy will rupture these bonds and cause loss of activity. Specific sites in the protein molecule which are 'active sites', i.e. which need to coincide directly with substrate molecule con- figurations, are no longer in the correct positions, leading to loss of enzyme action — denaturation.

It is possible to plot a graph of your results, even though you have not measured the starch concentrations in actual units. Plot 1/time (vertically) against tem- perature, where time is the number of minutes required for the starch to disappear totally. If the reaction was slow at certain temperatures, you can continue readings beyond 30 minutes.

Do not forget to discuss your ideas on how much value may be placed on your results.

21 To investigate the effect of substrate concentration on the reaction rate of an enzyme-catalysed reaction

APPARATUS Test-tubes and racks
10% starch solution
1% amylase solution as in the previous experiment
Water bath at 25°C
Dropping pipettes and teats
Stop-clock
White tile
5 cm³ graduated pipettes
Iodine in potassium iodide solution

METHOD Enzyme activity is variable from extract to extract, so you must first perform a pilot experiment to determine whether or not 0.5 cm³ enzyme extract, together with the smallest quantities of starch and water suggested, allow the reaction to be completed in about 3–5 minutes. If the reaction finishes too quickly, increase all the starch concentrations accordingly. Set up the following tubes:

Tube 1 1 cm³ starch solution and 4 cm³ water.
Tube 2 2 cm³ starch solution and 3 cm³ water.
Tube 3 3 cm³ starch solution and 2 cm³ water.
Tube 4 4 cm³ starch solution and 1 cm³ water.
Tube 5 5 cm³ starch solution and 0 cm³ water.
Tube 6 5 cm³ starch solution and 0.5 cm³ water — no enzyme to be added.

Set up the white tile with a series of drops of iodine solution as before. Add 0.5 cm³ of enzyme solution to the first tube, mix well and start the clock. Continue by adding 0.5 cm³ enzyme solution to each of the other tubes at 1 minute intervals. Withdraw a drop of the mixture from the test-tubes at timed intervals and add to a drop of the iodine solution on the white tile to test for the disappearance of the blue colour produced by starch.

Enter your results on a chart of tube number against time, as starch present or absent. Plot a graph of 1/time for total disappearance against concentration of starch. Calculate this concentration from the volume of 10% starch solution that you actually use, and allow for the appropriate dilution factor.

This experiment could also make use of a colori- meter if you have one. You would be able to get a time, or a value for 1/time, against concentration curve for each dilution, and compare them. In this case you must stop or 'freeze' the reaction at the moment of sampling. This is usually done by diluting greatly — thus removing the molecules so far from each other that they can no longer collide and react. Each time you sample, with- draw 0.1 cm³ and make up to 5 cm³ with distilled water. The iodine solution added must be accurately measured, i.e. 0.1 cm³. These samples can be labelled and kept until the end of the experiment when you can carry out all your colorimeter readings together. Read off your figures on a calibration curve (see notes on using a colorimeter in Experiment 34). Plot a graph of 1/time against concentration for each dilution. You should find that the rate of reaction increases with the amount of substrate, but possibly only up to a certain point. Remember that the amount of substrate affects the enzyme concentration.

Discuss your results in terms of enzyme–substrate complex formation. Michaelis' constant measures the affinity of enzyme for substrate — it is defined as that substrate concentration, in moles dm^{-3}, which gives half maximum velocity. Have your solution concentrations exhibited a maximum velocity, i.e. a velocity above which a further increase in substrate concentration produces no further increase in velocity?

22 To investigate the effect of enzyme concentration on the rate of an enzyme-catalysed reaction

APPARATUS   As for Experiment 21.

METHOD   Perform a test run as in Experiment 21, using the highest enzyme concentration, so as to make sure that the time required is suitable. Dilute your enzyme solution by setting up the following tubes:

Tube 1   5 cm^3 starch solution; 0.4 cm^3 water; 0.1 cm^3 enzyme solution.

Tube 2   5 cm^3 starch solution; 0.3 cm^3 water; 0.2 cm^3 enzyme solution.

Tube 3   5 cm^3 starch solution; 0.2 cm^3 water; 0.3 cm^3 enzyme solution.

Tube 4   5 cm^3 starch solution; 0.1 cm^3 water; 0.4 cm^3 enzyme solution.

Tube 5   5 cm^3 starch solution; 0 cm^3 water; 0.5 cm^3 enzyme solution.

Tube 6   5 cm^3 starch solution; 0.5 cm^3 control — no enzyme.

Incubate at 25 °C as before and follow the same procedures. Plot results as before. Similarly, do you find that the concentrations of enzyme used appear to produce maximum velocity? If not, what further experiments would you carry out to determine this?

23 To investigate the effect of pH on the rate of an enzyme-catalysed reaction

APPARATUS   1% solution of invertase (sucrase)
10% solution of sucrose (free from reducing sugars)
Test-tubes and racks
Stop-clock
Boiling water bath or beaker
25 °C water bath
Buffer solutions in a range of pH 5.8–8.0 (these are commercially

available as tablets for making up into solutions or can be made up from 0.2 M Na_2HPO_4 and NaH_2PO_4 according to textbook tables; see Appendix 1) Benedict's solution

METHOD   A pilot run must first be performed using buffer at pH 7 to make sure that the time needed to give a positive Benedict's test is convenient. Adjust the volumes of substrate and/or enzyme to suit the time available to you.

Set up the following tubes: in each of seven test-tubes place 5 cm^3 of one of the following buffer solutions: pH 5.8, pH 6.2, pH 6.6, pH 7.0, pH 7.4, pH 7.8, pH 8.0. Label the tubes accordingly.

Add 5 cm^3 of sucrose solution and 0.1 cm^3 of invertase solution (for recipes, see Appendix 1). Theoretically speaking, each pH should have two control tubes, one with buffer, sucrose and boiled enzyme, and the other with buffer, sucrose and water. However, if this is too time consuming, you may omit them, performing each control only once, with an arbitrarily selected buffer. Do not forget to mention this way of proceeding in your discussion.

Set up test-tubes containing 2 cm^3 of Benedict's solution in the boiling water bath. At suitable time intervals, withdraw a few drops of mixture from test-tubes 1–7 and add each to a different tube of Benedict's solution in the water bath. Note the presence or absence of reducing sugars. The presence of reducing sugars is shown by a colour change — a slight green tinge for very small quantities, through a yellow colour, to a brown precipitate, and finally a brick-red precipitate.

Decide on the stage to be taken as standard, e.g. the first appearance of a greenish tinge, or a definite precipitate. Whichever of the various stages you choose, note the time at which this first appears for each pH. Enter your results on a previously prepared chart.

Draw a graph of pH against total time taken for a positive result. Deduce the optimum pH for this reaction, i.e. the one which produced a positive result the quickest. Discuss what is happening in terms of enzyme structure, and the effect of pH changes on colloidal properties and electrostatic attractive forces around the molecule of protein that is the enzyme.

24 The use of redox indicators to show dehydrogenase activity

There are various substances which can act as indicators for redox reactions by changing their colour when reduced, i.e. by acting as hydrogen acceptors.

- Methylene blue is colourless when reduced, blue when oxidised
- 2,3,5-triphenyl tetrazolium chloride (TTC) is colourless, but turns pink when reduced
- 2,6-dichlorophenol indophenol (DCPIP) is blue when oxidised, and colourless when reduced.

Any of these substances may be used to detect actively respiring materials, or, alternatively, photosynthesising processes.

APPARATUS	Soaked maize seeds
	Soaked maize seeds killed by boiling
	White tile
	Test-tubes, labels
	Water bath at 40°C
	1% DCPIP solution or methylene blue
	Stop-clock
	Graduated 5 cm^3 pipettes
	Pestle and mortar

METHOD Lightly crush five soaked seeds in the mortar, and place in a test-tube labelled A. Repeat with the dead seeds and label the tube B. Add 2 cm^3 of DCPIP or methylene blue (for recipes, see Appendix 1) to each tube, and place in the water bath. Observe the colour changes every 5 minutes for half an hour. This is most easily done by removing the tube briefly from the water bath and holding it up against the white tile. If you want to have very exact measurements, you may use a colorimeter if one is available. Instructions for the use, and notes on the theory, of the colorimeter are given in Experiment 17.

You will find that the living seeds will decolorise the DCPIP, or the methylene blue, and the dead seeds will not. This reaction does not in itself indicate any specific activity, as many substances also decolorise DCPIP. However, combined with the lack of activity after boiling, this does indicate enzyme, and therefore dehydrogenase, activity. The particular dehydrogenase can only be determined by adding various substrates in turn to samples of the mixture, e.g. by adding succinic acid to find out whether the rate of dehydrogenase activity is increased. A colorimeter is essential for such a further investigation.

25 To find out where dehydrogenase activity occurs, using 2,3,5-triphenyl tetrazolium chloride (TTC)

APPARATUS	5 maize seeds soaked for 24 hours
	5 maize seeds killed by boiling
	Solution of 0.05% TTC (see Appendix 1 for recipe)
	Petri dishes
	Hand-lens
	Scalpel
	25 cm^3 measuring cylinder

METHOD Cut the seeds in half lengthwise. Place the living seeds cut-surface down in a petri dish containing 15 cm^3 of TTC. Repeat with the dead seeds. After 30 minutes, examine the cut surfaces with a hand-lens for red-stained areas. Draw a map of the cut surface, showing the relative positions of these areas. In this experiment the red-stained areas show where respiration, and therefore dehydrogenase activity, is actively occurring. Relate the position of such areas to the source of respiratory substrate and to the germinating embryo. Relate the pattern of activity, or its lack, in the control seeds to their treatment.

26 To investigate enzyme inhibition

Dehydrogenase activity is detected using 2,6-dichlorophenol indophenol (DCPIP). The substrate is sodium succinate

$$H_2-C-COONa$$
$$H_2-C-COONa$$

Its reaction with succinic dehydrogenase is inhibited by sodium malonate

$$H_2-C\begin{array}{l}COONa\\COONa\end{array}$$

A source of succinic dehydrogenase (which occurs in the Krebs cycle during aerobic respiration) can be germinating bean seeds. Soak bean seeds and allow them to germinate. Remove the seed coats and grind 20–30 seeds thoroughly in a little ice-water. Filter, and use the filtrate as a source of enzyme. Carry out a pilot run first using 1 cm^3 each of DCPIP, substrate and enzyme. Incubate at 25°C and note the time taken for the indicator to become colourless. Adjust the enzyme and substrate concentrations if necessary to give a suitable reaction time.

APPARATUS	Enzyme-containing filtrate
	Phosphate buffer pH 6.8
	1% solution of DCPIP
	0.1 M sodium malonate
	0.1 M sodium succinate
	Test-tubes and racks
	Rubber stoppers to fit the tubes
	25°C water bath

METHOD Set up the following tubes (volumes are given in cm^3; for recipes, see Appendix 1):

	Buffer	DCPIP	Succinate	Malonate	Enzyme
Tube 1	2	0.1	1	–	1
Tube 2	2	0.1	1	–	1 (boiled)
Tube 3	1	0.1	1	1	1
Tube 4	3	0.1	1	–	–
Tube 5	3	0.1	–	1	–
Tube 6	2	0.1	1	1	–

Tubes 2, 4, 5 and 6 are controls. Mix the contents of each tube thoroughly and stopper quickly. The change in colour is more rapid if most of the oxygen can be excluded. Incubate at 25 °C and note the time taken for the DCPIP colour to disappear from the experimental tubes, i.e. tubes 1 and 3. There should be no change in any of the other tubes.

The phenomenon demonstrated here is competitive inhibition. It can be seen that the two substrates are structurally similar. Both can be accepted by the active sites on the enzyme, but only succinate will result in a reaction. Malonate only serves to block the active sites. It would be expected therefore that a concentration effect would be observed. This would need further experiments in which varying concentration combinations of succinate and malonate are set up and the time of reaction observed. What would you expect to find? Is the rate proportional to the concentration of succinate?

27 To investigate the presence of the enzyme catalase in various plant and animal tissues

APPARATUS Test-tubes
Racks
Distilled water
Glass rods
Hydrogen peroxide solution ('20 volume') (be careful to keep this solution away from skin, clothes and heat; see Appendix 1 for recipe)
Boiling water bath
Pieces of liver, muscle
Pieces of potato, carrot etc.
A suspension of yeast
Germinating pea seedlings
Bunsen
Splints

METHOD Place in separate test-tubes small pieces of liver, muscle and crushed potato, and some yeast suspension. Divide up the seedlings as follows: radicle tips, upper portions of radicles, cotyledons and plumules. Place each portion in separate test-tubes and gently crush the tissue with a glass rod. To each of these tissues in turn add a few drops of hydrogen peroxide. Observe carefully. Test the gas given off with a glowing splint. Place similar test-tubes and contents in the boiling water bath and leave for at least 10 minutes. Cool thoroughly. Test again with hydrogen peroxide, and then with a glowing splint. Record your results in a chart, listing the tissues used and saying whether bubbles of gas were observed and whether or not the glowing splint was rekindled.

As boiling the tissues gave no positive result, i.e. no bubbles were seen arising, provided that they were cooled sufficiently, the reaction could be said to be due to the presence of an enzyme in the tissues which had been denatured by boiling. The live tissues gave positive results, i.e. much effervescence was seen after adding

hydrogen peroxide. Were there any detectable differences in the quantity of bubbles seen arising from one tissue rather than another? Even if bubbles were seen, was the splint always relit?

$$2H_2O_2 \xrightarrow{catalase} 2H_2O + O_2$$

Hydrogen peroxide is toxic to protoplasm. Dehydrogenase activity is very common in metabolising tissues. The ultimate hydrogen acceptor in aerobic tissues is oxygen, thus producing hydrogen peroxide. It is therefore necessary for catalase to be present to convert the peroxide to water and oxygen. You would probably find that actively respiring and growing tissues, e.g. root tips, muscle and, especially, liver, were more catalase active than others. Storage organs, e.g. potato, did not contain catalase in such large quantities. Relate the amounts of catalase that you found to the position of the organ involved, and its role in the metabolism of the organism. Why is crushing necessary — do you think catalase is intracellular or extracellular, and why?

28 To demonstrate the presence of the enzyme phosphatase in plant tissue

$$phenolphthalein\ phosphate \xrightarrow{enzyme} phenolphthalein$$
$$phenolphthalein \xrightarrow{Na_2CO_3} red$$

APPARATUS Broad bean seedlings, several weeks old
Pestle and mortar
Fine, clean sand
Distilled water
Phenolphthalein phosphate solution (0.1%)
10% sodium hydrogen carbonate solution
Buffer solution; pH 7
Filter paper and funnels
Test-tubes, racks
Water bath at 30 °C
Beaker of water, bunsen etc. for boiling water bath
Measuring cylinders

METHOD Cut several pieces of root tissues and grind with sand in the mortar. Add 12–15 cm³ of distilled water. Filter and use filtrate for testing. Prepare a similar extract of stem tissue. In a boiling tube place 2 cm³ of phenolphthalein phosphate solution, 6 cm³ of buffer solution and 2 cm³ of enzyme extract. Repeat with stem extract. Incubate at 30 °C for 20 minutes and then add 10 cm³ of Na₂CO₃ solution. If the enzyme is present and hydrolysis of the substrate has occurred, then a red colour will be produced. Make up two further tubes containing substrate and buffer as before but using root extract that has been boiled for 10 minutes in one tube and similarly treated stem extract in the other tube. Then repeat the incubation and testing procedures. The absence of any colour change in this control will demonstrate that an enzyme is responsible.

DISCUSSION Phosphatase enzymes will occur in any actively metabolising tissue. They convert such substrates as hexose phosphates, nucleotides and so on into the free base and phosphoric acid. This phosphoric acid can then be used in the synthesis of ATP, amongst other important reactions. Find as many examples as you can among the metabolic processes known to you. Can you think of any tissues that might not contain phosphatases?

29 To investigate the permeability of a membrane using dialysis tubing

APPARATUS Dialysis (Visking) tubing
Two three-way taps
1 cm^3 syringe
Two beakers of distilled water
37°C water bath
10% starch solution (reducing sugar free)
1% amylase solution
White tile
Iodine in potassium iodide solution
Benedict's solution
Clock
Boiling water bath, or beaker and bunsen etc.
Test-tubes and racks
Two glass rods
Length of fine string

METHOD Soak the Visking tubing in distilled water for some minutes to soften it. Cut into two lengths each about 6 inches long. Tie a knot in one end of each length, and place 10 cm^3 of starch solution in each. Attach the three-way tap to the open end and tie firmly in place. Test for leaks. Suspend the length of tubing over the beaker of distilled water by means of string and a glass rod. Make sure that there is sufficient water to come above the level of the starch solution.

Place the beaker in the 37 °C water bath. If your amylase is of plant origin, the experiment may be carried out at room temperature, with a thermometer placed in the beaker. To one of the lengths of tubing add 1 cm^3 of amylase solution. This is done by taking up 1 cm^3 of amylase solution in the syringe and fixing the syringe to an aperture of the three-way tap, turning the knob appropriately and then injecting the solution.

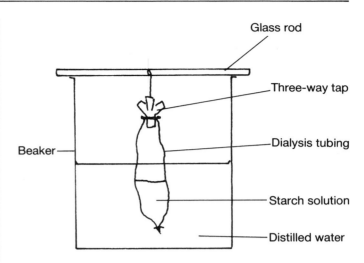

Start the clock. At 5 minute intervals, withdraw 0.1 cm^3 samples from inside both lengths of tubing using fresh syringes each time. Withdraw 1 cm^3 from the beaker of water surrounding the tubing. Put each sample in an appropriately labelled test-tube, and then place one drop of each sample on a white tile, and test for the presence of starch. Try not to allow any time to elapse between withdrawing the test sample and performing the test as the amylase will continue working.

Test the remainder of each sample for the presence of reducing sugars using Benedict's solution. Continue taking samples for 30 minutes and record your results in a chart. In the control you should find only starch inside the tubing, and no reducing sugars anywhere. (Bear in mind that starch is liable to break down to glucose spontaneously if left in solution.)

In the experimental tubing the amylase will have acted on the starch, which you should find gradually disappearing throughout the duration of the test. Ideally you should also carry out a second control using boiled amylase solution. Reducing sugars will be found in increasing quantities in the solution surrounding the tubing. Smaller molecules such as glucose are able to diffuse through the dialysis tubing and are hence found in the surrounding medium. Larger samples were taken from the beaker to compensate for the diluting effect of the greater volume of water in the beaker. Small samples were taken from inside the tubing in order not to reduce the total volume of solution inside more than absolutely necessary. Starch molecules are too large to pass through the pores in the membrane, thus mimicking the situation obtaining in the gut during digestion.

30 To investigate the amylase activity of invertebrate gut (e.g. locust or earthworm)

APPARATUS   1% starch solution (free from reducing sugars)
Invertebrate saline (for recipe, see Appendix 1; distilled water will do if saline is not available)
5 cm³ graduated pipettes or syringes
Iodine in potassium iodide solution
Fehling's or Benedict's solutions
White tile
Glass rod
Dropping pipettes and teats
Test-tubes, funnels and filter papers
Stop-clock
Dissecting needles
Boiling water bath, or similar form of heating
Labels for test-tubes
Large watch glasses

METHOD   Remove the gut from the earthworm or locust, and macerate with the dissecting needles in about 5 cm³ of water or saline in a watch glass. Filter. You are going to use this solution as an amylase enzyme extract, so think carefully about the controls that you will need. Ideally you should test your starch solution to show that there are no reducing sugars present.

If reducing sugars are present, make up some fresh starch solution (this solution hydrolyses fairly quickly and soon contains reducing sugars). You must also test your extract for the presence of reducing sugars.

Your locust or earthworm should have been starved for at least 24 hours before the experiment so as to empty the gut, but you must check. Place about 3 cm³ of starch solution in each of three test-tubes. To one test-tube add 1 cm³ of your extract, to the second 1 cm³ of distilled water and to the third 1 cm³ of boiled extract. These are your controls — no enzyme activity should occur using denatured enzyme, and no change should take place in the substrate using water instead of enzyme. Leave these tubes for 30 minutes at room temperature. Then test your extracts for the presence or absence of starch, and the presence or absence of reducing sugars. Write the details of these test procedures as part of your method — it is not sufficient to say 'the solution was tested for the presence of starch' unless you have already given the necessary details. Display your results as a chart, making sure that you give a key indicating the meaning of '+ve', '−ve' or '√', if you use these symbols. Otherwise indicate 'present' or 'absent'.

Your discussion should contain some idea of the structure of a polysaccharide and the mechanism of its hydrolysis to a simpler sugar that reduces copper(II) ions to copper(I) ions. Remember that there are some disaccharide reducing sugars, e.g. maltose and lactose, although all monosaccharides are reducing. This test procedure cannot therefore tell you whether your product is a monosaccharide or a disaccharide. The polysaccharide in a locust is probably starch. Although plant material, i.e. cellulose, is ingested, mechanical breakdown in the gizzard disrupts the cell walls and allows the enzymes access to the contained carbohydrates. The gut does not contain a cellulase.

Discuss the validity of your results. If the gut did contain some reducing sugars, the use of Benedict's solution (which is more sensitive than Fehling's solution) would help to determine whether they were present perhaps only as a trace, and became present in larger quantities as a result of enzyme action.

Are there any further experiments that would help to elucidate either the precise nature of the enzyme, i.e. specific only to starch, or a general carbohydrase, or the precise nature of the products?

31 To measure growth by means of an auxanometer

APPARATUS

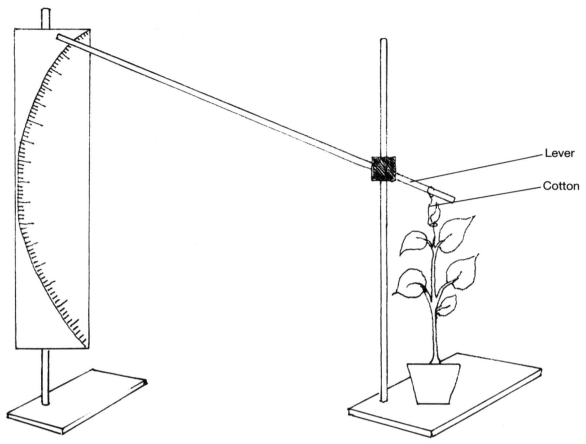

Lever

Cotton

Carefully connect the growing tip of the potted seedling to the pointer with cotton in such a way that the tip of the pointer rests at the uppermost part of the scale, at zero. Every 24 hours, take readings of the pointer's position. In the model shown the pointer magnifies by five times the amount of growth of the shoot tip (5 mm intervals therefore represents 1 mm growth). Record the readings in a chart, and plot actual growth in millimetres against time.

32 To measure the growth of a culture of yeast cells using the counting chamber or haematocrit

APPARATUS   2% sucrose solution
Suspension of yeast cells (dried yeast and water)
Haematocrit cell — counting chamber and coverslip
1 cm^3 pipettes graduated to 0.1 cm^3
Distilled water
Boiling tubes with cotton wool plugs
Racks

METHOD   Place 20 cm^3 of sucrose solution in a clean boiling tube (for recipe, see Appendix 1). Preferably sterilise the tubes first by heating in an oven, or rinsing with boiling water or alcohol. Swirl the yeast suspension to get as even a distribution as possible, and add 0.1 cm^3 of this suspension to the sucrose medium. Repeat this procedure as many times as you need to get sufficient tubes for the class. Stopper with a cotton wool plug. Take a roughly square piece of cotton wool, fold in the sides to make them even and roll the square up into a cylindrical plug. You may have to experiment a little to get the right size of cylinder for your tube:

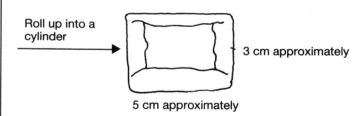

Roll up into a cylinder

3 cm approximately

5 cm approximately

Place the tubes of yeast suspension in a water bath or other incubator at 25°C. If an incubator is not available keep the tubes at as constant a temperature as possible. Growth will occur quite well at 20°C or lower, but will take a little longer. Shake carefully each day to aerate the culture. Remove a sample for counting as soon as the tube is set up, and take samples every 24 hours for further counts. The counting chamber method is described below.

There are various types of counting chamber (or haemocytometer, when used for counting red blood corpuscles) but all basically have the same pattern. Only the total volume may vary, so this you must check before starting. The counting chamber is a glass slide with deep grooves cut in it in such a way as to leave a square central area:

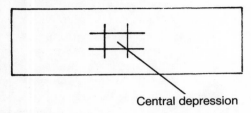

Central depression

This area is ground down so that when the coverslip is put on it is exactly 0.1 mm above the surface of the square. The square itself is 1 mm × 1 mm. When using the ×10 eyepiece and the ×10 objective, this square will fill the field of view. This is the value that may vary, so you can choose slides of larger or smaller area according to the size of the particles that you wish to count.

This millimetre square is divided into 400 smaller squares, as in graph paper, and every fifth line is triple-ruled as a guide:

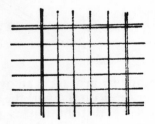

The volume of each tiny square is thus 1/400 mm³ × 0.1, i.e. 0.00025 mm³, and the total volume is 0.1 mm³.

Using a pipette with a fine nozzle, carefully place a drop of liquid from the well-stirred culture on the centre square and put on the cover-slip. For yeast cells it is probably best to count the ruled groups of 16 squares.

Use a systematic way of counting — decide to count all cells touching the bottom and left-hand boundaries *or* all those touching the top and right-hand boundaries. Include all cells within the given area

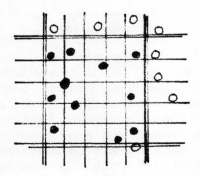

i.e. count all the cells shown in black in the diagram and leave the white cells to neighbouring counts. Remember to change the focus so as to count all the cells within the depth of the sample. If your particles are very small, use the highest power that you have and count the 0.00025 mm squares. Count about 100 of these. Whichever method you use, record your results as a chart of volume of square and number of particles. Then average your results; the variation from square to square is high due to uneven distribution.

$$\text{total number of particles per cm}^3 = \frac{\text{dilution factor (if any)}}{\text{volume in mm}^3 \text{ over one square}}$$
$$\times \frac{\text{total number of cells counted}}{\text{total number of squares counted}}$$
$$\times 10^3$$

If you find a dilution is necessary as the density of cells is too high to be countable, take 0.1 cm³ of your culture and place in 10 cm³ of distilled water. This will give you 1/100 dilution. Adjust, if necessary, until you get a suitable dilution.

Having made your counts over a period of days, you should find the increase in numbers levelling off. Remember that this method counts all cells, living and dead, and you will not find a drop in numbers, although the number of living cells will probably be dropping. Plot your results (a) on arithmetical graph paper — time (horizontally) against numbers (vertically) and (b) on log paper (if log paper is not available plot the logarithm of the numbers against time).

Remember to include in your discussion points about the accuracy of the counting method: how easy, or hard, it was to count every cell, errors due to dilution, uneven distribution in the tube, sampling errors and so on.

33 Measurement of size using a graticule

A graticule is a grid placed between two pieces of glass which is inserted inside the eyepiece of a microscope:

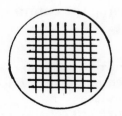

Eyepieces may be purchased already containing such a grid, and will come with a known calibration. Otherwise you must calibrate the graticule yourself.

This is done by means of a slide marked with a scale. A convenient scale is 10 × 1 mm. One of these millimetre divisions is subdivided, giving 10 × 0.1 mm units. The slide, called a stage micrometer, is placed on the microscope stage, the eyepiece graticule is inserted and the slide position adjusted. When one line on the slide lies exactly under one on the graticule, then a measurement can be obtained for each division on the grid; 1 mm is equivalent to 10^3 μm (micrometres), so each 0.1 mm subdivision is 100 μm. The calibrated graticule can then be used to measure the size of cells or specimens directly.

34 Measuring growth using a colorimeter

Estimation of cell numbers may also be carried out using a **colorimeter** to measure the degree of turbidity, i.e. the scattering of light from particles. The colorimeter may also be used to count red blood corpuscles and can be a method of estimating their response to various osmotic potentials. It is not a very accurate method for actual numbers — there are many errors — but as a relative method where errors are assumed to occur in the same way at each count, it provides a means of plotting a growth curve.

A calibration curve must first be obtained using known numbers of cells in several dilutions and measuring their turbidity. However, this curve will only apply to that one organism or cell in those particular experimental conditions, and so calibration curves are time consuming to construct. Low concentrations only must be used to get a linear response. The medium must not alter in its response to the colorimeter as growth proceeds, e.g. excretory substances may be present which alter the passage of light through the medium. In this case the cells must be centrifuged down, the medium removed, and the cells washed and resuspended in fresh medium before assaying. There must be no settling out of cells during the assay procedure.

35 Measuring growth by a dry weight method

This type of experiment can also be used to estimate growth using a dry weight method, and the results compared.

APPARATUS 10 boiling tubes with cotton wool plugs
2% sucrose solution
Yeast suspension
25 cm³ measuring cylinder
1 cm³ graduated pipettes
Glass rods
11 small weighing bottles (without caps, but numbered, and the weight of each bottle recorded)

METHOD Set up the boiling tubes with 20 cm³ of sucrose solution and 0.1 cm³ of yeast suspension as

described in Experiment 32. Be careful to keep the suspension well mixed to try to ensure that roughly comparable numbers of cells are added to each tube. This is a large source of error.

Take 5 cm³ of sucrose solution and place it in a numbered weighing bottle. Repeat with 5 cm³ of culture medium from one of the boiling tubes. Place these in an oven at around 96–100 °C and allow to dry. Remove from the oven, cool in a desiccator and weigh. Repeat the drying, cooling and weighing until two consecutive weights are equal. After 48 hours, repeat this procedure with the second boiling tube, omitting the sucrose solution control — the figure for this dry weight can be subtracted from all subsequent weighings.

This is more accurate than calculating the amount of sucrose in 5 cm³ of 2% solution — some may get lost in the handling and drying processes. When the weights of all the samples have been measured, record as a chart in g yeast cm⁻³ of solution. Plot as a graph against time.

36 The measurement of growth of a fungal colony

APPARATUS Petri dishes containing nutrient agar — malt or potato dextrose (these may be obtained ready prepared from commercial suppliers; recipes are given in Appendix 1)
Platinum wire loop
Rule, calibrated in millimetres

METHOD Expose some damp bread (*Mucor*) or citrus fruit (*Penicillium*, or *Aspergillus*) in the laboratory for a few days until good fungal growth is achieved. With a wire loop previously sterilised by heating in the bunsen flame (and allowed to *cool*) pick off, if possible, just one fruiting body, and touch the loop onto the centre of the culture plate. Replace the lid immediately, and incubate at 25 °C.

Measure the colony width in millimetres every 24 hours. Record your results and plot them as a graph. Discuss your results in terms of factors affecting growth. Can you distinguish a 'lag' phase? Is the curve sigmoid?

37 To investigate the effects of the lack of certain mineral ions on plant growth

This method makes use of a cultural technique known as hydroponics — growing plants in aqueous culture medium rather than in soil. It is thus easy to vary the contents of the culture medium, and to leave out mineral ions as necessary. A series of such culture media may be obtained from biological suppliers, usually in tablet or in powder form. One tablet is then dissolved in 100 cm³ of water to give the required solution. The exact recipes are given with the culture kits (see Appendix 1). They may vary, as there are several suitable recipes available. The salts usually involved are $CaSO_4$, $Ca_3(PO_4)_2$, $MgSO_4$, $NaCl$, KNO_3 and $FeCl_3$. You will end up with solutions lacking the following ions: Ca^{2+}, K^+, Fe^{3+}, PO_4^{3-}, Mg^{2+}, NO_3^- and Na^+. The last, an absence of Na^+, is optional since sodium is only required in minute amounts and is very rarely lacking in natural circumstances. A control tube — normal culture — contains all the ions.

One way of setting up the experiment is to use a series of gas jars, each with a cotton wool plug holding a seedling, and to exclude light from the jars with black paper. This will prevent the growth of algae in the culture solution. The algae would compete with the seedlings for nutrients and oxygen. It is now possible to buy special racks, each holding six large boiling tubes. The racks have solid sides, one of which may be slid back to allow the cultures to be examined.

The tubes are plugged with cotton wool, rolled gently round the seedling. A glass tube is pushed down the side of the plug and into the solution. Through this tube, air is blown daily to oxygenate the cultures. This can be done without removing the side of the rack. The cultures must be checked frequently for evaporation, and topped up if necessary. Small seeds, such as sunflower, wheat or possibly pea seeds, are best. Large seeds should not be used — they contain too much reserve food to give good results.

Charts are prepared as follows:

Criterion	Solutions			
	Normal	$-Ca^{2+}$	$-Mg^{2+}$	$-NO_3^-$ etc.
Length of shoot				
Length of root				
etc.				

The criteria to be judged are length of shoot, length of root, amount of lateral root growth, length of stem internodes, leaf size, leaf colour and general condition. These charts are filled in at suitable intervals, e.g. one,

three or seven days, depending on the rate of growth on the seedling. It will give a picture of the effect of the lack of a particular mineral ion on the growth of the seedling: does it have an immediate effect, or no effect until later on in the growth; which areas of the plant are affected? This can then be correlated with what is known about the role of that particular ion.

38 To investigate the areas responsible for growth in a radicle

APPARATUS   Germinating bean seeds with radicles about 1 inch long
Black marking ink
Fine pen, or cotton for marking lines
Ruler
Tray with damp cotton wool

METHOD   Mark the radicles with fine black lines at 1 mm intervals:

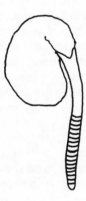

Place on the damp cotton wool and leave in a warm place. View after 24, 36, 48 and 60 hours. Draw the radicle, measuring the position of the lines accurately. Make a note of the area where most growth in length occurred at each time interval. Discuss your findings in terms of the regions of maximum cell multiplication, elongation and differentiation.

39 To show the influence of light of various kinds on the shoots of seedlings

APPARATUS   Wheat or barley seedlings germinated on wet cotton wool in small trays to fit in the phototropism apparatus (commercially available)

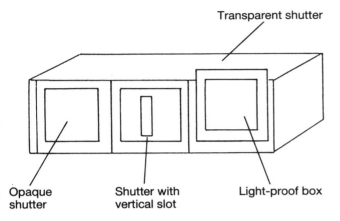

The apparatus includes six removable shutters to fit the compartments: one is opaque, one is transparent and one has a vertical slot allowing unidirectional lighting only. A fourth shutter allows only diffuse light to enter, the fifth has a blue filter and the sixth has a yellow filter.

METHOD   Place three trays of seedlings in the apparatus, put the first three shutters in their places in the compartments and leave the apparatus for 24 hours. Examine, and report your findings. If necessary, leave for a longer period. Then repeat the experiment with the remaining three shutters. Discuss the results first in terms of auxin production and its effect on the young cells of the shoot, and secondly in terms of the range of wavelengths excluded by the filters. Did certain wavelengths have more effect on auxin production than others?

40 To investigate the influence of gravity on germinating seedlings using a clinostat

APPARATUS   Cork board
Pins
10 germinating bean seedlings, with radicles and plumules well developed
Clinostat

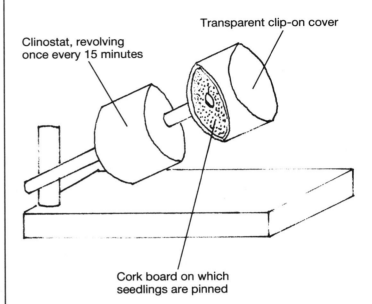

METHOD   Pin five of the seedlings to the cork board by placing the pin through the cotyledons in such a way that the radicles and plumules are pointing parallel to the ground. Pin five seedlings similarly to the clinostat. If you wish, on both the experimental board and the clinostat (the control) you may place the seedlings with their radicles pointing in various directions. If you do this, you must make diagrams to show the original positions of all the seedlings. Switch the clinostat on and leave it to rotate slowly four times an hour, for 24 hours. Place the clinostat and the experimental board in as nearly identical positions of light and temperature as possible. View after 24 hours, and make diagrams of the positions of all the plumules and radicles. If necessary, the experiment may be prolonged for another 24 or 48 hours in order to get clear results.

The clinostat rotating the beans on their axis will nullify the effects of gravity — you should find that the plumules and radicles continue growing in the same direction as they were placed at the start of the experiment. The experimental beans should show a negative response to gravity for the plumules, and a positive response for the radicles.

Discuss your results in terms of the effect and distribution of auxins in both shoots and roots.

41   To make a squash preparation of locust testis to show stages in meiosis

APPARATUS   Male locust; either a very young adult, or in last instar previous to moulting into adult
Acetic orcein stain (see Appendix 1 for recipe)
Bunsen burner
Slides and coverslips
Dissecting instruments and dish

METHOD   Your locust will be given to you freshly killed. Remove the head and, if you wish, the legs and wings. Pin it on its ventral side in a dissecting dish, and cover with water. Open up the insect by cutting up its mid-dorsal line. Turn back and pin the body wall. You should be able to see the testis as a single oval body lying above the gut in the abdomen. Remove onto a slide, and take off as much of the yellow fat body as possible. You should now be able to see the white testis tubules — remove two or three onto a fresh slide. Place another slide on top and squash them gently together. This will give you two slides ready for examination. Add a suitably sized drop of aceto-orcein to each and cover with a coverslip. Warm gently over a bunsen flame for a few seconds to improve staining. Examine, and draw the stages.

42   To make a squash preparation of the root-tip of a germinating broad bean

APPARATUS   Broad bean seeds, soaked for 12 hours
Pots of vermiculite
Microscope
Slides and coverslips
Hotplate at 50°C or a water bath with a suitable rack
Filter paper
Mounted needle, scalpel
Watch glasses
Acetic orcein (or propionic orcein)
1 M HCl

METHOD   Germinate the bean seeds in the damp vermiculite for two weeks. When the radicle of each is between 1 and 2 cm long, cut off the tip. This will encourage the growth of numerous lateral roots, which you will use for the squash preparation. Cut off a 2–3 cm portion of lateral root, being very careful not to damage the tip. Starting from the tip and working backwards, cut off four or five 3 mm portions, and put each in a separate watch glass. Mix acetic orcein and 1 M HCl in the proportions of ten parts of stain to one part of acid, and add enough of the mixture to each watch glass to cover the root portion.

Warm for 5 minutes on the water bath or hotplate. Unless the hotplate is accurately controlled thermostatically, it is better to use the water bath, propping your watch glasses on some suitable rack. The solution must *not* be allowed to boil. Place each portion of the root on an appropriately labelled slide in sufficient stain for the coverslip. Break up the root very gently with a needle, but disturb the relative positions of the cells as little as possible. Put a coverslip on top, and cover it with a folded piece of filter paper. Press down on the coverslip either with your thumb or with the wooden handle of a mounted needle. Try not to allow any sideways movement of the coverslip. Examine your preparation under the microscope. You are looking for two things:

1   Stages in mitosis:
● **prophase**: this stage is characterised by the presence of the nuclear membrane; chromosomes are forming but are irregularly distributed
● **metaphase**: no nuclear membrane; chromosomes arranged loosely along the equator of the spindle
● **telophase**: chromosomes in two distinct clusters; the beginnings of the cell plate are visible.
Identify and draw as many stages as possible. You will probably find most stages in the section taken nearest the root tip.

2   Stages in the development of differentiated cells from the apical meristem. Examining each of the serial portions in turn, look for and draw the following:
● **root cap cells**: relatively large nuclei, no vacuoles, some may be destroyed on the outer surface
● **zone of cell division**: actively dividing cells fairly cubical in shape; no vacuoles, nuclei again relatively large
● **zone of expansion**: cells more elongated, nuclei relatively smaller
● **zone of differentiation**: elongated cells; the characteristics of phloem and of xylem with spiral thickening may be seen.

43   To show that gametes are produced from heterozygotes in equal numbers using maize pollen

APPARATUS   Anthers of maize, heterozygous for waxy/non-waxy alleles (commercially available)
Microscope
Slides and coverslips
Iodine in potassium iodide solution
Mounted needle

METHOD   Tease the pollen grains from an anther onto a slide on which you have placed some drops of iodine solution. Carefully put on a coverslip and examine under the microscope, using the ×10 eyepiece and the low-power objective. Use the diaphragm fully open. After a few minutes in iodine, some grains will turn blue-black; some will be brown. Count as many grains as you can, recording the numbers of each colour.

DISCUSSION   The two alleles operating here are called waxy (*wx*) and non-waxy (*Wx*) or starchy. The latter allele causes the production of normal starch. This starch is made up of amylose and amylopectin. Amylose stains deep blue with I_2/KI solution, whereas amylopectin, a phosphocarbohydrate, stains reddish brown. This colour is usually masked in the presence of amylose. The recessive allele *wx* leads to the production of amylopectin only, and hence the red-brown colour can be seen. Your results should give you equal numbers of each type of pollen grain. Pooling of class results will give a larger sample and increase the possibility of an accurate ratio. However, you should perform a χ^2 test to find the accuracy.

Although the technique is fairly simple, there are some sources of error; faulty counting is possible. Some pollen grains are empty, and will show up as light brown. However, if your illumination is not strong enough (i.e. the diaphragm is not fully open), sufficient time is not allowed for the full blue-black colour to develop, or if the iodine solution is too strong, the empty grains could be counted as 'waxy'.

44   To observe the germination of pollen grains using a hanging drop preparation

44A   To make the hanging drop preparation

METHOD   Take a cavity slide and, using a mounted needle, make a thin ring of vaseline around the cavity:

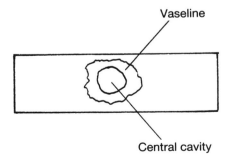

Take care that the vaseline does not intrude into the cavity and will not do so when flattened by a coverslip. Place a coverslip on the bench and in the centre place a small drop of the solution under investigation. Carefully take the slide and place it over the coverslip in such a way that the cavity in the slide is exactly over the drop. Press gently to adhere the slip to the vaseline. This is the stage at which you will find out if you have used too much grease! Now carefully invert the slide. The drop should remain attached to the coverslip and suspended within the cavity.

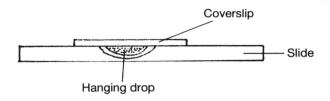

If you have no success at first, keep practising. Keep the size of the drop small and well-centred on the coverslip.

44B   To germinate the pollen grains

APPARATUS   Pollen grains from various sources
Cavity slides and coverslips
1 M sucrose, with a very little boric acid and yeast extract added (see Appendix 1 for recipe). Prepare dilutions from this in a range from 0.2 M to 0.5 M
Dissecting instruments and microscope

METHOD   Examine first each sample of pollen, noting its source and whether it is from wind-pollinated or insect-pollinated plants. Draw and annotate differences — size, surface appearance, shape, airsacs, sticky and so on. Prepare a coverslip with a small drop of your chosen dilution of sucrose. With a brush, dust a small sample of pollen onto the drop. Then proceed to make your hanging drop preparation. If the laboratory temperature is about 20 °C, you can leave the slide on the bench; otherwise place it near a radiator. Examine after an hour, and at half-hourly intervals for the next three hours. Each time, count the number of pollen grains germinated. Estimate the rate of growth of pollen tubes over the period, i.e. ×1, ×2 or ×3 the original grain size. Repeat using the other samples of pollen. Repeat again with the different molarities.

This is a difficult experiment to carry out; in the laboratory 0.3–0.4 M sucrose will probably give the best results. Boron has been found to be essential for the growth of some species of pollen, and yeast probably provides protein nutrient. A well-germinated sample could be transferred to another slide, stained with aceto-carmine (for recipe, see Appendix 1) and examined for the tube nucleus and the two male nuclei.

45 To make preparations of stages in the development of *Capsella bursa-pastoris* embryos

APPARATUS 5% potassium hydroxide (see
Appendix 1 for recipe)
Solution of iodine in potassium iodide
Plants of Shepherd's Purse (*Capsella bursa-pastoris*) with fruits
Watch glasses
Microscope slides and coverslips

METHOD   Select fruits in various stages of development from the apex of the plant (young forms) downwards to the oldest forms. Place each one separately in a watch glass in a few drops of potassium hydroxide. Tease out the ovules. Leave for 10 minutes. Then mount one or two ovules from each watch glass on a slide, in a drop of iodine solution. Cover with a coverslip, and press down gently with the handle of a mounted needle. This should squeeze out the embryo unharmed.

Draw each stage, and tabulate the differences between them.

46 To investigate the responses of small arthropods to differences in humidity

APPARATUS Woodlice, flour beetles or blowfly larvae
Choice chambers
Calcium chloride — a drying agent

METHOD The bottom portion of the choice chamber, which is constructed like a large petri dish, is divided into four sections. Fill two with water, and the other two with calcium chloride. Cover the base of the upper part of the chamber with muslin and fix with the elastic band. Drop 5–10 animals through each of the two holes in the top. Cover with light-proof material, or place in a light-proof box. Students should carry out their experiments in various areas of the laboratory, in order to minimise the effect of any other factors. Behaviour experiments are extremely difficult to control, and the absence of one factor for experimental purposes may cause yet other factors to become operative. Leave for 30 minutes to allow the organisms to settle, and record the numbers of animals in each of the two sections. Turn the top section through 180°, and repeat.

Turning the top section should nullify any physical factors such as a slight temperature gradient, a slope to the bench, draught and so on. A further control is to have some chambers with the right half filled with water, and some with the left. The main control is to put beetles into a chamber with the lower containers empty, and cover with light-proof material. Records are made in a similar way to the test chambers. Testing each area with cobalt chloride paper should prove whether or not there is a humidity difference. (This paper is blue when dry and pink when damp.) Several counts should be carried out on each chamber, but at least an hour should pass between each count. If time does not allow this, then the animals should be removed and fresh ones put in.

To assess the significance of any results, a standard deviation calculation should be performed. You assume for this purpose a 'null hypothesis', i.e. no difference between the sides of the chamber. This means that out of 100 animals, 50 will be found in each side. So long as more than 10 counts are made you can also assume that the distribution approaches the normal curve of distribution, and therefore that the mean is 50 and the variance is 25.

In practice, you may find that the control experiments show rather a lot of variance due to other quite minor factors, all of which are difficult to pinpoint. Averaging results from the whole class will help.

Biological rhythms may operate, so you may get

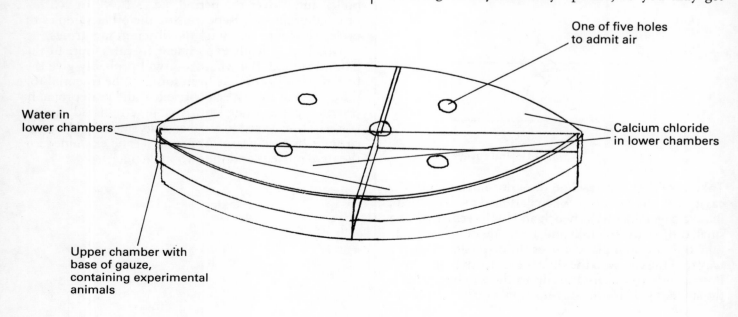

One of five holes to admit air

Water in lower chambers

Calcium chloride in lower chambers

Upper chamber with base of gauze, containing experimental animals

different results by testing in the early morning, or during the evening. Any previous treatment, e.g. whether the animals have come recently from a dry or a damp environment, will affect results. A dried-out animal will seek a damp environment. This may be nullified by keeping the animals in the laboratory in an optimum environment for several days before the test. Some animals may spend the majority of their time in one environment, but a definite period in another. This can be demonstrated by marking the animals, but you must be sure that the marking material used does not have an effect. Some paint solvents have been shown to reverse a tactic response. You should also carry out the same experiment, controls and all, in a totally light environment. This will show whether their response to humidity is the same in the light as in the dark.

10 PROJECT WORK

Project work has been defined by the Nuffield Advanced Studies workers as 'a practical investigation carried out by an individual student involving inquiry into some aspect of Biology, conducted largely on his/her own initiative'. Projects now appear, at least in an optional form, on most A-level syllabuses and in some cases they are obligatory.

'On his/her own initiative' means, of course, that although some time might be set aside in your busy 2-year schedule for class or individual discussion with the teacher about your project, the bulk of the work will be carried out by you in your free periods at school. Depending on the type of project you choose, it may also be necessary to do some work on your project in the evenings and at weekends. The work need not be purely experimental, but may involve some other form of investigation.

Your teacher will give you the original guidance as to your choice of topic. There will probably be a limited list of options already available, which are geared to the resources and equipment of the school. However, the more original the project is, the better. It must, though, be realistic in terms of the time available and the use of cheap or easily made equipment. You are therefore free to think up a topic for yourself provided that it is very carefully planned, and that it is vetted by your teacher so as to exclude procedures that are unrealistic or even dangerous.

The criterion to use is 'does the project contain something new' — at least at the standard reached in A-level biology. The 'new' need not be a totally fresh concept; it may be a well-tried technique applied to a new organism, or a change in an everyday piece of equipment for a particular purpose.

Setting out on your project will require the same technique as planning a physiology experiment, except that you will go into it in much greater depth and with more time and facilities at your disposal. Try to keep your project simple, and always have a clear aim formulated. This will be the first problem to solve — to find an area of investigation which contains some questions to answer and which is fairly easily available. This may be in your garden or your local park if it is ecological, or it may involve organisms that you can rear in the laboratory. The level of investigation can range from the overall ecological relationship between an organism and its surroundings down to the biochemistry of some aspect of an organism's metabolism.

It is not usually a good idea to work in pairs or in groups, since problems inevitably arise over whether one person is doing more work than another. But it would be possible for two, or even three, people to work on different aspects of an organism, e.g. the effects of light and temperature on a particular plant's growth rate.

Keep the aim of your project simple. Investigate only one factor at a time and never allow yourself to be side tracked; time is too short for following up any fascinating secondary aspects that you may come across. As your project is going to occupy you over most of your two years, events occurring as a result of seasonal changes can be studied. You may well arrive at two or three possible titles. You must then look at the available literature to find out what type of work has been done. This will help you to reject some of the alternatives, and possibly cause you to modify others. It may also be the source of new ideas.

Then plan out one or more of your options in some detail to give yourself an idea of the equipment you will need and the space you will take up in growing plants, rearing animals and so forth. This is the stage at which you should discuss your project again with your teacher, since he or she will have to plan out available laboratory space, use of equipment, sharing of glassware and so on for the whole class. This may result in your having to abandon some options as impracticable.

Having settled your project title, you must now plan your project in much more detail. This is to ensure that you follow a line of investigation that should produce results, that you will not 'run out of steam' halfway through and, even more important, that you will not be tempted to change your mind and start something new every few months. In many cases, your project title, together with a brief description of the expected procedures, has to be approved in advance by the examining board. However, should some unforeseen disaster strike your project at a crucial moment, credit is given for designing and carrying out your experiment, together with your discussion.

Your teacher will advise you on any legal or ethical problems that you might encounter in your project, e.g. making sure that no harm will come to any animal that you may include in your experiments. He or she will also advise you on your sources of reference; not only the school library, but also the local library, access to reprints, relevant television broadcasts etc.

Your plan should start with a list of contents followed by a short introduction saying why you selected that particular topic; write down any observation you might have made that triggered off a particular line of thought. Then go on to list the experiments you hope to carry out, the apparatus needed and the readings that you hope to make. This will enable you to find any equipment that you might need to adapt, or even to make, before you start. Things rarely go smoothly, and you must be prepared to modify your techniques or approach in the light of the experience you gain or the difficulties that you encounter as you go along.

You must keep a laboratory notebook. In this you should record the experiments that you perform on any particular day, and the results as you obtain them. You should also enter any hitches or problems that you meet, your thoughts on how to overcome them and things you wish to remember to do. List points that you wish to look up in the library, or anything that you would like to ask your teacher.

Aim to conclude your project with plenty of time left to write it up. Sometimes the date for submitting projects to the examining board is considerably earlier than the actual examination. Writing up can often take a lot longer than you expect. Good, concise laboratory notes will be a great help here. You may have taken photographs at various stages, and these will have to be mounted and included as part of your results.

Present your results in ways similar to those recommended in Chapter 8. Again the aim is to be as clear and concise as possible so that a reader can see immediately the information to be got from a set of results.

You may need to carry out some statistical evaluation, and this will again take time if you are unfamiliar with the mathematical processes involved. You may or may not be able to get clear-cut conclusions from your results. This is not necessarily bad. Discuss them succinctly but thoroughly and, if possible, summarise the main deductions.

When you are investigating the background literature to your project, it is a good idea to keep an exercise book, or even a card index, in which to record the titles of all the publications that you use for reference. This will make it easy to compile a bibliography which, together with acknowledgements of help that you may have received, will be the last section of your project.

APPENDIX 1: RECIPES

Experiment 1

Holtfreter's solution
Sold commercially as 'Instant Pond'. Used as a culture medium for *Daphnia* sp.
  0.02 g sodium bicarbonate ($NaHCO_3$)
  3.50 g sodium chloride (NaCl)
  0.10 g calcium chloride ($CaCl_2$)
  0.05 g potassium chloride (KCl)
  Add to 1 dm^3 distilled water and mix thoroughly.

Experiment 2

Sucrose solutions

Molarity of solution	Amount (in grams) of sucrose ($C_{12}H_{22}O_{11}$) for 1 dm^3 of distilled water)
0.20	68.4
0.30	102.6
0.35	119.7
0.40	136.8
0.45	153.9
0.50	171.0
1.00	342.0

Domestic table sugar may be used for these solutions.

Experiment 4

Saline solutions

% saline	Sodium chloride (g dm^{-3})
0.05	0.5
0.09	0.9
2.5	25.0

Oxalated blood
  20 cm^3 saturated potassium oxalate and
  30 cm^3 saturated ammonium oxalate per dm^3 of blood.

Experiment 5

Brodie's fluid
  0.3 g Evans blue
  1.0 g 'Stergene'
  40.0 g sodium bromide (NaBr)

2 M KOH (potassium hydroxide)
  112 g dm^{-3}

Experiment 8

0.5 m sucrose ($C_6H_{22}O_{11}$) solution
  171 g dm^{-3} distilled water

Lime water
  A saturated solution of calcium hydroxide ($Ca(OH)_2$), about 2 g dm^{-3} at room temperature.

Iodoform test
  Add a small quantity of iodine to your yeast sample. Add 10% potassium hydroxide drop by drop. You will need to warm slightly.
  10% KOH = 10 g dm^{-3}

Experiment 9

Commercial concentrated hydrochloric acid needs to be diluted about 12 times for 1 M HCl. Add about 80 cm^3 of concentrated acid *very* slowly to about 900 cm^3 of distilled water in a heat-resistant container. If the mixture becomes too hot, allow to cool before adding more acid.

1 M sodium hydrogen carbonate ($NaHCO_3$)
84 g dm^{-3}

Experiment 10

Bicarbonate indicator
This is normally made in a concentrated form and diluted 1 in 10 for laboratory use.

0.84 g of $NaHCO_3$ (sodium hydrogen carbonate)
About 1 dm^3 distilled water
0.2 g thymol blue ⎫ dissolved in 20 cm^3 of
0.1 g cresol red ⎭ absolute ethanol and filtered
Dissolve the $NaHCO_3$ in a 1 dm^3 flask with some of the distilled water. Add the dye solution, and make up to the 1 dm^3 mark with the remaining distilled water.

1 M HCl (see Experiment 9)
1 M NaOH (sodium hydroxide) = 40 g dm^{-3}

Experiment 13

$KHCO_3$ (potassium hydrogen carbonate) solution
(To supply carbon dioxide.)

% $KHCO_3$ solution	$KHCO_3$ (g dm^{-3})
0.25	2.5
0.50	5.0
0.75	7.5
1.00	10.0
1.50	15.0
2.00	20.0

Experiment 14

Solvent for chromatogram
900 cm^3 petroleum ether (use commercially available, BP° between 80 and 100°C)
100 cm^3 acetone

Experiment 18

Fehling's solution A
69.2 g of copper(II) sulphate ($CuSO_4$) per dm^3 of distilled water

Fehling's solution B
154 g sodium hydroxide (NaOH)
350 g sodium potassium tartrate
Dissolve in 1 dm^3 of distilled water. Keep solutions A and B separate; only mix just as the test is being made.

Benedict's solution
100 g hydrated sodium carbonate ($Na_2CO_3 \cdot 10H_2O$)
173 g hydrated sodium citrate
Dissolve in about 750 cm^3 of distilled water. You may need to warm gently. Filtering may also be necessary.
Dissolve 17.3 g of $CuSO_4$ (copper(II) sulphate) in about 150 cm^3 of distilled water. Slowly add this solution to the citrate and carbonate mixture. Stir constantly. Make up to 1 dm^3 with distilled water.

Iodine in potassium iodide solution
6 g KI (potassium iodide)
3 g I_2 (iodine crystals)
Dissolve KI in 1 dm^3 of distilled water and add iodine. Leave overnight, or perhaps for longer, for iodine crystals to dissolve.

Concentrated sulphuric acid (H_2SO_4)
Commercially available concentrated H_2SO_4 may be used as such, or *carefully* diluted one part in two with distilled water. (N.B. Always add acid *very* slowly to water, *not* the other way round. Cool continuously. Make sure the container is heat resistant.)

Schultze's solution (chlor-zinc iodine)
(N.B. This solution is POISONOUS.)

Solution A
20 g zinc chloride $ZnCl_2$
10 cm^3 distilled water

Solution B
1.0 g KI (potassium iodide)
0.5 g I_2 (iodine)
20 cm^3 distilled water

Add drops of solution A to the whole of solution B until a precipitate of iodine crystals appears and remains even after shaking thoroughly (about 2.0 cm^3)

Alcoholic orcin
0.5 g of orcin dissolved in 100 cm^3 of 90% ethanol

Acidified phloroglucinol
Dissolve 5 g of phloroglucinol in 100 cm^3 of 95% ethanol. Add concentrated HCl until a precipitate just begins to appear.

Aniline sulphate (POISONOUS)
1 g aniline sulphate (chloride may also be used)
Dissolve in 90 cm^3 of 70% ethanol
Add 10 cm^3 of 0.05 M sulphuric acid (made by diluting 1 M H_2SO_4 1 in 20 with distilled water).

Copper sulphate for Biuret test
10 g $CuSO_4$ (copper(II) sulphate) in 1 dm^3 distilled water

Concentrated nitric acid (HNO_3)
Commercially available may be used, or diluted 1 in 2 (see note on H_2SO_4) to give 9 M HNO_3

Dilute ammonium hydroxide (NH_4OH)
Commercially available is about 15 M
About 70 cm^3 made up to 1 dm^3 with distilled water (approx. 1 M).

Millon's reagent (POISONOUS)
Use a fume cupboard to make up this solution.
Put 2 cm^3 of mercury in a beaker and add 20 cm^3 concentrated HNO_3.

After the reaction has completed, in the closed fume cupboard, add 22 cm^3 of distilled water.

Sudan III

Saturate 100 cm^3 of 70% alcohol with Sudan III powder. You may need to place in a warm water bath to help the dye dissolve. Allow to stand overnight. Filter if necessary.

Experiment 20

10% starch solution
    100 g soluble starch
    1 dm^3 distilled water

Mix the starch with enough water to make a thin paste. Boil the remainder of the water. Pour the starch mixture into the hot water, stirring constantly to avoid lumps. This concentration is quite viscous and may be diluted 1 in 2 if necessary. (This solution must not be kept for longer than a few hours; reducing sugars appear.)

1% amylase solution
    10 g amylase powder in 1 dm^3 distilled water

Experiment 23

1% invertase (sucrase) solution

Supplied commercially as 'invertase concentrate' in solution. Take 10 cm^3 and make up to 1 dm^3 with distilled water.

10% sucrose solution (reducing sugar-free)

For this AR grade sucrose is required.
    100 g sucrose dissolved in 1 dm^3 distilled water

Phosphate buffer solutions

Solution 1
    0.2 M sodium dihydrogen phosphate
    $(NaH_2PO_4 \cdot 2H_2O) = 31.2$ g dm^{-3}
Solution 2
    0.2 M disodium hydrogen phosphate $(Na_2HPO_4) =$
    28.4 g dm^{-3} or if using the hydrated salt
    $NA_2HPO_4 \cdot 12H_2O = 71.6$ g dm^{-3}

Mix together in the following proportions according to the pH required:

pH	Solution 1 (cm^3)	Solution 2 (cm^3)	Distilled water (cm^3)
5.8	460	40	500
6.2	407	92	501
6.6	312	187	501
7.0	195	305	500
7.4	95	405	500
7.8	42	467	491
8.0	26	473	501

These quantities are for 1 dm^3 of buffer solution.

Experiment 24

DCPIP solution (1%)
    10 g 2,6-dichlorophenolindophenol
    1 dm^3 distilled water

Methylene blue solution (0.01%)
(For detecting dehydrogenase activity.)
    0.1 g methylene blue powder, or 1.0 of solution (as purchased)
    1 dm^3 distilled water. May be strengthened if dehydrogenase activity is high.

Experiment 25

TTC solution (0.05%)
    0.5 g 2,3,5-triphenyl tetrazolium chloride
    1 dm^3 distilled water

May be purchased commercially as a solution, in which case dilute according to the concentration of the purchased solution.

Experiment 26

0.1 M sodium malonate ($CH_2(COONa)_2$)
    14.8 g dm^{-3}

0.1 M sodium succinate (($CH_2COONa)_2$)
    16.2 g dm^{-3}

Experiment 27

Hydrogen peroxide (H_2O_2)
    '20 volume' may be purchased from chemists

Experiment 28

Phenolphthalein phosphate solution (0.1%)
    1 g phenolphthalein phosphate
    1 dm^3 distilled water

As this reagent is very expensive, a dilute solution is sufficient. The pink colour of free phenolphthalein in alkaline solution shows up very clearly in small quantities.

Sodium hydrogen carbonate solution (10%) ($NaHCO_3$)
    100 g $NaHCO_3$
    1 dm^3 distilled water

Experiment 30

Invertebrate saline
Clarke's version (many others are in use)
   6.5 g sodium chloride (NaCl)
   1.4 g potassium chloride (KCl)
   0.12 g calcium chloride ($CaCl_2$)
   0.1 g sodium hydrogen carbonate ($NaHCO_3$)
   0.01 g disodium hydrogen phosphate (Na_2HPO_4)
   1 dm^3 distilled water

Experiment 32

2% sucrose solution
   20 g dm^{-3} sucrose dissolved in distilled water

Experiment 36

Malt agar
   30 g malt extract (from chemists)
   15 g agar
   1 dm^3 distilled water
Heat to dissolve, dispense, if wished, into pour-plates or tubes, and autoclave at 10 lbs pressure for 10 minutes.

Potato dextrose agar
Boil 200 g of peeled, diced potatoes and mash thoroughly
Add 20 g dextrose. Mix well.
Dissolve 15 g of agar in 1 dm^3 water, by heating gently.
Add potato-dextrose mixture to agar solution. Autoclave to sterilize.

Experiment 37

Culture medium for hydroponics (Sach's)
1 Normal solution (i.e. complete)
    0.25 g calcium sulphate ($CaSO_4$)
    0.25 g calcium phosphate ($Ca_3(PO_4)_2$)
    0.25 g magnesium sulphate ($MgSO_4$)
    0.08 sodium chloride (NaCl)
    0.70 g potassium nitrate (KNO_3)
    0.005 g iron(III) chloride ($FeCl_3$)
    1 dm^3 distilled water
2 Calcium absent
    Substitute 0.20 g potassium sulphate (K_2SO_4) and 0.71 g sodium phosphate (Na_3PO_4) for the two calcium salts.
3 Iron absent
    Omit the iron(III) chloride.

4 Potassium absent
    Use 0.59 g sodium nitrate ($NaNO_3$) for the potassium salt.
5 Phosphorus absent
    Use 0.16 g calcium nitrate ($CaNO_3$) instead of the calcium phosphate.
6 Magnesium absent
    Use 0.17 g potassium sulphate (K_2SO_4) instead of magnesium sulphate.
7 Sulphur absent
    Substitute 0.16 g calcium chloride ($CaCl_2$) for calcium sulphate and 0.21 g magnesium chloride for magnesium sulphate.
8 Nitrogen absent
    Use 0.52 g potassium chloride (KCl) instead of potassium nitrate.

Experiment 41

Acetic-orcein stain
This is made in concentrated form, and diluted 1 in 2 with water just before use.
Reflux 10 g of orcein with 300 cm^3 of glacial acetic acid for about 6 hours. (Propionic acid may be used, and the stain is then propionic orcein.) Filter if necessary.

Experiment 44

Germinating medium for pollen grains
   342 g sucrose (table variety)
   0.01 g boric acid
   0.01 g yeast extract (commercially available)
   1 dm^3 distilled water
This gives a 1 M solution. Dilute appropriately to give the concentrations required.

Aceto-carmine stain
   2 g carmine powder
   90 cm^3 glacial acetic acid
   100 cm^3 distilled water
Add dye to acetic acid and mix. Add the water. Boil, cool and filter.

Experiment 45

5% potassium hydroxide (KOH)
50 g KOH dissolved in 1 dm^3 distilled water. Add pellets one or two at a time to the water in a heat-resistant container. Heat and fumes are generated, so cool mixture constantly.

APPENDIX 2: STATISTICAL TABLES

Table of χ^2

n is the number of degrees of freedom and p is the probability.

p n	0.99	0.95	0.90	0.50	0.10	0.05	0.01	0.001
1	0.0157	0.00393	0.0158	0.455	2.71	3.84	6.64	10.83
2	0.0201	0.103	0.211	1.39	4.61	5.99	9.21	13.82
3	0.115	0.352	0.584	2.37	6.25	7.82	11.35	16.27
4	0.297	0.711	1.06	3.36	7.78	9.49	13.28	18.47
5	0.554	1.15	1.61	4.35	9.24	11.07	15.09	20.52
6	0.872	1.64	2.20	5.35	10.65	12.59	16.81	22.46
7	1.24	2.17	2.83	6.35	12.02	14.07	18.48	24.32
8	1.65	2.73	3.49	7.34	13.36	15.51	20.09	26.13
9	2.09	3.33	4.17	8.34	14.68	16.92	21.67	27.88
10	2.56	3.94	4.87	9.34	15.99	18.31	23.21	29.59
12	3.57	5.23	6.30	11.34	18.55	21.03	26.22	32.91
14	4.66	6.57	7.79	13.34	21.06	23.69	29.14	36.12
16	5.81	7.96	9.31	15.34	23.54	26.30	32.00	39.25
18	7.01	9.39	18.87	17.34	25.99	28.87	34.81	42.31
20	8.26	10.85	12.44	19.34	28.41	31.41	37.57	45.31
25	11.52	14.61	16.47	24.34	34.38	37.65	44.31	52.62
30	14.95	18.49	20.60	29.34	40.26	43.77	50.89	59.70

For larger values of n, $\sqrt{2\chi^2} - \sqrt{2n-1}$ may be used as a normal deviate; since the probability of χ^2 corresponds to a single tail of the normal curve, divide the resulting probability by 2.

Relative humidity

Aqueous solutions of constant vapour pressure

Relative humidity (%)	Sulphuric acid solutions, 25°C		Caustic potash solutions, 20°C	
	Vapour pressure at 25°C (mm Hg)	% by weight (g H_2SO_4 per 100 g of solution)	Vapour pressure at 20°C (mm Hg)	% by weight (g KOH per 100 g of solution)
100	23.756	0	17.535	0
95	22.568	11.02	16.658	7.00
90	21.380	17.91	15.782	11.75
85	20.193	22.88	14.905	15.80
80	19.005	26.79	14.028	19.25
75	17.817	30.14	13.151	22.25
70	16.629	33.09	12.275	25.00
65	15.441	35.80	11.398	27.30
60	14.254	38.35	10.521	29.50
55	13.066	40.75	9.644	31.60
50	11.878	43.10	8.768	33.70
45	10.690	45.41	7.891	35.80
40	9.502	47.71	7.014	37.95
35	8.315	50.04	6.137	40.10
30	7.127	52.45	5.261	42.30
25	5.939	55.01	4.384	44.50
20	4.751	57.76	3.507	47.00
15	3.563	60.80	2.630	49.80
10	2.376	64.45		
5	1.188	69.44		

BIBLIOGRAPHY

Barrass, R., *The Locust; A Guide for Laboratory Practical Work*, Butterworths, 1968.

Bishop, O. N., *Statistics for Biology*, Longman, 1983.

Bold, H. C., *The Plant Kingdom*, Prentice-Hall, 1970.

Borradaile, I.. A , Eastham, L. E., Potts, F. A. and Saunders, J. T., *The Invertebrates*, Cambridge University Press, 1963.

Bracegirdle, B. and Miles, P. H., *An Atlas of Plant Structure*, Vols. 1 and 2, Heinemann Educational Books, 1971.

Bradbury, S., *The Optical Microscope in Biology, Studies in Biology No. 59*, Edward Arnold, 1976.

Brown, G. and Creedy, J., *Experimental Biology Manual*, Heinemann Educational Books, 1971.

Buchsbaum, R., *Animals Without Backbones*, University of Chicago Press, 1976.

Bullough, W. S., *Practical Invertebrate Anatomy*, Macmillan, 1981.

Burns, M. A., *The Arlington Practical Botany*, Vol. 1, *Plant Anatomy*, Vol. 2, *Plant Physiology*, Arlington Books, 1972.

Carleton, H. M. and Short, R. H. D. (eds.), *Schafer's Essentials of Histology*, Longman, 1961.

Clegg, A. G. and Clegg, P. C., *Biology of the Mammal*, Heinemann Medical Books, 1975

Fowell, R. R., *Biology Staining Schedules*, H. K. Lewis & Co., 1967

Freeman, W. H. and Bracegirdle, B., *An Atlas of Histology*, Heinemann Educational Books, 1978.

Freeman, W. H. and Bracegirdle, B., *An Atlas of Invertebrate Structure*, Heinemann Educational Books, 1982.

Grove, A. J. and Newell, G. E., *Animal Biology*, University Tutorial Press, 1983.

Hurry, S. W., *The Microstructure of Cells*, John Murray, 1966.

Marshall, P. T. and Hughes, G. M., *Vertebrate Physiology*, Cambridge University Press, 1980.

McGlashan, M. L., *Physico-Chemical Quantities and Units, Monographs for Teachers No. 15*, Royal Institute of Chemistry, 1971.

Monger, G. *et al.* (eds.), *Nuffield Advanced Biological Science Course*, Longman, 1985.

Roberts, M. B. V., *Biology – A Functional Approach*, Nelson, 1983.

Roberts, M. B. V., *Biology – A Functional Approach, Students Manual*, Nelson, 1979.

Robinson, M. A. and Wiggins, J. F., *Animal Types, I Invertebrates, II Vertebrates*, Hutchinson, 1978.

Romer, A. S., *The Vertebrate Body*, University of Chicago Press, 1977.

Romer, A. S., *The Vertebrate Story*, University of Chicago Press, 1959.

Sandon, H., *Essays on Protozoology*, Hutchinson Educational, 1968.

Saunders, J. T. and Manton, S. M., *Practical Vertebrate Morphology*, Oxford University Press, 1979.

Shaw, A. C., Lazell, S. K. and Foster, G. N., *Photomicrographs of the Flowering Plant*, Longman, 1979.

Shaw, A. C., Lazell, S. K. and Foster, G. N., *Photomicrographs of the Non-flowering Plant*, Longman, 1979.

Shaw, G. W., *Modern Cytological Techniques, Modern Science Memoirs No. 40*, John Murray, 1964.

Simon, E. W., Dormer, K. J. and Hartshorne, J. N., *Lowsons Textbook of Botany*, University Tutorial Press, 1981.

Simpkins, J. and Williams, J., *Advanced Biology*, Bell and Hyman, 1984.

Strafford, G. A., *Essentials of Plant Physiology*, Heinmann Educational Books, 1982.

Vickermann, K. and Cox, F. E. G., *The Protozoa*, John Murray, 1967.

Villee, C. A., Walker, W. F. and Barnes, R. D., *General Zoology*, Saunders, 1984.

Vines, A. E. and Rees, N., *Plant and Animal Biology*, Vols. I and II, Pitman, 1975.

Wallis, C. J., *Human Biology*, Heinemann, 1980.

Wells, T. A. G., *Three Vertebrates*, Heinemann, 1964.

Yapp, W. B., *Borradaile's Manual of Elementary Zoology*, Oxford University Press, 1963.

Young, J. Z., *The Life of Mammals*, Oxford University Press, 1975.

Young, J. Z., *The Life of Vertebrates*, Oxford University Press, 1981.

INDEX OF SPECIMENS